Shirley Hibberd

The amateur's kitchen garden, frame-ground and forcing pit

Shirley Hibberd

The amateur's kitchen garden, frame-ground and forcing pit

ISBN/EAN: 9783742892577

Manufactured in Europe, USA, Canada, Australia, Japa

Cover: Foto ©Thomas Meinert / pixelio.de

Manufactured and distributed by brebook publishing software (www.brebook.com)

Shirley Hibberd

The amateur's kitchen garden, frame-ground and forcing pit

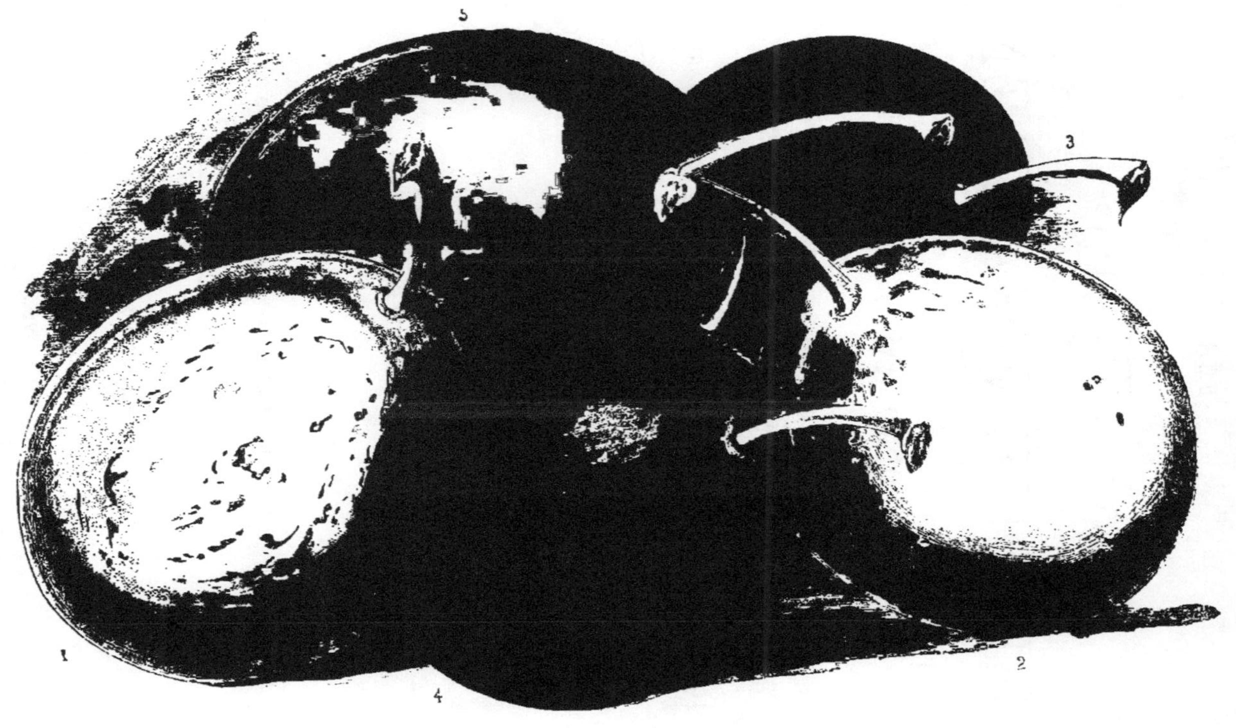
5
3
1
4
2

THE

AMATEUR'S KITCHEN GARDEN

FRAME-GROUND AND FORCING PIT:

A Handy Guide

TO THE FORMATION AND MANAGEMENT OF THE KITCHEN GARDEN AND THE CULTIVATION OF USEFUL VEGETABLES AND FRUITS.

BY

SHIRLEY HIBBERD.

Author of "The Amateur's Flower Garden," "The Amateur's Greenhouse," "The Amateur's Rose Book," "The Fern Garden," etc., etc.

ILLUSTRATED WITH COLOURED PLATES AND WOOD ENGRAVINGS.

LONDON:

GROOMBRIDGE AND SONS.

MDCCCLXXVII.

CONTENTS.

CHAPTER XVI.

CHAPTER XVII.

CHAPTER XVIII.

CHAPTER XIX.

CHAPTER XX.

CHAPTER XXI.

CHAPTER XXII.

CHAPTER XXIII.

CHAPTER XXIV.

CHAPTER XXV.

CHAPTER XXVI.

CHAPTER XXVII.

CHAPTER XXVIII.

CHAPTER XXIX.

THE AMATEUR'S

KITCHEN GARDEN.

INTRODUCTION.

"Here grow the humble cives, and hard by them,
The tall leek, tapering with its rushy stem;
High climbs his pulse in many an even row,
Deep strike the ponderous roots in soil below,
And herbs of potent smell and pungent taste,
Give a warm relish to the night's repast.
Apples and cherries grafted by his hand,
And clustered nuts for neighbouring market stand."

CRABBE. *Parish Register.*

THE subjects treated of in this volume might reasonably occupy much more than the space assigned them. But the convenience of the amateur gardener will probably be best consulted by presenting him, in one handy volume, as complete a treatise on the cultivation of vegetables and fruits as the space at command will allow. What may be lost by the adoption of a somewhat rough and ready mode of procedure, in place of the elaboration proper to a larger and more costly work, will be more than made up, it is hoped, by the usefulness to many of sound advice, conveyed, in the fewest possible words, on a department of gardening which ministers immediately and immensely to the comfort of home, as well as to individual health and enjoyment. What is known as the "kitchen garden" would greatly outgrow the limits of such a humble tome as this, if any approach to the "exhaustive" method were attempted; and as for the fruit garden, any number of volumes of any size might be filled with discourses on its occupants. But those who are well able to judge say, that such a volume as the present is greatly needed. The author indulges the hope that it will prove a creditable addition to the "amateur" series.

Those who are curious on the subject of garden literature will find, if they care to inquire, that books on the management of the kitchen garden are, to a great extent, repetitions of each other. In some respects this is inevitable; but there is much more sameness and imitation than we can fairly make allowance for, considering how plentifully such books are pumped out by the press, and the almost absolute lack of originality amongst them. The book in the reader's hands has its defects, no doubt—at all events, no pretensions are made to infallibility, or any near approach thereto—but it is no compilation: it is original in the fullest sense of the word, so far as it can be applied to such a work; and it embodies the results, in a comparatively small compass, of the work of a quarter of a century in gardens largely devoted to fruit and vegetable culture.

It must be clearly understood that this work is comprehensive, both as regards plan and details. It contains sufficiently full, and, it is hoped, sufficiently explicit instructions, to enable any one having command of the requisite land and appliances, to produce abundant supplies of all the kitchen garden productions ordinarily required in a substantial middle-class household, and that is the household most in need of help in respect of useful gardening.

CHAPTER I.

THE FORMATION OF THE KITCHEN GARDEN.

THE first principles to be observed in laying out a kitchen garden are so extremely simple, that they may be disposed of (as principles) in a few words. The ground should be rectangular, slightly sloping to the south, divided into convenient sized plots, with good walks of sufficient width between; it should be effectually drained; the soil a deep loam; there should be sheltering plantations on the north and east, substantial boundary walls on all four sides, and a suitable extent should be screened off by means of hedges or walls, to serve as frame ground, and rubbish yard, and a place of shelter for pot plants and other nursery purposes. Finally, there should be an abundant supply of water, the climate should be genial, and especially characterized by an equable temperature, not subject to severe frosts in the later days of spring, and exempt from the trying times of excessive heat and drought by which the summer is occasionally characterized in many parts of Great Britain, which as a whole, may be described as less than perfect for horticultural purposes.

The amateur need not take alarm at this brief sketch of essential primary principles, for vegetables and fruit are produced in plenty where none of them can be fully realized, and from first to last gardening in this country is a continuous conflict with difficulties. We look out of window on one of our own kitchen plots, which in shape approximates to a very long wedge, or a cross between a parabola and an isosceles triangle. From another window we view another plot which is of no shape at all, but comes nearest to a rhomboid out of joint, the sides and angles violently unequal, so that symmetrical division is impossible. The first piece is embellished with a brook that overflows half the ground when extra heavy rains occur, and is as dry as dust in a droughty summer; the other piece consists of undrained clay with water at a depth of eighteen inches six months out of the twelve, and the whole exposed to the bitterest east wind that ever blew in any part ot the home counties. We have other pieces much more favourably situated, but we are bound to say of these adjuncts to the home garden that we obtain from them a great variety and abundance of vegetables and fruits of the finest quality, the result simply of suitable management. In what the suitable management consists will be explained as we proceed; our object in referring to these gardens is merely to indicate at starting that we do not for our own use possess gardens representative of the essential primary principles that we have enumerated above. In all practical matters there is a compromise of some sort to be accomplished, and hence, in working out a theory or a scheme, allowance must be made for friction, the defects of material, and human fallibility.

It is well, however, to keep in mind all that is required, for much may be done by the exercise of skill and patience to remove or modify the various impediments to success that will have to be encountered as we go along. Whatever the soil or situation, the "laying out" should be a very simple matter. It may be prudent to plant a shrubbery and intersect it with winding walks and flower borders on one or on all sides of the kitchen garden. But whatever the kind of boundary taste or convenience may suggest, we must have rectangular plots, and symmetrical angular divisions where the work of the kitchen garden is to be carried on, and the amateur who enters upon the business with no experience to fall back upon, may be content for a time with grass walks or narrow ways marked with a few inches of coal ashes, and by the aid of these carry on the work until a definite idea is arrived at as to the most convenient and serviceable method of settling the configuration of the ground. In taking an old garden, you take the system with it, and generally speaking, it will be well to adapt operations to that system, even if it be a bad one, rather than to attempt a revolution, for that is sure to prove a costly business. Before altering an old garden, a prudent man will consider the cost, and the probability that it is better adapted to the locality, and to the circumstances of its owner than at first appears. At all events our advice to the amateur who takes a garden ready made is, make the best of it, and be in no haste to make important alterations, for they will cost money, and interrupt the work of production, and when accomplished may prove to be alterations only and not improvements.

In breaking up a piece of grass land, you have at least the advantage of your ideas of what a kitchen garden should be. You can make your boundaries and walks, and the forms and sizes of the several plots and plantations in accordance with your own theory of a perfect garden, so far at least as the extent of the ground, the nature of the soil, and other inevitable conditions will allow. Now in this case the two matters of vital importance are the boundaries and the drainage. In making the boundaries, it will be well to consider at the very first start to what extent will shelter be needful, and of what should it consist. A broad belt of wood or coppice affords the best of shelter against the keen east winds that in many parts make havoc of our own gardens in the months of March and April. If a site can be selected on the west or south of a sheltering hill or wood, the gain will be great in those seasons when "winter lingers in the lap of spring." But it may be that the land is exposed to all the winds of heaven, and in that case shelter will be of the utmost value. Dwarf walls and close boarded fences are generally considered valuable for purposes of shelter, but in truth their value is but slight. It is well to count the cost and probable efficiency of a "cheap" wall before determining on its adoption. To grow fruit satisfactorily is impossible on walls of four or five feet, and a boarded fence is of less value than a dwarf brick wall for fruit growing. But a cheap wall is a screen to shut out curious eyes, and it constitutes a moral if not a material barrier against thieves, who will often hesitate to get over a wall when they would not hesitate to mount a rough open fence, or even with the help of sacks overtop a hedge of holly. He who encloses his own land and has in view to grow good fruit, will be wise to build a wall of ten to fourteen feet high, the material stone or brick, with strengthening pillars, and a coping of six to eight inches. The minimum height for a wall to be of any use in fruit growing is eight feet. Such a wall should be nine inches thick, and have a coping projecting forwards. If from eight to fourteen feet, the thickness should be thirteen-and-a-half inches, and the coping six to eight inches. If from fourteen to twenty feet, the thickness must be eighteen inches, and the coping should project at least a foot. Hollow walls are formed by placing the bricks on edge alternately with their faces and ends outside, so that every second brick is a tie, and every course alternates in the order of facings so that every end comes over and under a full face. By this means a nine inch wall of great strength is obtained, and a considerable saving of bricks is effected.

When a live fence is preferred to a wall, the question will arise, what shall it be? Thorn is the quickest and cheapest, and if well arranged makes an effectual fence, but it is not well adapted for a garden. Common privet soon makes a dense evergreen boundary, useful alike for shelter and to impose a check on thieves, especially when it obtains a height of six or seven feet. The beautiful large leaved privet, *Ligustrum ovalifoliam*, is as fast growing and handsome a plant as can be used for a garden fence, and will cost but little more than the common privet. Everybody knows that holly is the finest of all boundary plants, but it should never be planted by a tenant at will unless the landlord is willing to pay for it, and in every case it will require the growth of years to thicken into a barrier and make a fair return for the money and labour invested in it. For general purposes, common privet is the very best of boundary plants for enclosing a garden, for it is not only evergreen and grows as close as a mat if planted thick enough, but it soon gets up to a useful height, so that no one can see through or over it. One of our pieces, which abuts on a road one side and an open meadow on the other, is fenced in as follows: Next the road an "unclimbable" iron fence and two rows of privet, with Lombardy poplars twenty feet apart, and standard Ligustram ovalifolium between the poplars. On the opposite side next the meadow, a strong five feet fence of oak posts and rails leaning over towards the meadow, and rendered additionally difficult of access by a deep ditch on that side. Within the fence two rows of common privet and Lombardy poplars twenty feet apart. On this side, there are no standard privets, as we desire as free a range as possible for the eye over the open country. On the third side, which is seen from the house and abuts only on a field path, there is a fence of posts and rails, poplars at twenty feet, two rows of holly next the rails, and one row of evergreen barbery, *Berberis aquifolium,* inside the hollies, forming a dense screen. On the fourth side is a mixed shrubbery, forming the boundary that way of the pleasure garden.

The boundaries being defined, we proceed to consider how far drainage is needed. It matters not what the staple may be, if it is water-logged periodically, and retains water for any length of time, drainage will not only improve it, but operate like magic in increasing its productiveness and rendering it suitable for many forms of vegetation that will not thrive on cold damp land. If it be possible, the whole of the drains should be carried under walks, and, if necessary, they should be taken direct, or as direct as possible to the natural outfall. In most cases a main drain formed of a pipe six inches in diameter should be laid along the lower side of the ground, opening to the outfall, and the other drains communicating with it should be formed of half pipe and sole, or three-inch whole pipe with sole attached, and all connections should be made by turning the pipe slightly in the direction of the flow in the main, because water does not easily turn at a right angle, and a quick removal without conflict is required. The depth of the drains will depend upon the set of the land and the nature of the outfall, but a depth of two feet is better than a depth of one foot, and a depth of three feet better still. The result will be more satisfactory, if the channels are cut by an experienced workman, and filled in over the pipes with chalk, or limestone, or shale, or brickbats. If you cannot command hard stuff for the purpose, use brushwood, for, when covered with earth and kept undisturbed, it is scarcely to be spoken of as a perishable substance, and it greatly facilitates the downward passage of water to the pipes. In heavy low-lying clay lands where moles abound, it is often necessary to lay shallow drains, because of the small fall obtainable. In such a case pipes of one inch bore are to be preferred, and the distance may range from twelve to twenty feet. In lighter soils, in which deep drains may be laid, they may be thirty to sixty feet apart, and the last-named measure answers well for dividing walks, so that walks and drains may go together, leaving sixty feet plots between, which may be again divided into beds and quarters. In marking out the ground, the purposes to which it is to be devoted must of course be taken into consideration.

Now it is of the first importance to determine to what extent it is likely fruit trees will be planted in the kitchen garden, because it is not desirable either to plant them where they will not thrive or to be perpetually shifting them about because you find them in the way. We are bound to say then, in the first place, that fruits and vegetables should, generally speaking, be grown in gardens or plots quite apart from each other. Now it is not at all needful for the amateur, who has but a small garden, to conclude he cannot grow a bit of everything in it because he can neither plant an orchard, nor devote broad tracts to asparagus, seakale, and the rest of the vegetable delicacies. The *most profitable way* is the best for him certainly, for he has not an inch of ground to waste; and the most profitable way, to begin with, is to keep the fruits and vegetables quite apart. It is common to see in small gardens a number of crooked and perverse apple trees dotted here and there in delightful irregularity, with crops of cabbage, peas, potatoes, etc., between and beneath them. Now that is the unprofitable way, and, therefore, the wrong way. The trees are constantly injured by the disturbance and destruction of their roots, and hence their ugliness, for they are perpetually making distorted growths, and losing the shapely limbs with which they began life in the nursery. On the other hand, the vegetables grown beneath them are robbed by the trees of their due share of rain and sunshine, and as regards the double tax upon the soil of the trees and vegetables, the end of it is that they starve each other. The tree that produces a peck of apples when it ought to produce two or three bushels, cannot be said to have the most judicious treatment. The question arises, do the peas, potatoes, etc., grown within its shadow and amongst its roots, pay for the defect of the fruit crop. Let everyone so circumstanced answer the question in the face of experience; it will be found that the attempt to get both fruit and vegetables out of the self-same plot of ground is a mistake, because it is an unprofitable mode of managing things.

It may be said that if we are careful and considerate, the trees need not suffer so much as to injure their health, or seriously lessen their productiveness. If we could always be sure that garden work would be done in a careful and considerate manner, there might be a plausible defence set up for the violation of principle we have now before us. But we never can insure the quality of garden work from first to last. Men who know better, will actually go grubbing amongst the roots of fruit trees, and labour hard to cut great roots away, because they interfere with the planting of rhubarb, or cabbages, or something of that sort. When work is done on a wrong principle, we cannot expect from an unthinking workman what a workman of some quality refuses us, that is the careful and exceptional mode of procedure needful to prevent a breakdown in a case where first principles have been violated. Thus we come back to the proposition, that fruits and vegetables should be kept apart, generally speaking.

In the smallest garden the separation is easily effected. Where there's a will there's a way, and every separate case must be considered and disposed of on its merits.

Suppose for the sake of a hypothetical solution of the difficulty, that we put all the fruits at one end, and all the vegetables at the other, and make it a law as severe as that of the Medes and Persians that neither shall invade the other's department. That we will say is solution No. 1. In working it out, we shall plant the trees in rows at sufficient distance apart, with rows of black currants and raspberries in between, for these fruits thrive in partial shade. The boundary lines of the fruit plot we shall plant with red and white currants and gooseberries, for these require more air and light than black currants and raspberries. This ground is not to be dug, for digging is a destructive practice where fruits of any kind are growing. If it be said we have not provided for the strawberries, the answer is that they travel about, and require a new plot every three years at least, and an open spot among the vegetables will suit them admirably. The wise way is to plant a row or two of strong runners every year, and every year destroy a row or two of the oldest.

But there are several ways of saving the fruit-trees. Instead of planting them all at one end, we may plant them all round the boundary. How about the apples that hang over the road? Think of that in time. If they are likely to be safe, plant the trees near the roadway to hang over and beautify it, and also to utilize the sunshine there which you obtain for nothing, for it is of sunshine chiefly that fruits are made. But on the inner side of the supposed belt of fruit-trees, you must have some protection to prevent the happy peasant who may chance to dig the ground from going too near the currant and gooseberry trees, which we will suppose form the inner boundary next the vegetable plot. Now a safe and sure, and easy and convenient, way of disposing of this difficulty is to construct a walk And the end of it will be a combined vegetable and fruit garden, with none of the absurdity of trees everywhere in the way, and always exposed to insult and injury. This is solution No. 2.

It is now time to offer a third proposition. Employ as

many fruits as possible for ornamental purposes, and thus utilize for the good of the household the sunshine of the lawn, the croquet ground, the entrance court, and the shrubbery. We are now upon delicate ground, and gentility might stop the way. It must be repeated, that every separate case must be considered on its merits. Let us, therefore, go on, and leave it to the reader to judge if our proposals are in any way applicable to any particular case.

It must be understood at starting, that, while some kinds of fruit are decidedly ornamental, others are as decidedly not so. All the most valuable household fruits, apples, pears, cherries, and plums, are decidedly ornamental, and adapted to embellish the lawn and shrubbery, and give shade to the summer-house and the croquet ground. There are several kinds not usually regarded as proper to the fruit garden, that would be both useful and ornamental, as for example the Siberian crab, which is one of the most beautiful of trees, and its pretty fruit makes a good preserve. All the varieties of nuts are handsome, and make nice lovers' walks. For particular positions, the Purple-leaved Filbert is well adapted, the leafage being of a rich bronzy green colour, and the nuts of excellent quality. Those who wish for ornamental trees that will contribute to the comfort of the household, may easily find them, and we are quite sure no one will dispute the proposition that decorative horticulture might derive considerable aid from the trees and shrubs that belong technically to the fruit-garden.

As a rule, bush fruits are not ornamental. The raspberry, black currant, and gooseberry are the most tolerable in respect of appearance, and may be allowed to come within view of the walks in the remoter parts of the pleasure garden. The black currant makes a good dividing fence, and as it need not be pruned at all, soon gets up and becomes a dense leafy screen, and as it comes into leaf early, and sheds its leaves late, it is, for practical purposes, almost an evergreen. The red and white currants must have an open sunny spot, and it is worthy of observation that they endure punishment at the root better than any other trees in the world, and so they may be taken into a compromise of another sort, and be planted on the boundaries of open plots in the kitchen-garden.

We seem to have travelled a long journey without walks. They are generally made first instead of last. We have not the slightest objection to the formation of the walks in the first instance, for until we have them, we cannot properly speak of the ground as a garden, but the boundaries and the drains are really of more importance; you may actually wait years before making proper walks, and suffer but little inconvenience, but defence, shelter, and removal of surplus water are essential to production; given these requisites, and the cultivation may go on prosperously. But when walks are made, they should be well-made. Mere tracks on which two or three inches of coal ashes are laid will serve for dividing lines, but the main walks should have a good depth of hard stuff for a foundation, and a good body of gravel or shell, or whatever is the best material the district affords, for a top crust, and they should be wide enough for the traffic, and slightly convex on the surface. It is of the utmost importance that all kinds of ground work should be well done, and nothing contributes in a more decisive way to the enjoyment as well as the usefulness of a garden as well-made walks and neat edgings. A kitchen garden of any size should at some convenient point afford access for carts with a good yard for pitching, and sufficient shed room where all small matters can be kept tidily and safe from rats and mice. The seed-room is a suitable place for a few garden books, a boxful of tallies, and convenience for writing labels and casting up accounts, and such other matters of clerkship as properly pertain to the work of the garden. As this book will be wholly written in our seed room, we can speak experimentally of the value of such a place, removed from the household into the midst of all the paraphernalia of practical gardening.

For the finishing of walks we must encounter the difficult subject of edgings. One way out of the difficulty is to do without edgings. The old and well-tried edging of box is of course as good as ever. Some people lean to strawberries, others to chives, and a few to parsley. If we were to eke out this paragraph, we should be in danger of heart break, and therefore we shall make three remarks in haste and close up. Nine tenths of all the tiles made for edgings answer admirably, until heavy rain is followed by hard frost, and then they split into fragments and have to be swept up as rubbish. Our triangular tile made by Mr. Looker of Kingston-on-Thames, is perfect, but it is inelegant and rather costly. When well laid, this tile is immoveable and imperishable. There cannot be a doubt that in a majority of cases a plank on edge fixed to

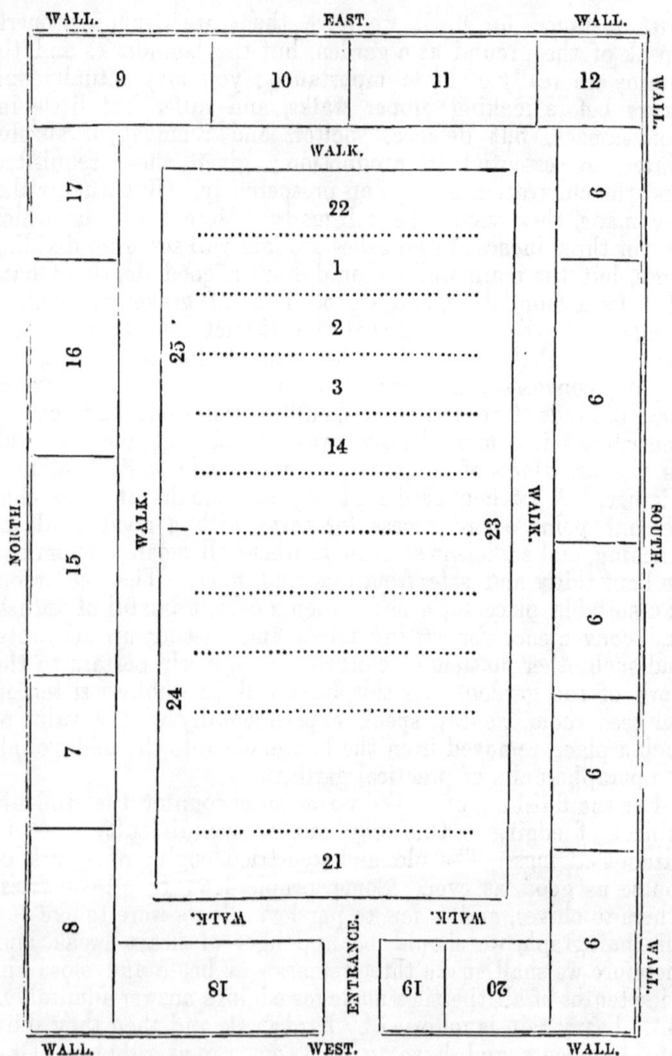

PLAN FOR A KITCHIN-GARDEN.

Length 160 feet; width 110 feet.

posts driven down at distances of eight feet or so, is the best possible edging for a kitchen garden. The paltry lath sort of stuff we sometimes see is not to be considered plank on edge. We want planks one inch thick, and four to nine inches broad, and they should not be sunk into the ground at all, but the border should be made up to them. The top edge may be rounded, and that is all the fine art possible, unless it is determined to pitch or paint them. Finally a substantial stone moulding is the proper thing, and happy, in one sense at least, are those who can afford it.

It is necessary now to illustrate the foregoing remarks with a few examples. It must be remembered that a small garden well managed is much to be preferred to a large garden kept in a discreditable state. In regard to mere production, the first will beat the second both in quantity and quality, and indeed it is surprising what a small plot of well cultivated land will produce. The subjoined plan represents a plot comprising about $\frac{7}{10}$ths of an acre; only one entrance and one walk round are provided. If necessary, a walk can be carried through the centre from west to east, and another across the centre from north to south, to divide the whole into four equal parts; the border next the wall all round is ten feet wide, the walk five feet, the central plot eighty feet from north to south. On the border 4, 5, 6, 7, 8, 9, etc., may be planted to skirt the wall, bush and pyramid apple, pear, and plum trees, and again on the central plot next the walk all round may be planted similar trees, with an occasional run of black and red currants, gooseberries, and raspberries between. Standard trees are not admissible, and there must be no trees at all in the interior of the central plot, for we want all the air and light obtainable there for the production of first class vegetables.

Our arrangement of the ground will possibly not suit anybody, but we shall nevertheless proceed to plant and crop this garden. The strip marked 1 is to be devoted to raspberries; 2, red and white currants; 3, gooseberries; the border 4, late raspberries; the border 5, black currants; the border 6, late strawberries; the border 7, early strawberries; the border 8, successional strawberries. The wall *looking* south, that is to say the wall on the north side of the garden, to be covered with peaches, nectarines, and apricots; the wall looking north, with plums and Morello cherries; the wall looking east, with pears; the wall looking west, with early cherries and figs.

We now provide for a few vegetables. On the border 9 is a good place for early rhubarb ; 10 will suit for kale, 11 for globe artichokes ; 12, 13, and 26, summer saladings ; 14, asparagus ; 15, early peas ; 16, early lettuces ; 17, spring seed-beds ; 18, second crop of peas ; 19, early horn carrots ; 20, early kidney beans ; 21, sweet herbs that are often required, and parsley ; 22, corresponding border of herbs, but comprising sorts not often required, and such as are to be cut for drying ; 23, autumn seed-beds ; 24, kidney beans ; 25, successional lettuce.

There still remains a space between 21 and 14 for peas, potatoes, cauliflowers, and other successional crops, for which thus far, we have only partially provided. But we may stop at this point, and it may be well to remark that as we mentioned potatoes, we should consider the main crop for winter supply quite out of place in this garden. A few first earlies of the finest quality may be grown, but the substantial family supply should be derived from another piece of ground without, or from the nearest market ; this garden is too small for potato growing, if a considerable variety of produce of fine quality is to be derived from it.

The fruit and vegetable garden represented in the accompanying plan has been designed for the production of a supply of the choicest as well as of the commoner kinds of fruits and vegetables sufficient for a moderate-size household. There is nothing fanciful about it, for a complicated design was not desired, but it is so admirably adapted for the purpose, and so complete in all its details, that a brief description of it, with the aid of the plan, will be appropriate in this place.

The garden is formed on an estate of about twelve acres, within thirty miles of London, and, as the space could not well be spared for an orchard, it was determined to make the kitchen garden large enough to accommodate a fair proportion of all the fruit trees usually planted in gardens. Against the walls we planted apricots, peaches, nectarines, pears, cherries, figs, and plums, and by the side of the walks pyramidal trees of all the fruits mentioned above, with the exception of the apricots, figs, peaches, and nectarines. The supply of fruit is consequently in favourable seasons most abundant for at least eight months out of every twelve, and there is no lack of vegetables throughout the year.

WEST.

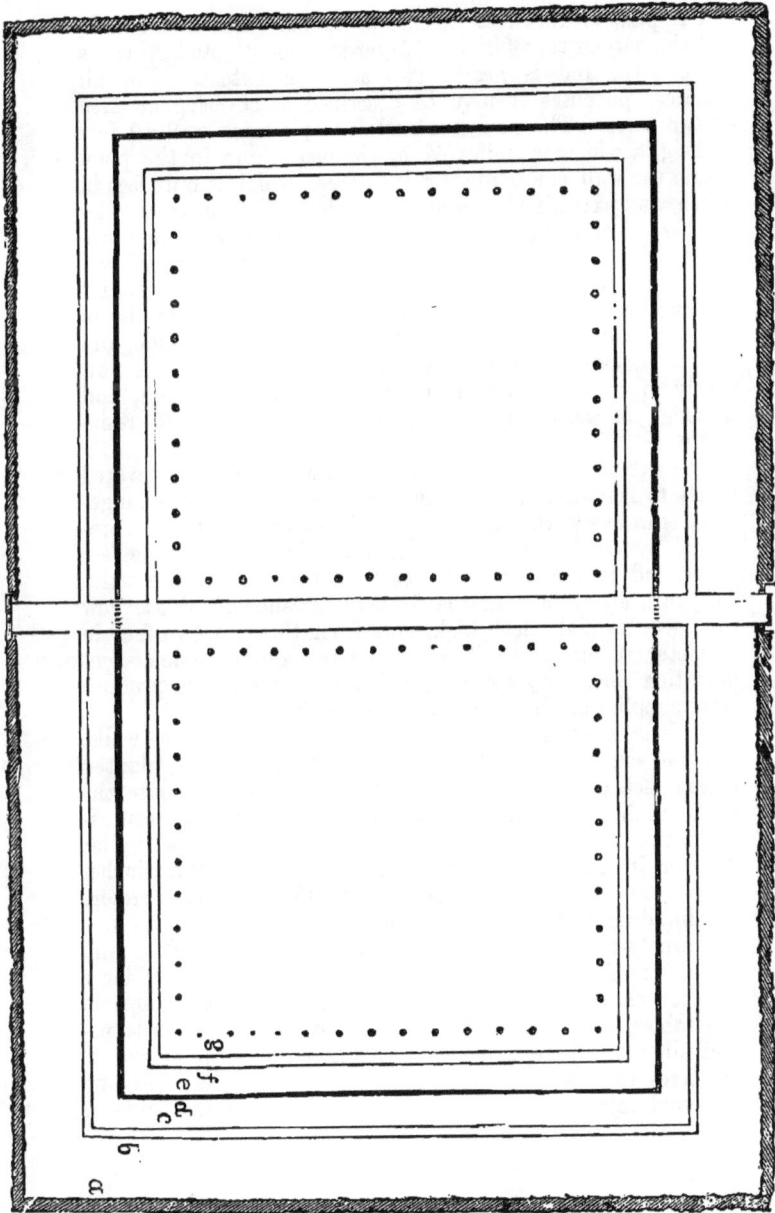

NORTH.

EAST.

a Boder. *b* Walk. *c* Border. *d* Fruit-wall. *e* Border. *f* Walk. *g* Pyramid or Espalier Trees.

MODEL FRUIT AND VEGETABLE GARDEN. (Scale, 2) yards to 1 inch).

The plan is drawn to a scale of twenty yards to one inch, and the garden therefore is 116 yards in length, and 80 yards in breadth, and is nearly two acres in extent. For all practical purposes it may be described as covering an area of two acres. The garden is enclosed by a brick wall 10 feet in height, which is indicated by the black lines in the plan. Inside the wall is a border for fruit trees, which is nine feet in width, and extends all round the garden. Within the border is a three-feet gravel walk, and the central area is divided into two spacious quarters by a pathway nine feet wide, to allow a cart to pass through the garden. Outside the wall is a border all round of the same width as that inside, then a walk also of the same width, and a strip or border eighteen feet wide, and this is enclosed with a good quick-set hedge, which is now nearly four feet high and about thirty inches through, and a hedge of this kind is found quite sufficient to resist cattle.

The two central quarters are, as shewn in the plan, devoted partly to fruit-trees and partly to vegetables, and the arrangement is in every way satisfactory. The trees, which are represented by the dots alongside the walks, are planted nine feet apart, and four and a half feet from the edge of the walk. They are all trained in the form of pyramids, and are now from five to eight feet high, and from three to five feet in diameter at the base. The two quarters afford ample accommodation for ninety-six trees, which are sufficient to produce large supplies of the several kinds of fruits.

Fruit-trees are of course planted on both sides of the walls. The two south aspects afford room for thirty-six trees, planted fifteen feet apart; the two north aspects accommodate the same number, planted at the same distance; the two west aspects, twenty-two trees; and the two east aspects a similar number, in each case the trees being fifteen feet three inches apart. The number of trees against the walls is therefore one hundred and sixteen; and of pyramids in the open quarters ninety-nine; making in all a total of two hundred and fifteen trees; and notwithstanding the comparatively large number, they do not materially interfere with the crops of vegetables, the bush fruits, and the strawberries. A three-feet alley is left next the wall, to enable those who attend to the trees to pass along without treading upon the crops, and to avoid injuring the roots. The other part of the border is devoted to early crops and such things as do not root deeply. The central quarters are devoted to the more important main crops, and the strips outside are set apart for the coarser vegetables, such as potatoes, cabbages, turnips, and a portion of the crops of winter greens and broccolis.

The selections of the various kinds of fruits are unusually good; for whilst due regard has been paid to securing of each fruit a supply extending over as long a period as possible, none but sorts of first-class quality have been planted. The two south aspects are divided into four parts by the two entrances to the garden, and the thirty-six trees with which they are planted are as follows:—twenty peaches, eight nectarines, three early cherries, three early plums, and two figs; the latter are planted one at each corner, on the south aspect at the north side of the garden. The varieties of the several fruits are:—

1 Peach, Early Grosse Mignonne.
1 ,, Early York.
2 ,, Grosse Mignonne.
4 ,, Royal George.
3 ,, Noblesse.
3 ,, Bellegarde.
2 ,, Barrington.
2 ,, Walburton Admirable.
1 ,, Gregory's Late.
1 ,, Desse Tardive.
2 Nectarine, Hardwicke.
1 Nectarine, Hunt's Tawny.
1 ,, Balgowan.
2 ,, Elruge.
2 ,, Violette Hâtive.
1 Cherry, Belle d'Orléans.
1 ,, Black Tartarian.
1 ,, Frogmore Early Bigarreau.
1 Plum, July Green Gage.
1 ,, De Montfort.
1 ,, PerdrigonVioletHâtif
2 Fig, Brown Turkey.

One of the east and one of the west aspects are planted with pear-trees, eleven to each. The varieties on the west aspect are:—

1 Pear, Beurré de l'Assomption.
2 ,, Jargonelle.
1 ,, Gansel's Bergamot.
1 ,, Beurré Hardy.
1 Pear Beurré Superfin.
1 ,, Comte de Lamy.
2 ,, Beurré Bosc.
2 ,, Beurré Diel.

The east aspect is devoted to later kinds as follows :—

1 Pear, Duchesse d'Angoulême	2 Pear, Beurré de Rance.
1 „ Catillac (stewing).	2 „ Glou Morceau.
1 „ Beurré de Jonghe.	1 „ Josephine de Malines.
1 „ Uvedale's St. Germains	2 „ Easter Beurré.

The second west aspect is devoted to apricots, cherries, and plums :—

1 Apricot, Hemskirk.	2 Cherry, May Duke.
1 „ Large Early.	1 „ Late Bigarreau.
1 Cherry, Black Tartarian.	1 „ Late Duke.
1 „ Governor Wood.	1 Plum, Purple Gage.
1 „ Frogmore Early Bigarreau.	1 „ Coe's Golden Drop.

The second east aspect is devoted chiefly to apricots with a few plums. The varieties are as under :—

1 Apricot, Large Early.	2 Apricot, Royal.
4 „ Moorpark.	1 Plum, Transparent Gage. D.
1 „ Pine-apple.	1 „ Reine Claude de Bavay, D.
2 „ Peach.	

Against the two north aspects are planted twenty-eight plums and eight cherries. The varieties of the respective fruits comprise the following :—

2 Plum, De Montfort, D.	2 Plum, Angelina Burdett, D.
2 „ Perdrigon Violet Hâtif, D.	2 „ Coe's Golden Drop, D.
1 „ Denniston's Superb, D.	1 „ Victoria, K.
4 „ Green Gage, D.	2 „ Late Green Gage, D.
1 „ Huling's Superb, D.	1 „ Reine Claude de Bavay, D.
2 „ Purple Gage, D.	2 „ Ickworth Imperatrice, D.
1 „ Prince Englebert, K. D.	5 Cherry, Morello, K.
2 „ Jefferson's, D.	2 „ Black Tartarian, D
3 „ Kirke's, D.	1 „ Late Duke. D.

The Pyramidal trees comprise forty-three apples, thirty-three pears, fourteen plums, and six cherries; the varieties being as follows:—

1 Apple, Devonshire Quarrenden, D.
1 ,, Red Astrachan, D.
1 ,, Kerry Pippin, D.
1 ,, Adams' Pearmian, D.
3 ,, Cox's Orange Pippin D.
3 ,, Fearn's Pippin, D.
2 ,, Ribston Pippin, D.
4 ,, Blenheim Orange, D. K.
2 ,, Sykehouse Russet, D.
2 ,, Cockle Pippin, D.
3 ,, Court Pendu Plat, D.
1 ,, Braddick's Nonpareil, D.
1 ,, Sam Young, D.
2 ,, Winter Pearmain, D.
2 ,, Keswick Codlin, K.
1 ,, Lord Suffield.
1 ,, Forge, K.
2 ,, Hawthornden, K.
1 ,, Small's Admirable.
2 ,, London Pippin, K.
1 ,, Rymer, K.
2 ,, Alfriston, K.
3 ,, Wellington, K.
2 ,, Norfolk Beefing, K.
1 ,, Royal Russet, K.
1 Pear, Doyenné d'Eté.
1 ,, Beurré Giffard.
2 ,, Beurré de l'Assomption.
2 ,, Williams's Bon Chrétien.
1 ,, Jargonelle.
1 Pear, Louise Bonne of Jersey.
1 ,, Naquette.
2 ,, Gansel's Bergamot.
1 ,, Beurré Superfin.
2 ,, Beurré d'Amanlis.
1 ,, Comte de Lamy.
1 ,, Beurré Bachelier.
2 ,, Duchesse d'Angoulême
2 ,, Beurré de Jonghe.
2 ,, Passe Colmar.
3 ,, Beurré Rance.
1 ,, Beurré Six.
1 ,, Doyenné de Comice.
2 ,, Easter Beurré.
2 ,, Josephine de Malines.
2 ,, Van de Weyer Bates.
1 Plum, July Green Gage, D.
1 ,, Early Rivers, K.
1 ,, Early Orleans, K.
1 ,, Oullin's Golden, D.
2 ,, Green Gage, D.
1 ,, Gisborne's, K.
2 ,, Prince Englebert, K.D.
1 ,, White Magnum Bonum, K.
1 ,, Red Magnum Bonum, K.
2 ,, Victoria, K.
1 ,, Woolston Black, D.
1 Cherry, Belle d'Orléans, D.
1 ,, Early Red Bigarreau.
2 ,, Kentish, K.
2 ,, Belle Magnifique, K.

The varieties in all the above lists are arranged in the order of attaining maturity.

CHAPTER II.

THE AMATEUR IN THE KITCHEN GARDEN.

Earth's increase, and foison plenty,
Barns and garners never empty;
Vines, with clust'ring branches growing;
Plants with goodly burden bowing;
Spring come to you, at the farthest,
In the very end of harvest,
Scarcity, and want, shall shun you;
Ceres' blessing so is on you.

The Tempest, IV., 1.

CONTACT with the brown earth cures all diseases, mitigates all troubles and anxieties, smooths the wrinkles that city cares have engraved on the face; and restores, even in the later days of a man's life, some touches of the joy that made gold and honey and music, and ever-changing aspirations and fancies of the simplest facts, and, indeed, of all the facts of human existence in the happy days of youth. Do you remember the doll's garden the girls made next to yours, and took up your sprouting mustard seed to make a hedge all round it to keep the dog out? Do you remember wondering which side up to place the scarlet runner seed, and the frantic delight with which you saw green shoots appear on the willow sticks you stole from the gardener's shed, and employed to make a terrific palisade to your own garden when there were three clumps of crocuses in flower, and some wall-flowers almost out, and a rose tree nearly dead through being five times transplanted, and the girls broke in again and called you greedy for having all the tops of the pine-apples swathed in wool and planted in front of the cottage you had made out of a cigar box? You *do* remember these things? Of course you do; you will never forget them; but this garden you are now thinking about will bring the flower of youth to beautify your grave experiences, and *health,* the foundation of happiness, will come as a distillation from the earth and its leafy garniture. The fable of Antæus is an epitome of the life of man, and illustrates, in its own heroic way, the spiritual and material tonic that may be derived from farming and gardening.

SOILS.—In determining what to grow and how to manage, you will have to face this difficulty—that no garden, however favourable in a general way the soil and climate and surroundings may be, is equally adapted for all the kinds of vegetables and fruits you will wish to derive from it. The consequence is that you will have to effect compromises and make shifts, and in the end, perhaps, make yourself content with inferior products of some kinds, while, let us hope, you will have plenty of superior products of other kinds to compensate abundantly. Moreover, it matters not how well versed you may be in geology and chemistry and the requirements of plants, you will have to learn much on the spot, and you will have to respect the *genius loci*, and be in no haste to regard as nonsense the "wise saws" of your neighbours who may tell you that yours is a wonderful land for parsley, but won't do for asparagus; or that it suits cauliflowers beyond all expectation, but will not produce potatoes fit to eat. A deep sandy loam will suit almost every crop you can think of as proper for a kitchen garden, and deep retentive clay may be made one of the best soils in the world by means of hard work and judicious manuring and cropping. If you are located on clay, you ought to embrace every opportunity of carting in at a cheap rate lime-rubbish and sandy road drift. If on peat, lime-rubbish and clay will be valuable materials, and bone the best of manures. If on chalk or gravel, clay, turf, pond-mud, and fat manure will be of immense advantage. There is scarcely a soil to be found that does not need the occasional help of good stable manure, but it certainly does tend to make light soils lighter, so that it is possible in some cases its employment may be less advantageous than others.

But it is nevertheless a golden rule that to use manure in excess is scarcely possible, and the market gardens in the neighbourhood of London may always be pointed to in illustration of the rule. It is scarcely an exaggeration to say that for every load of vegetables taken off the ground a load of good stable manure is put on. The waggon that goes to market with a load of cabbages calls on the way home at some brewery or omnibus yard for a load of manure, and thus the supply is sustained at little cost, and the fertility of the land is kept at a high pitch.

In the management of the soil scientific knowledge is of some value. For example, chemistry tells us that the potato contains a considerable proportion of potash, salts, and phosphates. Geology tells us that sandy soils, which consist largely of silica, are often deficient of those minerals, while granitic soils are usually rich in potash, and limestone soils are rich in phosphates. What shall we do, then, to prepare our sand for the production of potatoes? Good stable manure will help it immensely, and, wanting that, phospho-guano may answer admirably, and, wanting that, muriate of potash and superphosphate may suffice. The most useful of what are called "artificial manures" are phospho-guano, superphosphate of lime, bone-dust, kainit (a cheap, rough kind of potash); muriate of potash, a better and apparently more expensive manure, that in many instances would prove cheaper than kainit; nitrate of soda, and common salt.

It is worthy of remark that deep fertile soils in first-rate condition are not in the least degree benefited by "artificials," whereas on thin poor soils that have been badly managed they frequently—indeed commonly—produce results that may be described as more than satisfactory and that actually approach the wonderful. Everything depends on what is done and how it is done, but this may be averred with safety, that it will always pay well to manure the land liberally and keep it in the highest possible condition of productiveness. To be afraid to bury money in the soil is to forfeit your right to take money out. The deep strong clays and loams need the help of good stable manure, but artificials will be of little service to them, except to thin the crop and so ensure more room for the plants that survive. It is a fact to be borne in mind that artificial manures, even if of so mild a nature as ivory dust and superphosphate, kill a considerable proportion of seed; so that it is advisable to put these fertilizers out of the immediate reach of the young plants, for it is better to thin them ourselves than have them thinned by a process of poisoning. The mode of application we find answer best is to have the artificials powdered on the soil in the trench as the digging proceeds, as they are then covered with soil, and the plants do not reach them until they are strong enough to derive benefit from high living.

Earth-work is generally well understood by the class likely to be employed in the rougher kinds of garden labour. We shall suppose the reader to regard the handling of the spade as *infra dig.*, and this will save expenditure of space in describing the noble art of turning the turf topsy-turvy. It will soon be discovered by the observant amateur that human nature has a greater liking for scratching than for digging, and hence to ensure for a piece of ground what a gardener would call a "good doing" is not an easy matter. But there is great virtue in stirring, notwithstanding Hood's assertion that it is the action of a spoon. It is rather the exception than the rule for the kitchen garden to be as deeply stirred and knocked about as it ought to be. Ordinary flat digging answers for most crops, but a certain extent of ground ought every year to be trenched, so that in the course of five or six years or so, all the plots devoted to rotation cropping may be turned over to the depth of two spits. If the crop to be put on will allow of it, a good body of manure should be put in the trench, between the two spits, as the work proceeds, but it may be advisable to put the manure at the bottom of the trench below both spits, or to trench without manure and finish by pricking in a coat of manure on the top. If gigantic parsnips, carrots, and salsify are wanted, put the manure at the bottom; if fine peas, beans, cauliflowers, broccolis, and cabbages are your desire, put the manure between the two spits; if the ground is intended for a seed bed, prick the manure into the top crust about half a spit deep. It is a common experience of those who enter into possession of old gardens to find the growth of everything stunted and the soil apparently worn out. Nine times in ten, or even ninety-nine times in a hundred, when this is the case, the land may be rendered capable of almost anything by the simple process of trenching and putting a good body of fat manure between the two spits. In all probability the kind of tillage that has been followed has been founded on scratching instead of digging, and hence the second spit, perhaps the whole body, of soil from a depth of six inches downward is in the state of maiden earth, never touched by plough or spade, with all the elements of fertility still locked up in it as in the times far back when the soil was made by the deposition of grain upon grain at the bottom of the sea. As the value of trenching depends on the quality of the subsoil, it follows of course that where the subsoil consists of unkind stuff it may not be advisable to bring it to the surface. In very many such cases bastard trenching, in which the second or under spit is broken, but is not thrown up, improves the ground considerably, and it may happen that a subsoil of a most unpromising appearance and texture proves of the greatest value when mixed with the surface soil, and exposed for a time to the atmosphere. A mixture of soils generally results in the production of a staple more fertile than either were separately; but caution must of course be exercised, whenever the subsoil is not obviously suitable. In the case of a deep yellow loam or nut-brown clay showing a tendency to mellow into loam, there can be no question for doubt, and the spirited cultivator will ensure that some of the second spit shall see the daylight.

Garden Tools and Implements may be multiplied *ad infinitum* by anyone who happens to be so unfortunate as to have a taste for such things. Our garden museum contains examples of ingenious contrivances for accomplishing all possible, and some impossible, garden operations, from the spudding out of a dock or daisy to the gathering of a single leaf from the topmost branch of the tallest tree. We have carefully observed the fate of the many strange inventions it is our good or ill luck to make acquaintance with from time to time, and we find that as a rule they go to the museum, and are clean forgotten, while the work of the garden goes on satisfactorily with the aid of the old-fashioned and vulgar implements. You will probably want a couple of spades, a couple of steel digging forks, three-tined and four-tined; a few commonplace rakes and hoes, a line and reel, long-handled and short-handled clipping shears; a hedge-slasher, a pickaxe, a heavy bill, a straight edge and plumb-line, a long and short ladder, and a few of the most commonplace carpenter's tools. The common Dutch hoe and the draw shave-hoe are indispensable, the latter being a most effectual weeding implement, its action being to cut a thin slice off the ground, which removes weeds by a close cut over their roots. As you go on you will discover what tools are wanted, and your handy man will be loud enough in his reminders. Our concern is chiefly to warn you against wasting your money in "gimcrack" things that are made for fid-fad purposes, or that your workmen will never take to, though their ingenuity and usefulness may be obvious. We have lately seen an experiment in wheelbarrows illustrative of the last remark. A gentleman who makes his hands dusty by working in the garden bought a grand iron wheelbarrow. It held twice as much as a common wooden wheelbarrow, and required only half as much strength to propel it, so cleverly was it pivoted on the axle and adjusted to the hands. But his man would never use it; the old wooden barrow was always in use, while the economizer of strength and time became ingloriously rusty, and was at last found lying heels upwards in the rubbish yard, battered, full of holes, and in all respects in the same state of dilapidation as the kettle that is taken from a cinder heap to be tied to a dog's tail.

A few specially useful implements will be figured further on; but this appears the proper place for a suggestion on the artistic arrangement of garden tools, where they happen to be sufficiently numerous to make a picture.

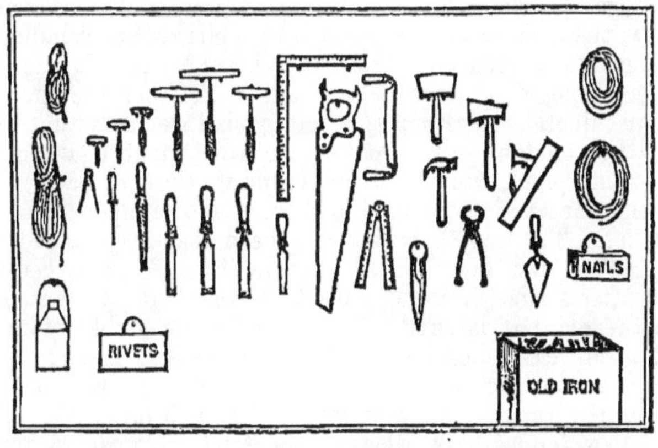

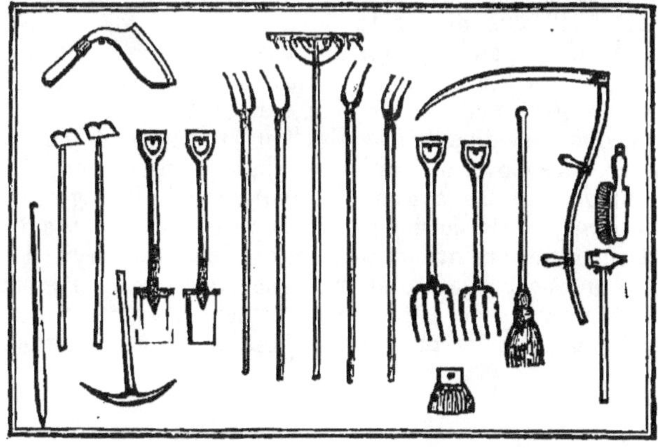

THE ORDER OF CROPPING, or the "Rotation" of crops, is of much less importance in gardening than in farming. If a starving system of cultivation be followed, the crops must be moved about, and even then they are not likely to be worth harvesting. But in proportion as the ground is at every opportunity well dug and liberally manured, the necessity for observing a distinct order of cropping becomes less and less necessary. The principle of rotation is simple enough. We grow on a piece deep-rooted and somewhat exhaustive crops, such as parsnips, potatoes, carrots, and salsify. For these we will suppose the ground was trenched two spits deep, and had a winter's frost upon it before the crops were sown. We may be content to flat dig next year one spit deep, putting in a dressing of manure and laying out the land for seed beds and saladings. Next year it may serve for peas, cauliflowers, and celery; the next for kidney beans, beets, collards, and saladings; the next to be trenched for another lot of roots. It was formerly supposed that while a plant took from the ground certain mineral constituents, it left behind elements that rendered the land unfit to produce the same plant again until some other plant, which could appropriate those objectionable elements or excreta as food, had been grown upon it as a refresher. The hypothesis has long been abandoned as ridiculous. The land does indeed become "tired" of a certain plant after a time, if we may use the term; but the reason is that the plant it is tired of, has taken all it could obtain of certain silicates, phosphates, and other mineral matters, and there is not enough of these elements of plant-growth left to sustain the same plant any longer. This brings us to the idea of a fallow. By allowing the land to "rest," a fresh supply of silicates, phosphates, etc., is obtained for it, for the air, and the dew, and the rain, and the sunshine are continually breaking down the mineral constituents, the very pebbles are slowly dissolved and the organic matter in the soil decays, and in due time this "clover-sick" or "turnip-tired" soil will again produce clover or turnips, or whatever else it may have been tired of in past seasons. Manuring and stirring obviate the necessity for fallowing; and the more heartily these renovating operations are carried on, the less necessary is it to observe any system of rotation. The potato is, in a greater degree than any other garden plant, benefited by being moved about from place to place, or, if possible, grown on ground that never produced potatoes before. But we know plots of land that have been cropped with potatoes without a break for thirty years, and produce as good crops as ever, having no more help than fair digging by a field labourer, whose children scrape up manure from the roads for it.

The modern mode of fallowing is a compromise full of instruction for the gardener. The farmer cannot afford to let the land rest, so he grows a "fallow crop," it may be of turnips, for which the ground is well prepared both by plough and manure cart. To grow good turnips the hoe must be plied briskly, and the practice clears away weeds. In due time the leaves of the turnips cover the ground, and kill whatever weeds have started since the final hoeing was done, and thus the land is cleaned. But the turnips are fed off by folding sheep upon them, and thus the surface is well trodden and manured, so that when ploughed again it is in fine condition for whatever purpose it is next to be devoted to. Another mode of fallowing consists in sowing a fast growing green crop, and, when it has attained considerable bulk, it is ploughed in. As a considerable portion of the constituents of a crop are derived from the atmosphere, this method of procedure enables us to incorporate with the soil the carbonic acid, the ammonia, we may even say the sunshine, the plant has obtained through the agency of its leaves for its sustenance. To dig in weeds when full grown, but before they run to seed, is of necessity an improving process, and it will often be found advantageous to grow spinach or any other quick green crop and dig it in as manure. This practice is especially useful in districts remote from towns where manures are costly and difficult to obtain. Whatever plant grows rapidly to a considerable bulk, and costs but little in the first instance, is the best for the purpose. Such manuring, however, cannot be continued for ever, for it adds nothing to the mineral constituents of the soil.

In the foregoing remarks stable manure is referred to as the most important fertilizer of its class. Such is the truth, and the statement needs no modification. But the cow-byre, the pig-sty, the poultry shed, and the sheepfold are capable of supplying useful manures, and the business of the cultivator is to get what he can and make the best of it. Organic *debris* of any and every kind may be regarded as a possible fertilizer, and not the least important is the waste of the garden itself, which should be dug in as soon as possible, instead of being left, as it usually is, to decompose in a heap and diffuse obnoxious and injurious odours through the neighbourhood. We should like to punish some of the folks who lay up near public roads great heaps of cabbage stumps and other such offensive rubbish to generate a poisonous effluvium and sicken every passer-by. All such refuse should be buried a foot or so deep in a trench at least once a week to prevent accumulation, and to give to the earth those sulphureous gases which poison the air when fermentation takes place above ground. Cabbage stumps should be systematically burnt, and the ashes used as manure.

It may happen that when hotbeds are made up there remains a considerable bulk of long stable manure, which orthodox practice requires to be laid up in a heap to rot before it is fit to be put on the ground. Now, you need not be fettered by orthodoxy. There is a certain stage in the decomposition of a large bulk of stable manure when it gives out an indescribably obnoxious odour. It should be clearly understood therefore that rank or, as it is called, "green" manure may be dug into the soil not only without injury, but with advantage, provided only that it is done judiciously. Let it be carried on to the ground on which cauliflowers, broccolis, and other brassicas are to be planted, and there cut trenches two feet deep, and put a foot depth of the rank stuff in every trench, and put a foot of soil on, and leave the remainder in a ridge on the south side, and plant. You will have grand cauliflowers, and, when they come off, the land will be in a fine condition for the next crop.

Seed Beds.—Whatever the extent of an amateur's operations, he should at least understand the making of a seed bed, and the sowing of seeds, and the management of pits and frames. The rule with gardeners is to waste seed and jeopardize the crop by sowing too thick. It is very difficult to cure them of this bad habit, although they have abundant opportunities of observing the ill effects of overcrowding. To sow thick enough for a crop is of course always necessary, but because of the tendency to injurious waste an admonition in favour of "thin seeding" should be always ready to be dinned into the dull ears of the man who loves his own ways too much, and is vexatiously slow to learn. Seed drills of several kinds are made for garden use, and are of great service.

Better than any seed drill, however, is the capacity to use hands and eyes in sowing seeds so that there shall be a good plant without waste or over-crowding, and it is only by practice this capacity can be acquired. In preparing ground for seeds and in cleaning the surface between rows of young plants in the seed bed, a scratcher of the kind here figured will be found extremely useful. It is obtained by bending the tines of a common manure drag or fork, and it is advisable to get a smith to prepare it, to ensure having the tines sufficiently and uniformly bent.

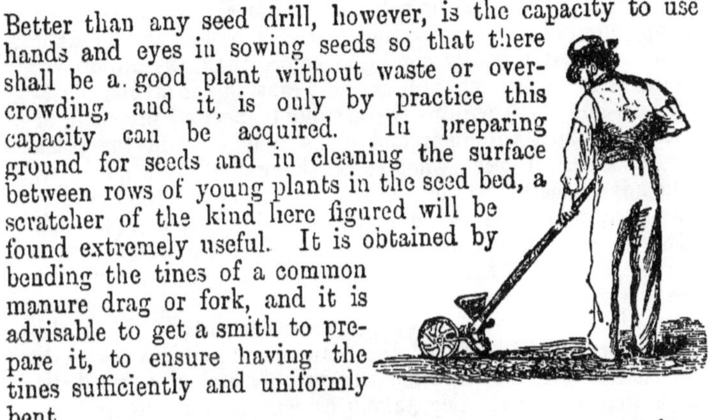

Seeds are sown in many ways. In any case we want for a seed bed a well-pulverized soil, dry and warm, and of necessity seed can be best sown during dry weather. The settled width

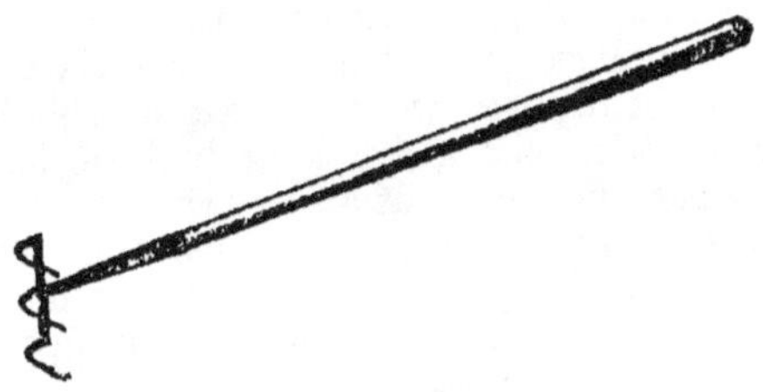

of a seed bed is four feet, because by leaning over one can reach the middle of it easily. But seeds may be sown in single rows across the ground, and that is a good practice in a large garden where the work is done somewhat roughly. To draw a drill we put down the line and scratch to it with the corner of the hoe, then sprinkle the seed and draw the earth over it by using the edge of the hoe. The depth of the drill is regulated by the size of the seed, and the books give a rule that every seed should be buried at its own depth, which is nonsense. The smallest kitchen garden seeds may be put in drills an inch deep, and they will come through as well as if covered with a mere dusting, and generally speaking make a better plant, because they will escape being eaten by birds and being roasted by sunshine, when just beginning to germinate.

As a matter of course, it will not pay to sow small seeds on lumpy ground; the surface must be well broken and brought to a somewhat powdery condition before the drills are drawn. With large seeds such as peas and beans this is of less consequence, but these require the ground to be well prepared, or many of them will miss and make ugly gaps in the rows. Broadcasting of seed is not to be thought of by a gardener. The advantage of drilling is too great to allow of such a hap-hazard system. When the plant is in drills, it can be thinned, cleaned, and watered with a minimum of labour, and it has a tidy appearance. A compromise between the machine and the inexperienced fingers may be effected by means of a wooden rake with teeth placed at a suitable distance apart. Draw the rake lengthways of the bed, then across, and put in a few seeds at each square; or draw lengthways only and sow two drills at a time from the alley, taking care to drop as few seeds as possible at a proper distance apart.

TO MAKE A HOTBED is easy enough, but to manage one to the greatest advantage requires some amount of skill and experience. It is almost useless to begin with a small quantity of stuff, unless the bed is required merely to start a few seeds or strike a few cuttings. For whatever, except the most trivial, purpose it may be required, we must have suitable frames and lights, or good brick pits and a large bulk of long manure that has not been fermented at all, or has only been once fermented in the heap made in the first removal from the stable. It should contain plenty of fibre, and therefore, if already short and somewhat rotted down, mix with it a good body of waste straw, hay, turf, or any such rough vegetable fibre. It must be moist enough, but not wet; if dry and chippy it must be sprinkled with water when turned with the fork to induce a steady fermentation throughout the whole of the mass. We will suppose we are going to make a bed for a three-light frame to grow melons or cucumbers. We begin with six to twelve one-horse loads of stable manure in which there is plenty of straw visible. As a rule eight loads will be required. This is carted on to the ground and turned into a long low heap, being sprinkled, if dry, layer by layer. In the course of a few days it will heat tremendously. It is now turned again, and if still rather dry and flaky is again sprinkled. In the course of a week it is likely to be in prime condition for making up the bed. The ground is, of course, marked out to suit the frames, and on the selected site the manure is spread and piled; but it should extend a full yard every way beyond the frames, and be well divided and broken by the fork in the process, and be again sprinkled if need be; but if you make it pasty wet your work will all go wrong. When spread and piled in a flat oblong mass, we put on the frames, treading on the manure as little as possible, and leave the affair for a day or two. Then we put into the frames the soil for the hillocks, and if the heat rises nicely and not fiercely, we put out the plants, and we regulate the ventilation and the watering, and, indeed, all the management, by the fermentation. If that rages vehemently, we must leave the lights tilted day and night until a sweet heat prevails; but if the heat rises slowly, we must shut up and be patient and hope for the best. It will soon be discovered, but it may as well be notified in advance, that whatever tends to compress the manure, such as treading on it, putting soil on it, and so forth, promotes the activity, and at the same time shortens the life of the fermentation. It is good practice to have a large body of stuff and let it settle down in its own way, with the least compression possible consistent with the work that must be done. We have grown as fine melons as were ever seen or tasted with the aid of grass-mowings and waste straw, fern, and other dry litter only, without a particle of stable manure. This will show the importance of mastering the hotbed business, for it is our cheapest mode of creating an artificial climate, and one moreover that answers admirably for such leafy plants as melons and cucumber, because of the great advantage to them of an atmosphere impregnated with ammoniacal vapours.

PITS AND FRAMES are of immense service for the preservation during the winter of cauliflower plants, endives, lettuces, and sweet herbs; for raising in spring saladings, new potatoes, and brassicas for planting out; for the growth by the aid of sun heat only of melons, cucumbers, tomatoes, capsicums, and aubergines in summer; for growing mushrooms and raising seeds of many kinds in the autumn. A frame ground is one of the most important adjuncts to the kitchen garden. We want much more than the climate will give us to make life bearable, and a bit of glass is a grand help towards a winter salad and an early summer cauliflower. There is nothing like good brick pits for the solid work, and well-made frames for moving about. Beware of having either too large for convenient use. The enormous lights occasionally met with are things to be avoided, for not only does it require the strength of a giant to handle them, but they must be more or less twisted in the process, and we have always found that unwieldy lights are soon worn out, while those of convenient size last any length of time if fairly taken care of. On this subject, however, a chapter will be given further on.

It is proper, perhaps, that we should say a word here about the many kinds of frames and protectors that have been patented of late years. It has been our misfortune to try them all, and we should repent the waste of time and money had we not gained experience, which enables us to advise our readers to consider twice before they embark once in any of these things. Well-made pits and frames are always tidy and weather-proof; the patent things that are founded on bricks and tiles are apt to be always out of joint, and it is sometimes impossible to give air or get anything from their insides, whether a lettuce or a handful of violets, without breaking more glass than the lettuce or violets are worth.

> "How various his employments, whom the world
> Calls idle ; and who justly, in return,
> Esteems that busy world an idler too !
> Friends, books, a garden, and perhaps his pen,
> Delightful industry enjoyed at home,
> And nature in her cultivated trim
> Dressed to his taste, inviting him abroad—
> Can he want occupation, who has these ?
> Will he be idle, who has much t' enjoy ?
> * * * * *
> Proud of his well-spread walls, he views his trees,
> That meet, no barren interval between,
> With pleasure more than even their fruits afford ;
> Which save himself who trains them, none can feel.
> These therefore are his own peculiar charge ;
> No meaner hand may discipline the shoots,
> None but his steel approach them."
>
> COWPER.

CHAPTER III.

PITS AND FRAMES.

AMONGST the numerous structures now to be met with in gardens, there are none possessing a greater degree of utility than pits and frames. They are of the utmost value for hardening off bedding plants in spring, for the cultivation of cucumbers, melons, primulas, cinerarias, and other soft-wooded plants required for the embellishment of the conservatory during the summer and autumn, and for preservative purposes during the winter.

In all constructive works in the garden the measure of a man of ordinary stature and strength should be taken into consideration, and especially is this necessary in the construction of pits and frames. If these structures are too wide, there will be some difficulty in giving the plants the attention they require, and, if the lights are too large and heavy, it will be impossible to move them about without unduly taxing the strength of those who have to handle them, or by having two men to do work which ought to be performed by one. The measure of a man's strength is in this case an important matter, and helps to show us that the ancients with their spans, cubits, and fathoms, were at least as wise as regards measurement as those who would introduce into general use the mètre, the millimètre, and the centimètre, which form part of a system of measurement based upon astronomical facts that very few can realize. In building pits we have to consider how far a man can reach, and what weight he can conveniently lift, and, when we have done this, we shall not have much difficulty in determining the size and construction of the pits.

The most convenient form of pit is the ordinary lean-to. It is of the most simple construction, comparatively inexpensive, and is well adapted for the cultivation of every class of plants that can be grown in a pit. The exterior walls may be formed with bricks, wood, or turf, but for neatness and durability there can be no doubt brick walls are the best. The pit represented in the diagram is five feet wide, outside measure, three feet high at the back, and one foot and a half high in front. This affords sufficient fall to carry off the rain quickly, and by this means prevents the plants being injured by drip, so long as the lights are in thorough repair. One peculiarity about the walls is their being of two thicknesses. The wall to

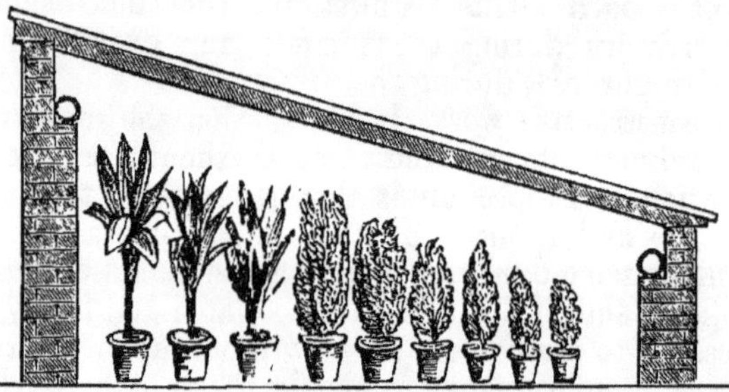

LEAN-TO HEATED PIT.

within twelve inches of the plate is nine inches in thickness, and the top part is four and a half inches in thickness. By this means a wall of great strength is built, some little saving of materials is effected, and a most effectual support is secured for the hot-water pipes, in case it should be considered needful to heat the pit at any time. One of the greatest advantages resulting from this mode of constru ction is the placing of the pipes where they, practically speaking, take up no space whatever. The wall-plate to which the rafters are fixed should be two inches in thickness and an inch or so wider than the wall, for the purpose of carrying off the water clear of the wall. In practice it is best to form the wall-plate by dividing a deal four inches by twelve into four pieces, two by six inches, less the reduction; each strip will thus be in working. The rafters to carry the lights should be three feet six inches apart from centre to centre, and be four inches in depth by three inches in width, and have a strip of wood an inch square fixed down the centre to form a rebate on each side to receive the lights. The rafters should be either let into the wall-plates or be fixed with a screw in a manner that will admit of their being readily removed whenever necessary. Especially needful is portability in the garden of the amateur, where alterations are as a rule constantly being made. The principal point is to make the joints to fit nicely, and to fasten rafters down with screws previously well greased to prevent their rusting.

The sashes must be five feet four inches in length, and three feet five inches in width, to fit a frame of the width above mentioned, with rafters three feet six inches apart. The wood-work should be two inches in thickness, and each light have three sash bars, and be glazed with glass nine and a half inches wide; and by allowing one inch for the outside framework, and a third of an inch for each of the sash-bars, it will be found that glass of the size recommended will fit without requiring to be cut, and all waste avoided. The length of the squares is not of so much importance, but those twelve inches in length will have the best appearance, as the length will be proportionate to the breadth.

We now come to the span-roof form. This is drawn on a smaller scale, as the lights are in two, and a greater width of frame can be allowed without the lights being too heavy to move about. This frame is seven feet wide, one foot high at the sides, and two and a half feet high in the middle. The lights are three feet nine inches in length, and have the handles fixed at the bottom instead of the top, but in other respects

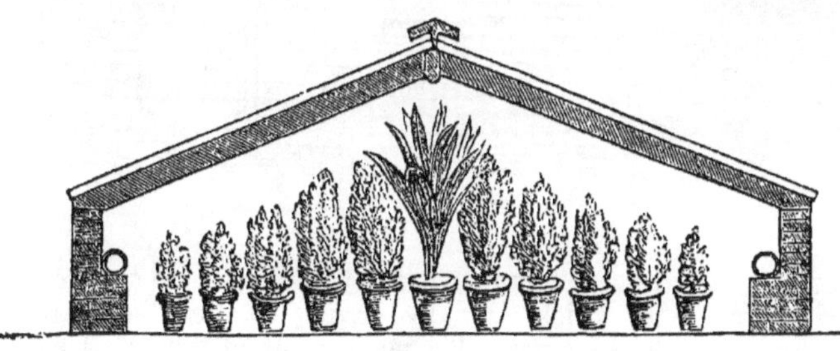

SPAN-ROOFED HEATED PIT.

they are made in precisely the same manner as those for the lean-to. There is a difficulty in handling the lights of a span-roof which does not occur with those of the lean-to. They cannot be drawn out of the way when watering, but must either be held up with the hand, or a wooden support, or be lifted bodily away. The centre-piece against which the lights abut is simply a strip of board six inches in depth and two inches in thickness. For frames of four or five lights no support will be required for the ridge-board, but for frames of greater length it will be necessary to have uprights about ten feet apart, and these should, as far as practicable, be placed immediately under the joints.

We now come to the consideration of the primitive turf-pit, the cheapest and not the least valuable of all garden structures. This will be found of considerable value for hardening bedders, and for wintering plants that require only moderate protection. They should be put out of sight, as they are by no means attractive at their best, and, when in a dilapidated state, they are positively unsightly; hence the necessity for keeping them in the background. When turf pits are made for utilizing old lights, the size of the latter must be taken into consideration, and the dimensions of the pit regulated accordingly. In any other case the dimensions should be the same as recommended for the lean-to brick pit, or rather smaller. It will perhaps be better to have the pit four feet six inches in width instead of five feet, and the lights

TURF PIT, NOT HEATED.

three feet in width. The walls will not, of course, be so strong as those made of brick, and, by having smaller lights, the strain will not be so great. To make a pit of turf that will not tumble down as soon as it is finished, mark out a space, and at each corner drive into the ground a post about six inches square, and in the line of the walls at back and front drive posts three feet apart, one at each end intermediate between the two corner posts. These posts should be three by six inches, and fixed with the broadest part across the wall.

The wall-plate should be nine inches in width, and two inches thick, and be fixed to the uprights by means of long screws. The turfs must be cut twelve inches long, nine inches wide, and three inches thick, and in building the wall they must be packed as firmly as possible. The rafters, which must be similar to those of the brick pit, should be fixed to the plate immediately over the uprights.

The lean-to and span-roof brick pits of dimensions given above have been designed expressly for dwarf growing plants in pots; but, if they will be required for cucumbers or melons during the summer, they must be twelve inches deeper at the back and front. The increased height may be obtained by sinking the floor of the pit twelve inches below the ground level, and this course can be strongly recommended excepting when the soil is naturally cold and wet. There will be no saving in brickwork, because the wall must be of precisely the same height, and the gain of having the floor below the level consists in the greater facility with which the frost can be kept out in the winter, and in the neater appearance of the pits.

Most useful and comparatively cheap span-roof pits may be made with wooden sides instead of brick walls. Deals of good quality and nine by three inches are most suitable for the formation of the walls, as they are strong, do not warp, and are most effectual in keeping out the cold. Boards one inch thick are most generally employed for making sides to frames, but, unless they have tie pieces about five feet apart, they soon become twisted and crooked. But the three inch deals make the most substantial walls, and last a long time, provided they are properly painted at intervals.

Nothing has been said about the length of the pits, because that must be regulated by the accommodation required and the space available. As an indication of the space required for the accommodation of a given number of plants, it may be said that fifty plants in three-inch pots may be arranged in a square yard without overcrowding. Those in larger pots will of course require space in proportion; and it will be most easy to determine the space required for any given number according to the size of the pots. In making calculations, it will be needful to take the measurement of the pots from the outside of the rim, and also to take into consideration the character of the growth of the plants it is intended chiefly to cultivate.

In heating pits, three-inch pipes should be used, and if one pipe of this kind will not suffice, a flow and return may be fixed along each side.

For some years past we have had in use a cheap contrivance of our own which we have designated the A frame. Frames of this kind can be made by the village carpenter, or by any

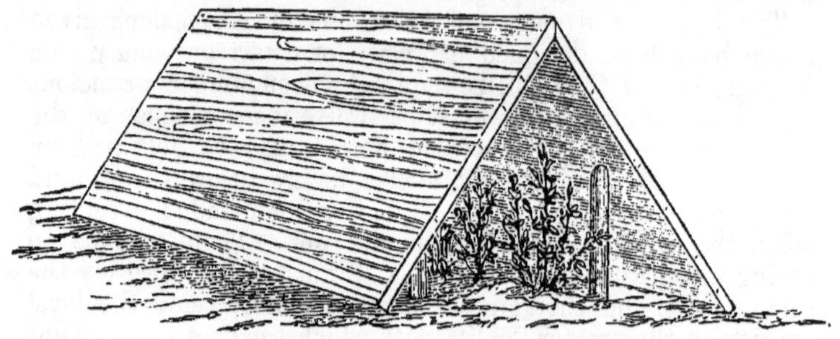

A FRAME FORMED OF LOOSE PLANKS.

amateur who is handy in the use of tools. We will begin by extemporizing a frame. Take a couple of planks nine to twelve inches wide, and place them on each side of a row of potatoes, so as to form a miniature span-roofed protector. If they do not come together nicely, drive in a few posts for them to lean upon. Every evening, except when warm showers are likely to fall, bring the planks together over the potatoes, and every morning

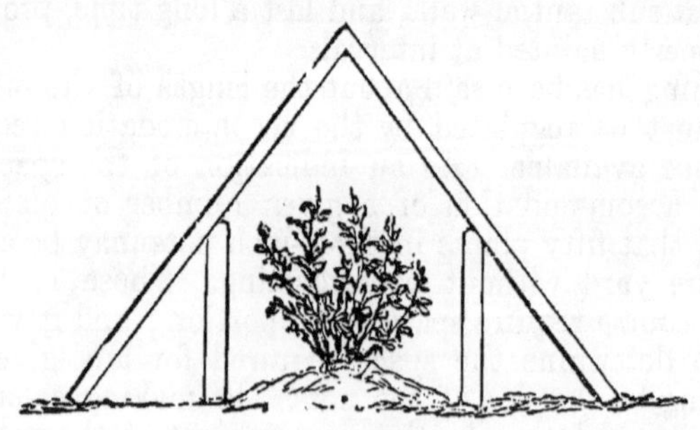

SECTION OF A FRAME FORMED OF LOOSE PLANKS.

lay them back on the ground, that the plant may enjoy light and air. This rough contrivance will save your selected row from being ravaged by spring frosts, and will do much to hasten their growth, and, if kept in use through April and May, will render the crop fit to dig three weeks earlier than a row of the same sort on the same ground wholly unprotected. To improve on the idea, have light frames made with cross-pieces to strengthen them, and cover the frames with cheap canvas, or have the frames open and cover as needful with mats or lengths of canvas cut to size and kept always ready. A section of such a frame will be like the letter A, and hence the name. The cost of a lot of such frames made in convenient lengths would be so trifling that one season's use would pay for them; as a matter of course, they could be made so as to last for years, and it would be a shame not to take proper care of them.

A FRAME WITH CANVAS COVERING.

Consider the use of such things. As already suggested, early potatoes may be hastened three weeks or so by their aid. Seeds sown early may be hastened in like manner, and seeds sown late, though not needing protection from the frost, may not the less be helped by being kept moist and dark, for the frames may of course be kept on by day as well as by night if needful. So, again, newly planted cauliflower plants and such-like usually need to be shaded and sheltered, and here is your ready-made shade and shelter all in a lump, to economize watering and prevent exhaustion by east wind or hot sun or frost. But winter will come, and the frames will be not the less useful then. A row of fine celery may be destroyed by frost, or, if taken up, may be considerably deteriorated before it is eaten. But the A frame will save it and keep it. The important point is to determine the size, remembering, of course, they will have to be frequently lifted, and that the larger they are consistent with easy lifting the better. A breadth one foot on the side will be useful, but fifteen inches adds to the usefulness, while adding very little to the cost of the frame. If frames of light timber, fifteen inches on the side, are put together at an angle of about fifty degrees, there will be space within for sheltering a plant twelve inches high, and if made in twelve feet lengths, a man can move them without difficulty. They should be closed at the ends, of course, for they are to be protectors in every sense of the word.

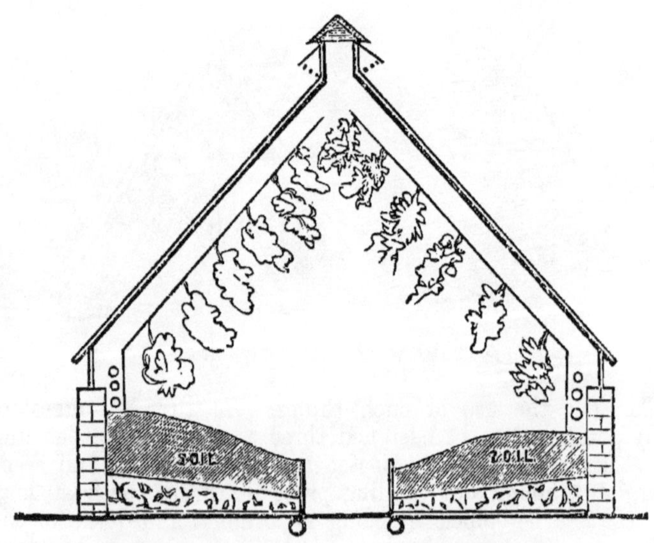

SPAN-ROOF HOUSE FOR VINES AND STRAWBERRIES.

CHAPTER IV.

SELECTING FOR THE KITCHEN GARDEN.

THE tastes and requirements of households differ so much, that to offer any general advice on selecting for the kitchen garden is of necessity a somewhat difficult task. But it must be attempted in the interest of the amateur who is anxious to bestow his labour and money to the best advantage, and has had but little experience to aid him in the making and managing of a kitchen garden. Speaking generally, it may be said that the gardener's business is never fully learnt; that indeed may be said of many other occupations; but it is peculiarly the case in one that takes a different complexion, more or less, in every locality, and which is also influenced by the march of improvement and by changes of fashion. The gardener, however rich in experience, may always learn something by observation; the better for him, for after all a state of finality as regards the acquisition of knowledge may be considered the equivalent of intellectual death.

There are two points of primary importance to be kept in view always—the capabilities of the garden, and the requirements of the family. As for the first, considerations of the soil and the climate will to a considerable extent enable us to order the system of cropping advantageously, and avoid serious mistakes. But the means at command, or in plain English, the money, must be considered also, for many difficulties may be overcome where expense is a matter of secondary importance, that it would be sheer folly to battle with unless aided by a sufficient purse. It must be understood then, that it is a rare event to find a garden in which all kinds of kitchen garden crops, well-managed, thrive with equal luxuriance, where only the nice points in management consist in producing good supplies of subjects that are in the least degree adapted to the local circumstances. A deep, fertile, sandy loam will suit a greater variety of vegetables and fruits than any other soil, but something good may be scraped off a sheer sand, and wonders may be done with clay, even in respect of plants that clay is altogether unfit for. In our own case we grow potatoes and asparagus of the finest quality on undrained clay by the comparatively inexpensive process of planting on ridges and using lime rubbish largely as a manure, the staple soil being deficient of calcareous matter. There is considerable advantage in securing from the garden a sufficiency of everything it should produce, for, as a rule, home-grown fruits and vegetables are better than can be purchased. Moreover, if the management be right, home-grown produce is the cheapest, whatever the cynical and the superficial may say to the contrary. Those who talk of cabbages costing half-a-crown each when grown at home, and in that case being inferior to twopenny cabbages from the market (and there are people who make an affectation of superiority when talking such nonsense), have simply everything to learn, and therefore should only be listened to for the amusement their folly may afford. But it will often happen that certain requisites may be more advantageously purchased than produced, and then the capabilities of the district as regards market supplies will have to be considered. In places where there is no difficulty in obtaining market vegetables, it will often be found advantageous to trust to the greengrocer for early peas, asparagus, mushrooms, potatoes, winter saladings, and even turnips; but first class main-crop peas, cauliflowers, seakale, summer salads, turnips for summer and autumn use, potatoes for use in June, July, and August, summer cabbages, broccolis for cutting in spring, winter greens, onions, celery, and such small but useful things as sweet and savoury herbs, should be grown if possible. On heavy land all kinds of brassicas are likely to prove profitable; on a good sandy soil asparagus will be at home; on sand, chalk, or peat potatoes are likely to prove fine in quality though perhaps small unless aided with suitable manures. Beans and peas like strong lands.

The question of climate is full of interest. In one of our gardens, which is sheltered on every side by means of dense hedges and plantations, it is a rare occurrence for anything to suffer from frost in the month of May. In another garden not a furlong distant, but open to the east, the havoc made by frost in May would be simply ruinous were the cropping not ordered with especial care to avoid losses. In the first garden, early bush fruits, asparagus, early peas, early spinach, and other good things are produced in plenty, whereas in the second, to labour for such things would be to organize disappointment and prepare for an annual waste of money, labour, and land.

To ensure a constant succession of things in season, and have always enough and no great glut at any time, necessitates a certain amount of forecasting. In one sense, gardening is founded on forecasting, but, as respects the matter now before us, it is rather complicated. It is pleasant to be enabled to send a friend a few nice cauliflowers or mushrooms or grapes, but it is not pleasant, and therefore not desirable to be burdened with a great glut of some particular thing, and, as you begin to tire of it, discover that there is nothing provided to take its place, that while you have been labouring, perhaps, to provide ten times more peas and potatoes than you can consume, you have made no arrangements to secure delicious broccolis in autumn, and have forgotten such useful roots as beets, carrots, parsnips, and such-like. There is no part of the scheme of a kitchen garden that requires such careful forecasting as the supply of the table during April and May. In the event of a cold spring, the garden will not supply a scrap of vegetation from Spring-sown seeds until far into June, when the first supplies of round spinach will be ready, and early peas, perhaps, will immediately follow. From the turn of the year, we may have collards, sprouts of many kinds, green kale and sprouting broccoli being the chief, and in April, the broccolis that have stood the winter will turn in and keep going to the end of May, and at the same time there should be a sufficiency of winter spinach, and the sprouting broccoli should hold out to quite the end of May. The fame of sea-kale and asparagus is enhanced by the fact that they come in at a time when there is not much else to be obtained, and hence the importance of doing them well and ensuring a sufficiency.

In selecting from catalogues of seeds, endeavour to hit the happy mean between too few and too many sorts of any particular thing. You may be inclined to grow a great many sorts, and you may be well warned in time that those who grow *collections* are bound to have bad sorts as well as good ones; whereas, on the other hand, those who grow *selections* may err the other way, and select too few. The case can be best illustrated by reference to the potato. You may have a dish say of the old Fluke, and it may be so snow white, so handsome, so nice with brown gravy that you may resolve to grow the Fluke potato only. If you carry out that resolve, you will soon find it to be a mistake. If you selected the Regent for your sole resource, the mistake would be none the less definite. But to those two excellent varieties you might add Ashleaf, Lapstone, Late Rose, and Magnum Bonum, and you would have a good selection certainly, though it might not be the best possible. In a season when potato disease prevails, the grower of one sort may have absolutely nothing to lift, while the grower of half a dozen or more sorts may have the good fortune to lift an unusually heavy crop, for the wet weather, that destroys some kinds of potatoes, may cause extra production of other kinds. The case is nearly the same in respect of peas, for although we do not know of a pea disease, we do know that a cold spring may destroy the earlier kinds, and really benefit the second earlies and main crops. But varieties are not only of relative merit *inter se,* they are of relative merit also as affected by peculiarities of soil and climate. Be not in haste to criticise the wisdom of the locality, but rather ascertain its purport and conform to it until you can see your way to a higher wisdom, for it is easier to learn than to unlearn, and the experiences of a clown are, generally speaking, tinctured with a finer spirit of truth than the guesses of the philosopher who fancies he can regulate the world by *a priori* considerations, although they may be based on truths that are, to his certain knowledge universal and eternal. As to the selection of mere novelties, you must use your own discretion. Nine-tenths of the best things in our gardens have been trade novelties, and more good things in the shape of novelties are to come yet. But while all your needs are fairly provided for in sorts well established, you may, if you prefer the cautious way, take time to consider in respect of novelties whether you will speculate or wait. It must be at your own discretion, for, in a general way, no one can advise.

All that is said here in regard to selecting vegetables applies with equal force in the selection of fruits. Mere collections are rather to be avoided than sought by those who simply desire to be well supplied for everyday purposes. There are, and ever will be collectors, and the writer of this pleads guilty to the folly of collecting, having been engaged in the pastime upwards of a quarter of a century. But this book is not written for the special benefit of collectors, and it is but proper here to say that in every class of vegetables and fruits are to be found varieties that enjoy considerable fame, and as a rule those varieties have become famous by their merits, and therefore have the first claim on our attention. In the chapters that follow the best varieties, in every class, will be named; and we may close this paragraph with the remark, that, whenever it is found that some particular variety is known by many names, it should be noted as desirable, for a multiplicity of synonyms is a proof of merit—it will not pay to give a bad thing a number of names. The writer of this could tell of a trading firm, that for several years in succession offered the British Queen pea every year under a new name; a bad or even second-rate pea would not bear such an incrustation of trickery; but this old variety is so good that, when people discover they have been cheated, they are not inclined to complain, because the remembrance of the delicious peas they have eaten awakens a generous feeling, which is averse to putting the naughty seedsman on his trial. First-class houses are of course above this sort of thing; they are not indeed infallible, and happily do not pretend to immunity from error, but they never catalogue a novelty until they have grown it for several years, and in fact they cannot, for before offering a novelty, it is necessary to secure a large stock to cover the cost of advertising, and to do this necessitates a thoroughly severe trial culture, in the course of which the peculiarities of the variety are likely to be thoroughly mastered. Those who are well versed in garden varieties find an immense amount of amusement in comparing novelties with the kinds they are represented as superseding, but it is a pastime quite unsuited to beginners, who had better be content with such things as have attained to celebrity through qualities approved by many witnesses, through a long succession of seasons and under a great variety of conditions.

CHAPTER V.

PEAS AND BEANS.

"Good Master Peaseblossom, I shall desire you of more acquaintance."
Midsummer Night's Dream, III. 1.

AS we must begin somewhere, and a scientific arrangement of subjects is impossible, peas and beans may as well take the lead in the chapters on special culture, because, in the estimation of many, they are the most important of all kitchen garden crops. Their near botanical relationship suggests a similarity of requirements, and wherever one is found to prosper, it will be strange if the conditions should prove unsuitable to the other.

THE PEA, *Pisum sativum,* is one of the most important of our summer vegetables, and the esteem in which it is held justifies the utmost liberality and spirit in its cultivation. The immense number of its varieties affords evidence of the popularity of this wholesome and savoury esculent, and may suggest to the cultivator that some discrimination is required in making a selection, when only a limited number of varieties is intended to be grown. It cannot be said, however, that the varieties of latest introduction are wholly superfluous, for in respect of improvement in recent years, the pea has kept pace with the potato, and a number of sorts that were held in high esteem only from ten to twenty years ago—to go back no further—have been quite superseded by later sorts of extraordinarily fine quality. A large proportion of the finest garden peas in cultivation were raised by systematic cross breeding by the late Dr. Maclean of Colchester, who devoted many years of his valuable life to this interesting and useful labour. Another successful worker, who has acquired well deserved fame in this department, is Mr. Thomas Laxton of Stamford. Many of the most celebrated sorts of peas are simply improved strains of old varieties, secured by careful selection on the part of the seed-grower, and oftentimes the strain or stock so secured acquires a character which places it many degrees in advance of the market type, or general average of the parent. Hence, it is not only important to obtain the best sorts of peas, but the best strains or stocks of the best varieties.

THE SOIL.—Peas are highly nutritive, and, when properly cooked, are as wholesome as any vegetable in our gardens. Being richer in phosphates than most other table vegetables, they are particularly adapted for invalids, and especially such as are deficient of nervous energy, the mineral constituents of peas ministering directly to the nourishment of the nervous system. The inorganic elements amount to about three per cent. of the entire bulk in ripe peas, but in green peas somewhat less. The principal inorganic elements are potash and phosphoric acid, and therefore it is only in soils rich in potash-salts and phosphates, that peas can be grown profitably, unless by liberal and systematic manuring the deficiency of the soil in those essential elements is compensated for. The importance of keeping the soil rich in these ingredients will be understood when we say that one bushel of seed peas contains about the following quantities of the several elements, namely, of—

Phosphoric acid	9	ounces
Lime	2	,,
Magnesia	1½	,,
Potash	10	,,

The pea will thrive in any soil of average good quality, provided it has good cultivation. The ground should be in every case deeply dug, and for all the second early and main crop sorts be liberally manured; the best mode of employing the manure being to lay it at the bottom of the trench. For the first early sorts it is advisable to manure less liberally than for those that come into pod later in the season, because a luxuriant growth is antagonistic to precocity of production, and in the case of the first earlies, the object of the cultivator is to gather a dish at the earliest date possible, even if the plants are less luxurious, and therefore less productive than they would be if encouraged by heavy manuring. It should be understood, however, that although manuring does somewhat delay the season of production, it is scarcely possible to manure too liberally for robust-growing sorts of fine quality; for although the first gathering from them may be obtained less early by a week or so than from the same sorts grown on poor ground, yet in the end high cultivation will pay the best by the superior quality and greater quantity of the produce, and the greater length of time during which the plants will continue in bearing.

The best manures for this crop, after farmyard dung, which is undoubtedly *the* best, are guano, superphosphate, kainit, and gypsum, which may be employed together in a mixture, and dug in when the ground is prepared, at the rate of half a ton per acre. If one comprehensive manure is required, there is nothing better than phospho-guano, which may be employed at the rate of five hundredweight per acre, if dug into the ground, or at a fourth of that rate, if sown in the drills. In any and every case where artificial manure is employed, care should be taken to prevent the manure and the seed meeting. A sprinkle of earth will prevent this. The tendency of artificials is to kill the young plants, hence they are said to save the cultivator the trouble of thinning.

SOWING.—The earliest peas should be sown on ridges, and the main crops in trenches. In other words, the first earlies require the warmest and driest position that can be found for them, and the more luxuriant and later sorts require heavily manured land in positions favourable to the retention of moisture. In every case close cropping is to be avoided as an unprofitable procedure, hence the custom of growing spinach, and other smallish subjects between early peas is commendable, as necessitating a sufficient space between the rows of peas to insure a free circulation of air. The dwarfest sorts, however, admit of being sown in close order, but the space between the rows must be increased in a direct ratio with the heights of the varieties. Our custom has been to extend the pea crop over the largest extent of ground possible, so as to have room between the rows for plantation of cabbage, cauliflower, and other summer crops, the tallest sorts of peas being fifteen to twenty feet apart in the rows, and the dwarfer sorts at least five feet. The practice commonly prevailing of sowing tall peas so close that there is scarcely room left for the gathering of the crop is simply a waste of labour, land, and seed, for where the vines mix and entangle the produce is miserably small, and, if the crop has to contend with drought, it soon becomes hopelessly mildewed.

In sowing the seed, drills two inches deep should be drawn with the hoe guided by the line, and the seed sprinkled in the drills with careful regularity. The early and wiry-habited sorts may be sown rather thickly, but tall robust kinds should be fully two inches apart. In districts favourable to early production the first early sorts are sown in November and December, but in places where the soil is deep and damp, and the climate unfavourable, it is sheer waste of labour to sow until the middle of February at the earliest, and, generally speaking, the middle of March is as early as the seed can be sown advantageously. The earlier the better everywhere, of course, but a sowing of peas made a week too soon will scarcely pay for the ground it covers, hence in cold districts experienced cultivators wait for favourable weather, without respect to the almanac, for the good reason that a late sowing that has had no check will in the end overtake and surpass in productiveness earlier sowings that have been two or three times pinched by frost, or dessicated by the east winds. Sowings of the second early and main crop sorts should be made from the middle of March to the end of May, according to requirements, and if these are sown in trenches prepared as for celery, at a distance of about fifteen feet apart, they will produce double the crop, and last double the time in bearing than the same sorts would if sown upon the level in a close piece with only enough space between for gathering.

First Early Peas are frequently unprofitable in small gardens and on heavy damp soils. But where circumstances are favourable, they pay in proportion to their earliness, and in districts where gardening is carried on with spirit, there is something like a race amongst the gardeners for the first gathering of green peas. During upwards of twenty-five years trial culture of peas, with, on many occasions, more than fifty varieties on the ground at one time, we have only once gathered a dish worth having in the month of May. This occurred in the year 1868, when the spring was characterized by unusual heat and drought, and the late peas failed entirely. In that year we gathered on the 23rd of May *good* dishes of *Sutton's Ringleader, Taber's Perfection, Sutton's Champion, Poynter's Early, and Dickson's First and Best.* On our cold clay, first early peas do not pay as they ought one year in five, but second early and late sorts, and especially marrow peas of the finest quality, are a splendid sample, and last a long time.

There are many ways of expediting the growth of first early peas without exposing the crop to the destructive winter weather. One good method is to sow the seed on turves, laid grass side downwards, in a frame or pit in November, December, or January. The plant is made as hardy as possible by abundant ventilation in favourable weather, and by being kept as near the glass as possible. Sometime in March the turves are carried to ground prepared for them and carefully laid in lines, and lightly moulded up with the hoe, and if favourable weather follows, the plant takes hold of the ground above, and green peas may be safely reckoned on in the ensuing month of May. But "there's many a slip," etc.; the keen east wind, the untimely snowdrift, the casual frost, may work sad havoc with the tender plants, and whoever practices this method of procedure should be prepared with protective measures in case of unfavourable weather, while the plant is as yet not well established in its new position. One precaution consists in putting stakes to the rows at the time of planting, and they should consist as much as possible of short thick brushwood, such as the smaller stuff from hornbeam and alder loppings, or even of fir or other evergreen trees. The shelter this kind of stuff affords is remarkably effective, and as a matter of course it soon affords support also, for the peas take hold as soon as they begin to grow.

Another good method is to sow in troughs or boxes, and without doubt the best form of box is that described by Mr. Maw of Broseley in the *Gardener's Chronicle.*

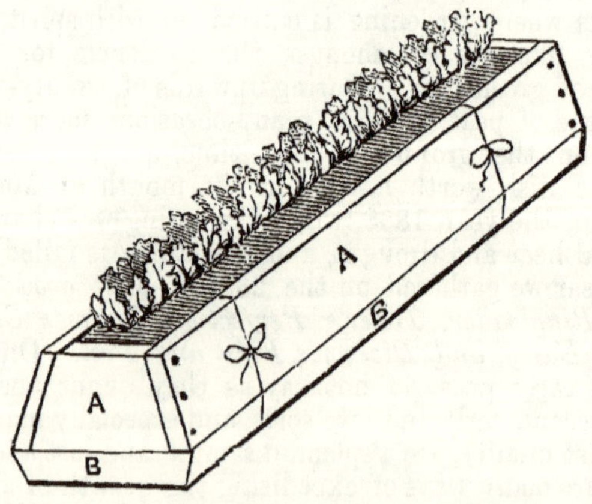

A A (drawn 1-6th the actual size) represents a wooden frame or box, with loose bottom B B, made of rough ½-inch boards, and of the following dimensions—2½ inches in vertical depth, 2 inches wide at the top, 3¼ inches wide at the bottom, and 3 feet long, inside measurements. The bottom is simply a loose ½inch board, about 4½ inches wide, temporarily attached to the box by two pieces of string. The box is filled with light rich soil, and the peas sown from the narrow side.

The transferring of the ready-made row of peas to the open ground is a simple process: a drill, rather deeper than is necessary for sowing peas in the open ground, is worked out with the hoe, and the boxes, each containing a yard of peas, are placed end to end in it. The strings which attach the body of the box to the loose bottom are released, and by slightly raising it on one side the bottom board is easily slipped from under. The frame, from being bevelled, readily delivers itself from its contents, and the row of peas is left *en masse* in the drill without the soil being broken or disturbed, or any check being given to the peas.

These narrow seed-boxes really occupy but very little space. They can be stacked two deep (the edges of the bottoms of the upper layer resting on the top edges of the sides of the lower layer), and a cold frame of 6 feet square would contain 40 lineal yards.

For the earliest crop little more than half the seed that would be sown in the open ground is required, as the boxes are under protection till past injury from birds and slugs.

The plan that has obtained favour on our trial-ground is the very old fashioned one of raising the plants in pots. The best size pots for the purpose are 16's or 9½ inch. They are filled to within two inches of the top with light rich compost, and the seed is sown thickly and covered with an inch and a half of soil. A cool frame or pit is the proper place for them. If sown in November, and carefully managed so as to keep them stout and hardy, they will be in fine condition for planting out in March. A piece of well prepared ground in a warm sheltered spot must be ready for them, and the planting should be done by turning out each ball complete into a hole made to receive it, and closing in neatly so that the plants shall not know they have been disturbed. The rows should be at least four feet apart, and the clumps two feet apart in the rows. They can be conveniently and effectually protected by turning over them the pots they were raised in, which can be left on the ground for the purpose. A quart of seed will suffice for seventy pots of 16 size, sufficient for a running length of 140 feet, or seven rows of 20 feet each, enough for any family from the first week in May to the middle of June, when sound early sorts from open ground sowings will come in to succeed them.

STICKING should be performed early, for the stakes not only support, but in some degree shelter the plant. In any and every case, if support of some kind can be provided, the plant will be more thrifty for it, and will yield a better crop. In putting the ordinary stakes to peas, the usual practice is to lean them in over the plant; but it is better to lean them out to encourage the plant to spread. for the abundant admission of light and air will render it fruitful to the ground line. But when the stakes lean out, they must be the more firmly driven into the ground, because they do not support each other. They should not lean out much, but just enough to encourage a somewhat spreading growth.

In districts where stakes are costly, wire netting and poles and lines are used instead. Mr. Voyce of Horley, in Surrey, manufactures a cheap wire rissel or trellis, and most of the London dealers in wirework have similar contrivances. The pole and line is an effectual mode of supporting peas and runner beans, and must be described. Larch poles six feet long should be procured if possible, but of course any slim poles will answer nearly as well. Drive them in about nine feet apart. A cord of the thickness of a common lead pencil will be required for such strong growing peas as *British Queen*, *Ne Plus Ultra*, and *King of the Marrows*, but a lighter and cheaper cord with shorter stakes will do for the three and four feet peas. The first run of the line should be at three inches from the ground, and the next at three inches more, after which the distance may be six inches from line to line, and there must of course be a turn round every pole, and the line must not be drawn quite tight because of its contraction during wet weather. The sparrows will not be able to do much mischief to peas supported in this way, as they require a good foothold to hack the pods open to get the peas.

It remains to be said that where there is plenty of room and appearances are not of great consequence, peas of all kinds, no matter how tall, may be very well grown without supports of any kind. We have given up staking as a waste of time, and (except when growing tall sorts for trial) restrict the selection to sorts that rise only three or four feet. These are sown in rows, eight or more feet apart, and are earthed up early, and made to lean one way—the way of the prevailing wind, and they do so well that we should scarcely care to put stakes to them, if the stakes were given for the purpose. Nevertheless we repeat that where stakes and time are available, they should always be used as producing a better plant and a finer sample. When the rows of peas are close, they should run north and south, but when a proper distance apart it does not matter which way they run.

THE ENEMIES OF PEAS are few in number, but great in power. Mice will eat the seed as soon as sown, and sparrows will eat the plant the instant it rises out of the ground. Chopped gorse sown with the seed will prevent the ravage of mice, for the spines of the gorse will prick their noses and defeat them. A cheap and simple method of checkmating both mice and sparrows is to sprinkle the seed and shake it in a pan with a little red lead. If ever so thinly coated with this poison, the little marauders will refrain from touching them—they will not even look at them. To protect when above ground, get a piece of deal board, about seven or eight inches wide and three-quarters of an inch thick, out of which make a number of bats, the shape of which is shown in the cut; and, after putting five small nails or tacks round the outer edge, place one at each end of every row of peas, and if the rows are long, place one or more at certain distances along the rows; then get some white worsted, and, beginning at the first bat, tie it on to the lowest nail on either side, then take it on to the corresponding nail in the next bat, give it one twist round, and so on to the end of the row, then bring it back on the second nails, and so on till there are five rows of worsted. This forms a complete arch over the peas, which no sparrow will venture under. Besides it has a very neat and tidy appearance; in fact, its very neatness helps to keep the birds away, for it has something of the trap or net look about it, and so the birds are outwitted and the crop

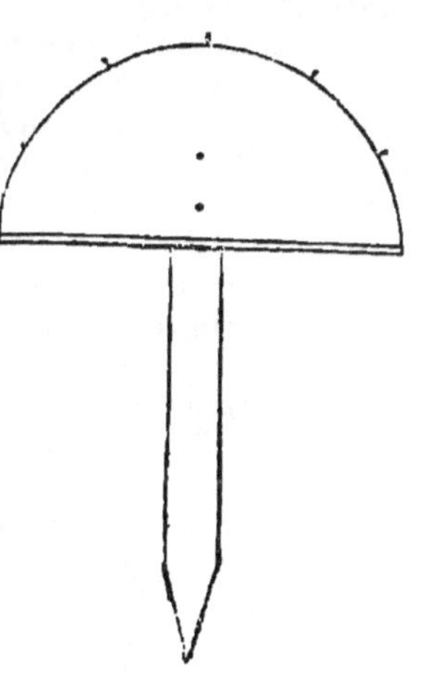

saved. Some may argue that it is extravagant to put five rows of worsted to one row of peas; not at all so, for by one person taking one end and one the other, they may be shifted from one crop to another as they advance, and so last a whole season. If the bats are dried and painted when the season is over, they will last for years.

On the first indication of mildew, it may be well to supply the plant with abundance of water or, better still, liquid manure, which may save it, and prevent the spread of the plague.

To protect the young plant from sparrows, proceed as follows:—From the time the plant has made a fair start, until the pods begin to swell, the sparrows take no notice of it. But now they again assail it, and with wondrous vigour. In a district where these impudent marauders abound, the entire crop may be taken by them, unless protective measures be resorted to. Now there is nothing so effectual as fine twine with strips of white paper attached. A few stout stakes should be driven in at about twelve to twenty feet apart, and the kite tails stretched upon them, just loose enough to swing freely to the wind. If put up too soon, the sparrows get used to them, therefore do not bring them into use until the crop is really in danger, when they will be sufficiently alarming to scare the enemy, and the terror will last until the last pea is gathered. It is a good plan to keep men constantly at work digging, planting, etc., on ground covered with peas where sparrows abound, from the time the peas begin to pod.

Where rats abound they feast upon peas night and day, and may be destroyed by shooting them from an ambush.

Late Peas are more precarious than early peas, as they are peculiarly subject to mildew. The sorts that pay best to sow in June and July are not the late, but the early and second early sorts, such as *Kentish Invicta, Wonderful, Advancer*, and *Alpha.* Prepare for the sowing well manured trenches twelve inches wide and eight inches deep. Put nine inches of manure in the bottom of the trench, and cover with six inches of soil, and sow. The plant will thus be in a trough, and may be liberally watered in dry weather, both to promote a strong growth and prevent mildew.

Where space is at command, there is no better plan for late peas than to place the rows a good distance apart, and plant other crops between: from nine to twelve yards is not too far. They will then have room for a proper development, and one row so placed will be as productive as two of the same length if they are close together.

THE SELECTION OF PEAS must be regulated by the require-

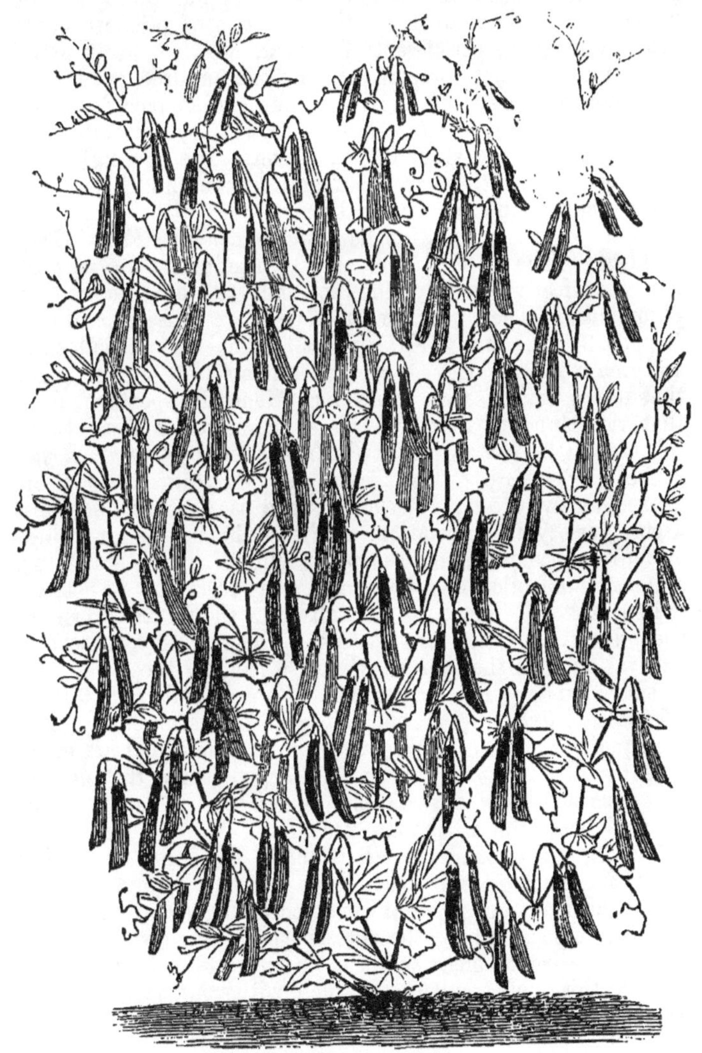

DR. MACLEAN PEA.

ments of the palate, and the circumstances of the garden. Those who object to peas of a sweet flavour will prefer the smooth white and blue seeded varieties; while those who love a rich buttery pea will lean to the wrinkled marrows. Having grown and made note of all the varieties of peas we could obtain during the past twenty-five years, we thought it would be an easy matter to prepare a list of one hundred good sorts, but were astonished on referring to our garden records to find that there are not more than about sixty firstrate and thoroughly distinct kinds in cultivation. The first earlies tell their own tale; they are comparatively unproductive, and many degrees inferior in quality to the later sorts. The earliest pea in cultivation is *Ringleader* or *First Crop*, 2½ feet. The best of the early white class is *Sangster's No.* 1, 3 feet; a really fine pea, but ten days later than *Ringleader*. The earliest marrow peas are *Advancer*, 2 feet, *Alpha*, 3 feet; and *William* 1*st*, 4 feet. Of second early and main crop varieties, we have many that are so good, that improvement seems impossible. Generally speaking, those that rise three to four feet are most useful, and of these, *Wonderful*, 2½ feet; *James's Prolific*, 4 feet; *Princess Royal*, 3 feet; *Premier*, 4 feet; and *Dr. Maclean*, 4 feet; are conspicuously good. The last named is perhaps the most useful variety in cultivation, as the seeds may be sown three or four inches apart, and the plant will fill up by branching, and bear well-filled and handsome pods from top to bottom. Where stakes are plentiful, the tall sorts should be grown for their fine quality and long lasting. There is no finer sort in cultivation than the *British Queen*, 6 feet, for those who love a tender, buttery, sugary pea, but *Waterloo Marrow*, 6 feet; *Ne Plus Ultra*, 5 feet; and *King of the Marrows*, 6 feet; are equally worthy of a place in a garden where peas are much in demand. Laxton's *Omega*, 2½ feet, will take the place of Ne Plus Ultra where stakes are scarce; it is the most generally useful of all the late peas.

The Bean, *Faba Vulgaris*, is one of the most nourishing vegetables known, and although it does not enjoy universal favour, for many people regard it as both vulgar and uneatable, this is compensated by the enthusiasm of those who proudly rank themselves amongst eaters of "bean feasts." It is unfortunate for this noble esculent—for such, with your permission, we regard it—that it is often served in a vulgar manner, and the most constant lover of beans will admit that when allowed to grow old, and then badly cooked and served with coarse bacon, the bean is not a thing to be desired. Let us do justice to the bean, that we may see it on the table as green as grass, tender, and slightly meally, without being in the least old, and accompanied with real parsley-butter as green as the beans, and with the true flavour of the parsley preserved to the utmost.

THE SOIL.—The bean requires a good soil, and it is an extremely exhausting crop, and therefore should be prepared for, or at least followed by, liberal manuring, for it takes out of the soil tremendous quantities of potash, phosphorus, lime, and sulphur. The seed is sown from November to the end of June, and consequently soil and situation must be selected to suit the several sowings. Those sown to stand the winter should be on a somewhat light and dry soil, and in a sheltered situation. Those sown in February and March will do better on a deep and heavy soil, as they will be in bearing in the hottest part of the summer. In any case the ground must be well dug, and sufficiently manured, and although shelter will assist the autumn and winter-sown crops, beans will never thrive under trees, or in any half-stifling spot, where air and light are deficient.

SOWING THE SEED.—It is a waste of seed, of ground, and of quality of produce, to sow the seed too thickly. It is usual to sow in double rows, thus—

a
b

The small-growing sorts may be in double rows two feet apart, and the drills may be two-and-a-half inches wide from *a* to *b*, and quite two inches deep. The large-growing sorts, such as *Windsor* and *Longpod*, may also be in double rows, but the breadth from *a* to *b* must be four inches, the distance from double row to double row must be three feet, and the seed must be set full three inches deep. Of late years we have practised sowing in single rows, as we grow for summer use only the largest varieties of Windsor bean, and we are satisfied that the extra space afforded the plants is amply repaid in the increased abundance and fine quality of the produce. As to distance apart, we never could get our men to sow thin enough, and so in our early morning walks in spring we go through the rows and pull half or two-thirds of the plants out, and leave them on the ground to perish. The amateur who manages things in his own way entirely, will find that the largest sorts of beans will pay well in single rows, three feet apart, and the plants eighteen inches asunder in the rows. If they come up too thick it will always pay to transplant them; but they must be carefully lifted with a trowel when they have made three or four rough leaves, and the work should be done in dull or showery weather.

SUMMER CULTURE.—The production and quality of beans are greatly enhanced by a proper course of culture, and the sowing of the seed is to be regarded as only one step towards success. When the plants are two inches high, the ground should be sown with gypsum and then hoed over, care being taken to avoid injuring the young plants. About a bushel per rood of gypsum will suffice, and its effects will be almost magical, more especially on ground that was previously well prepared by deep digging and manuring. It is not a good practice to give water to the growing plants, but in the case of long-continued drought it might be wise to open narrow V shaped trenches between the rows and fill them with water every evening for a week, or even a fortnight, at the time when the plants are advancing into flower, and then to close the trench and give no more. As the flowers open, the black-fly will probably appear. Strange to say, although this fly sucks the juices of the plant, it is not often injurious to an extent to cause anxiety, although, of course, we prefer to be altogether without it. As the fly usually affects the top of the plant, because, we may suppose, of the tenderness of the tissues there, it is a good practice to pinch out the tops and burn them. It is usual to pinch out the tops as soon as the plants are fairly in flower and the young beans are visible at the bottom; but, if there is no fly present, the pinching is not necessary, and is even objectionable when rudely performed, as it often is. The object of the topping is to prevent the production of an extravagant number of beans of comparatively poor quality, which may be expected if all the flowers are allowed to open and fructify. The books say, "two or three inches of stem should be broken off;" but it would be better to say, pinch out the tops as far down as they can be severed with the thumb nail, as soon as the pods are seen emerging from the lowest of the flowers. This will take off about an inch and a half, and the plants will remain vigorous. Severe topping lowers their vigour, for the leaves are their lungs, and the "hacking" process is always guarded against by the prudent gardener.

EARLY CROPS.—If beans are required at the earliest possible moment, and the season for early sowing out of doors has been lost, we must have the aid of glass, and sow for transplanting. A gentle hotbed will start the seed nicely, but a strong heat will produce weak plants scarcely worth putting out. Sow on grass turves, laid grass-side downwards, or in boxes or pots, taking care to let the young plants have plenty of light and air, to keep them stubby from the first. The roughest of contrivances for shelter will suffice to push the seed forward and help the plants until the time comes for putting out. Select for them a warm south border; get them out as early as possible, choosing mild, showery weather for the transplanting, and plant them in shallow trenches, filling in round their roots with old rotten manure in a powdery state, or old leaf-mould, or whatever else of a similar nature may be at hand, to coax the tender roots into action speedily.

The green plant is a first-rate fodder for milch kine, and therefore if an extra breadth of beans is grown, they may be drawn as needed to amuse the cows, and give the grass land a better chance for haymaking.

SECOND CROP.—On several occasions we have had a second crop of beans from the same plants, having encouraged the suckers to rise by cutting down the stems that bore the first crop. It is only in a long, hot, showery season that the suckers rise sufficiently strong to produce anything, and then, so far as our experience enables us to say, they make but a poor return for the ground they occupy. It is well, however, for the cultivator to know all that may be done, and it is a fact that in a favourable season a second crop may be taken from the same plants.

As remarked above, the bean is rich in phosphates and alkalies, and hence is an exhaustive crop. There is nothing better in the way of manure than good stable dung, half-rotten, and the ground should be deeply broken up; but guano may be employed with advantage, and the best mode of procedure is to sprinkle a little at the bottom and on the sides of every trench as the digging proceeds. The gypsum or plaster of

Paris recommended above should be spread on the surface and hoed in among the young plants. In one thousand pounds weight of beans, which we may reckon as the produce of half an acre of ground, there will be of mineral matters; phosphoric acid, 10lbs.; lime, 3lbs.; magnesia, 2lbs.; potash, 14lbs.; common salt, ½lb. It follows, therefore, that a heavy loam or clay land, rich in alkalies and phosphates, is the proper soil for beans when a large and fine production is required; but almost any soil may be rendered suitable by judicious manuring, and, as a rule, the best special manure available is phospho-guano.

IN SELECTING SORTS it is well to remember that there are some very bad ones in the market. The *Red Seeded* and the *Red Flowered* are about the worst that we are acquainted with, and we caution the amateur against the latter in particular, because it is occasionally advertised as an ornamental plant, producing an abundance of the most delicious beans. The truth is, it is one of the ugliest, least productive, and obnoxious-flavoured vegetables that ever found its way into an honest man's garden. The *Mazagan* is a poor thing, though dwarf and early. For early production, *Early Long-pod* is the best for mere production; the *Long-pod* class are the most profitable, and answer admirably where beans are grown for sale, the true *Johnson's Wonderful Long-pod* being of excellent quality and tremendously productive. Having tried all the sorts many times, we have adopted two, and never grow any others. These are, *Early Long-pod*, to sow in November, January, and June, for early crops of delicate beans, and *Green Windsor*, to sow in January, February, and March, for supplies of the handsomest and best-flavoured beans obtainable. We give the last-named plenty of room, and put the rows four feet asunder, and never fail to have a long-continued and abundant supply of the finest beans in the world.

THE KIDNEY BEAN, *Phaseolus vulgaris*, is universally appreciated, and peer and peasant are almost equally interested in the cultivation. In English cookery the ripe seeds are much less used than on the continent, where, for haricot dishes, the small white-seeded sorts, in a dried state, are in constant request. It is a question if the ripe seeds of any kidney beans (*Phaseolus*) are altogether wholesome; we incline to the belief that they possess properties which render them objectionable as food, but there can be no question about the green pods, as we are accustomed to eat them, carefully cooked, of a fine green colour, and tender as the slice of butter that the prudent cook will never fail to place on the top of the smoking pile when they have been drained and dished for table. An invalid may eat a dish of French beans or scarlet-runners late at night without danger, and that is a peculiar test of the wholesomeness of the dish; for, with the exception of spinach, there is scarcely any other vegetable that a weak stomach dare encounter when the mid-day hours have passed.

Kidney beans will grow fairly, and produce useful fruit in the most trashy soils and unpromising situations. There is scarcely a plant known to the cultivator of vegetables that will endure long-continued drought with so little harm as the dwarf French bean; and as to our old familiar friend, the scarlet-runner, it is no uncommon thing to see it thriving in a sort of cinder-bed, heavily shaded by trees, in the garden of the cottager whom the love of beer has seduced, and in whose garden, therefore, "the thorn and the thistle grow broader and higher." But the capabilities of a plant to endure insult are not sufficient to justify careless cultivation. For that, indeed, it should be shown that good treatment renders the kidney bean unproductive, while a hap-hazard life is conducive to its prosperity. It so happens, as a matter of fact, that this plant enjoys good living, and never fails to make an ample return for it. The lesson is consequently patent—it must be well grown in order to attain complete development, and make its owner happy by its bounteous dower of delicious fruit. A deep, fertile loam suits the kidney bean to perfection. The situation should be open, sunny, and sheltered. The plant is one of the most tender, and though it bears drought in a remarkably satisfactory manner, cold and excessive moisture soon bring it down to the dust or mud. The soil for runners should be especially well prepared by trenching and manuring, but the dwarf kidney beans do not so much need manure, though they will always pay for it, if in other respects they are managed in a sensible manner.

Now, as everybody grows these plants, it may seem an over-stretch of nicety to talk about "sensible manner," but we are bound to begin finding fault with everybody, by saying that everybody sows the seed too thick, and leaves too many plants on the ground. The weakest-growing sorts of kidney beans known will cover a square foot each plant, and therefore we may properly allow for the weakest a space of two feet between the rows, and of one foot between the plants. It is quite a common practice to leave the strong-growing sorts four to six inches apart, so we have a fair case for grumbling, even at the first start. The distances are to be determined by a consideration of the habit of the variety and the strength of the soil. On our fat loam, in a moist valley, we find that the Long-podded Negro dwarf bean may be in rows three feet apart, and the plants two feet asunder in the row, and then we can scarcely get amongst them to gather, so completely do they cover the ground. As for runners, we always leave them half a foot apart at least, and might leave them double that distance with the certainty of a good plant, and have the stakes heavily garlanded soon after Midsummer-day. It is well to sow in deep drills, even if they are a day or two longer in coming up than they would be if sown shallow. Cover the seed three inches at least, and be patient. Your neighbour, who covers with a mere dusting of soil, will have plants before you do, but in a run of years the deep-sowing system will win, for we do not merely need to see the plant sprout, we also desire to see it grow on without a check, and flower and fruit freely.

The best day in all the year for sowing kidney beans is May-day. Where an early supply is wanted, it is customary to sow in pots and boxes in March and April, and keep them in pits and frames until the plants can be put out. It is by no means wise so to act, and, as a rule, the man who sows in the open on the 1st of May will have the advantage of one who takes a lot of trouble to gain a week or so in the first gathering of fruit. The earliest sorts of dwarf beans may be sown in open borders about the middle of April with a fair prospect of success, especially if the rows can be protected by means of such a contrivance as our A frame, or by common bell-glasses or flower-pots in the event of cold weather occurring after the plants have begun to push through the ground. The crop may certainly be hastened by the adoption of simple measures of protecting or coaxing, and, indeed, early supplies of dwarf beans may be obtained most easily by sowing at the end of March, in frames, and giving air cautiously on fine days, more and more freely, until in the end the lights are removed altogether. But our anxiety has always been, not to obtain early, but *late* crops of kidney beans; and for this simple reason, that when they first come in, vegetables are plentiful, but, as they are going out, vegetables become scarce. Thus, in the earliest days of French beans and runners, there are at command cauliflowers, peas, spinach, broad beans, and new potatoes. Rapidly these drop out of the list, and, as the season advances, kidney beans and marrows are almost the only vegetables of a delicate kind available. For just this reason we do not usually sow until the 1st of June, and we never miss sowing two or three sorts—the common scarlet-runner being always one—about the 15th or 20th of June. In southern counties, and especially on light soils, sowing may be made as late as the first week in July, but on our cold soil that is too late, for just as the plants should be in full bearing, the fogs, frosts, and heavy rains take the shine (with the fruit as a make-weight) clean out of them.

All the sorts that require stakes pay better for staking than trailing, provided only that stakes can be obtained for moderate labour or reasonable outlay. There are a few valuable varieties that rise only three or four feet high, for which mere refuse brushwood will suffice. But if it is out of the question to stake the running sorts, they may be kept in a compact state of growth by constant pinching away of the points of the shoots, which should be done simultaneously with the gathering of the pods as often as possible. It is by this mode of procedure that the scarlet-runner is kept in a dwarf state as a field crop, and not by the sowing of a dwarf sort, which many people believe the market-gardeners to possess, and keep to themselves. In the books we find it recommended to pinch back all running sorts, even when they are well staked; but this is neither necessary nor desirable, for they bear more abundantly if allowed to grow to their full height unchecked, and therefore the cultivator may give them the tallest stakes he can afford, and consider the ladder a needful agent in the gathering of the crop. When string is used for training runner beans, it should be slack enough to allow for contraction in wet weather. When runner beans are grown on hot, dry soils, the seed should be sown in manured trenches, to facilitate the operation of watering; for if ever water is given to this crop, it must be in considerable quantities, with an interval of a week or so between the several supplies. The dwarfest sorts, however, are far better adapted to starving soils than any of the runners. The roots of all the sorts may be preserved during the winter in sand for planting out in May, precisely as dahlias are treated; but as seed is cheap, and produces a fruitful plant as rapidly as roots, the saving of the roots is a shere waste of time, and should be practised only by those who want amusement.

The gathering of the crop is really an important part of the general management of kidney beans. If allowed to hang too long, the pods become stringy, and tough, and tasteless, and the plants cease to produce as they should do. It is really better to gather all the produce on the instant of its becoming fit for use, and throw it away, than allow any accumulation on the plants of mature pods, because the maturing process puts a stop to bearing; and at the close of the season, when well-managed kidney beans are invaluable, those that have been allowed to ripen seeds are absolutely worthless. But the reader will ask, impatiently, perhaps, if he may not save a few seeds, as his father, grandfather, and great-grandfather did? Yes, certainly; save a few, by all means, if you wish, but do it properly, both to ensure a maximum of green pods and a maximum of ripe seeds; in other words, to obtain all the plant can give you, instead of half or two-thirds its proper produce. To solve this problem is most easy. If you wish to save a little seed, leave a few plants, or a row, according to requirements, altogether untouched. Let them have plenty of room for the enjoyment of the sunshine, but do not remove from them a single green pod—in other words, let them ripen every pod they produce from the very first, and you will have seed of the finest quality. From those you gather green pods, gather all, and you will have an enormous production, lasting until the cruel autumnal frosts make a miserable havoc of the plantation.

About fifty sorts of kidney beans have been grown in the experimental garden at Stoke Newington. It is equally agreeable and surprising to be able to say that a considerable proportion of them are good, but, as a matter of course, very few are needed in any private garden. We have made a selection of varieties for several classes of cultivators, and hope they will be useful, though unaccompanied with descriptions, which in this case appear to be unnecessary.

DWARF KIDNEY BEANS.—The best for forcing, and to sow on warm slopes for early crops, are *Sion House* and *Sir Joseph Paxton.* The best for main crops, a handsome plant, and prodigiously fruitful, is the *Long-Podded Negro.* The following are also good: *Mexican, Salmon, Fulmer's,* and *Dun-coloured.* The following are not worth growing, except for some special purpose: *Newington Wonder, Dwarf Battersea, Black-speckled.*

INTERMEDIATE KIDNEY BEANS.—The *Paris Market*, rising only three to five feet high, is invaluable for its abundant production of large, handsome, tender beans. The *Canterbury* dwarf rises about three feet, and is the better for being staked.

TALL-RUNNER KIDNEY BEANS.—The two best and handsomest of this class are *Giant White* and *Common Scarlet.* These should be grown in every garden, the white being singularly beautiful and highly productive. The best of such as we may call curious varieties, is the *Blue* or *Purple-podded,* which grows about five or six feet high, producing dark bronzy leaves, violet-coloured flowers, and pods of a violet-purple colour. It is moderately productive, and the pods make an excellent dish, being green and tender when cooked. All the white and yellow-podded runners are to be avoided, except by those who have become accustomed to their use, and understand how to cook them. The best of them, both for exhibition and the table, is the *Yellow-podded Algerian.* The following are good, and well worth growing, though of secondary importance: *White Dutch, White Lady, White Scimitar, New Zealand, Liver-coloured, Black-seeded, Painted Lady,* or *York* and *Lancaster.* The last is extremely pretty.

CHAPTER VI.

BRASSICAS.

"Good worts! good cabbage"
Merry Wives I., 1.

THE brassicas are the most useful of all our kitchen garden plants, as they are in use at all seasons, and may be produced with more or less success in every soil and climate of Great Britain. It must be a mournful case where the soil will not produce a cabbage that will pay for the labour and the land, and as regards gardens generally, the cauliflower may be regarded as affording a fair test of the capabilities both of the soil and the management. Brassicas include an immense variety of garden vegetables, all of which assimilate closely in requirements, and for the most part demand only the most ordinary care and average conditions. They are all partial to a strong soil, and may be manured to almost any extent with advantage, and yet on poor land, without the aid of manure, a very welcome dish of coleworts or kale may be grown with the least imaginable trouble, and with less risk of damage by heat, drought, frost, rain, wind, and vermin, than any other crop. In a well managed garden, brassicas of some kinds are always on the ground, and they are employed to occupy gaps and fill up spaces profitably, being never out of place and very rarely out of season.

THE CABBAGE *(Brassica oleracea.)*

SOIL.—The finest cabbages are grown on deep fertile loams and clay lands that have been long cultivated. The land should be heavily manured for them, and if farm-yard muck is scarce, guano and wood ashes may be used instead; deep digging, and indeed good work throughout, are requisite to the production of a clean and useful crop, for cabbage should grow quickly to be sweet and tender, and free from disease and vermin. In rough garden and allotment cultivation, the long manure fresh from the stable or cow-byre is to be preferred to manure rotted down, and any kind of green refuse may be added; the coarse stuff being put at the bottom of the trenches, when the ground is made ready for planting. In light dry soils, it is good practice to plant in trenches drawn as deep as possible with the hoe, and at once filled in with fat manure. As a matter of course, the ground is to be first prepared by deep digging and manuring, and this additional work is to form a nice bed into which the plants will strike roots at once, being of course aided with water, for in poor soils a quick start is of great value, and a small quantity of rotten manure will go a great way if employed merely to fill up the surface drills into which the plants are to be inserted.

Cabbages and Potatoes are often grown together on outlying plots, and the surplus of both are found of service in feeding cows, pigs, and poultry. It is the most profitable way of occupying a piece of spare ground, and if the two crops so are moved about that they do not come on precisely the same spaces from year to year, there need be no change of routine for a life time. We occupy several plots in this way, and manage to shift the crops as indicated in the subjoined diagram, in which "P" represents the potato and "C" the cabbage.

1876	P		C		P		C		P		C			
1877		P		C		P		C		P		C		
1878			P		C		P		C		P		C	
1879				P		C		P		C		P		C

To make an end of all difficulty about distances, we select only the strongest growing variety of potatoes, and put them in rows four feet asunder, and when they are lifted in September the ground is still covered with cabbages in rows four feet asunder. At every planting of cabbages, the ground is trenched between the potatoes and heavily manured, but the potatoes are planted in shallow trenches only two or three inches deep, and are moulded up from between, to keep them well above the surface, and no stable manure is used for them, but a light dressing of guano and Amies' patent manure, mixed in equal quantities. In this routine, the potatoes are planted in February and March, and the land is at once made ready between, and cabbages from seed sown in August or September of the previous year are planted out, the sorts being such as *Enfield Market, Large York*, etc. They are cut as required, the stumps being left with as many leaves on as possible, and they produce a prodigious quantity of secondary smallish cabbages all through the winter and spring, and thus remain on the ground until it becomes absolutely necessary to clear them off, and then they are burnt with other rubbish, and the ashes with guano added are used for top-dressing potatoes.

SUMMER CABBAGES.—For delicate summer cabbages, sow in February or March in a frame or cool greenhouse, and prick out the young plants on a bed of light rich soil in a spare frame as soon as they are large enough to handle. From this bed transfer them to rich land when they stand about three inches high, and give water freely if the weather is dry, to prevent any check. They may be planted one foot apart, in rows two feet asunder, and as soon as any are fit for use, every alternate plant should be first taken. The best sorts to grow for this purpose are the smallish quick hearting kinds, such as *Barr's Dwarf, Small Early York*, and *Hill's Incomparable.* A good supply of early cabbages may be secured by planting out in spring from a sowing made in August, a certain proportion being left in the seed bed to heart where sown. But spring sowing with good cultivation will generally produce a better article, because more quickly grown.

MAIN CROP.—With good management, one sowing every year is enough, but it may be advisable to sow twice. In any case the most important sowing is made some time between the 20th of July and the 10th of August, and from this sowing plants are obtained both for autumn and spring planting. The seed-bed should be well made, the drills should be a foot apart, and the seed sowed thickly in the drills. From the seedling stocks thus raised plants may be drawn at almost any time, until they become too large for removal, so that in suitable weather spare spaces may be filled with cabbage, to keep the ground always earning money. It may be necessary to supplement this principal sowing with another in March, and from this the plants will be put out in the same way as the other. In selecting for these two sowings, it will be advisable to select for sowing in the autumn the large growing sorts, such as the *Red Dutch, Large York, Battersea*, and *Enfield Market;* whereas for the spring sowing the smaller kinds are to be preferred. The distances at which they are planted will depend upon the sorts and system of cropping followed, but as a rule, the largest sorts will require to be two and a half feet apart, and in rows three feet apart, and the smaller kinds about half this distance.

COLLARDS, or COLEWORTS, are small cabbages that are usually drawn before they heart, but if left to heart, become compact dark green cabbages, about the size of a common Dutch cheese. The best of the class are *London Colewort*, and *Rosette Colewort*, and these are the most useful of all known cabbages for the supply of a good table, while at the same time they are much less profitable than larger cabbages, and therefore not to be recommended for the cottager's garden. Collards may be sown at almost any time, but it is sufficient for most purposes to sow in March, and again in July, August, and September. From these sowings plantations can be made as convenient, but in every case the plants should be put out as soon as possible after they become large enough to handle, and should be aided with water if the weather is dry at the time. They may be planted close, with a view to draw every alternate plant first, and on this plan may be in rows a foot apart, and the plants six inches apart in the row. If judiciously drawn, they will supply pretty little collards for a time, and finish their career as small delicate cabbages, in rows two feet apart, and the plants one foot apart in the row. The tender sprouts of all kinds of cabbages may be regarded as collards, for the main character of this vegetable is that it is of a deep green colour throughout, whereas a proper cabbage has a solid and whitish heart. There is nothing in the way of cabbage so elegant or so welcome flavoured as a well served dish of collards of a deep green hue, tender, marrowy, and fragrant.

BORECOLES.

BRUSSELS SPROUTS are the most aristocratic of all the borecoles. Universally as this fine vegetable is esteemed, many amateur gardeners make mistakes in its management, and hence produce buttons far inferior to those commonly seen in the baskets of the London greengrocers. Now, although tastes differ, we can safely say that this is the best autumn and winter green we possess, and especially worthy of being extra well grown, because the result of good culture will be handsome produce in such plenty as to prove that the liberal system is the most profitable.

The object of the cultivator should be to secure strong plants as early in the summer as possible. Therefore, the seed should be sown on a well-prepared seed-bed in February, or early in March, and the plants should be put out as soon as large enough to be lifted, and showery weather should be selected for the operation, or lacking rain, the plants should be shaded for a time, and regularly watered. A poor soil will not produce this vegetable in a state to be worth gathering; therefore, prepare for the plantation a deeply dug and well-manured plot. Our mode of procedure is to plant potatoes in rows four feet apart, and put out the Brussels sprouts between them two feet apart in the row. When the potatoes are taken up, the sprouts have the full breadth of four feet, and they very soon afterwards nearly meet across the rows, and it may be understood by the fact that we obtain our supplies of buttons from gigantic plants.

But we can do better than this, and now proceed to describe the better way. We make a sowing of seed in the first week of August, and as soon as possible thin the plants to three or four inches apart, and leave them to stand the winter. As early in March as weather will permit, we transplant them into the potato plot on a similarly good piece of ground in rows three or four feet apart, and they soon make a tremendous growth, and supply fine buttons in enormous quantity from the end of August until the month of March following. This practice answers perfectly on our cold damp soil, five miles north from London, and we take care to provide for the seed-bed a sheltered nook on the highest part of the ground. Were we located north of the Trent, we should sow in July to stand the winter in the open, and again in August for a few hundred plants, to be aided with some cheap protection. Whatever conduces to the early and luxuriant growth of this useful vegetable must be adopted as profitable, unless it is a very extravagant affair indeed. We expect to find our plants four feet high, and literally studded with round buttons the size of a small orange some time in the autumn, proportionate to the time at which the seed was sown.

Now, perhaps the reader would like to know what sort we grow, for there are many in the market. Well, we always order "imported seed," and find that other so-called improvements are either no better or some degree worse. There are other varieties of sprouts, such as the *Feather-stemmed savoy*, and the *Dalmeny sprouts*, but they are of little value; of Brussels sprouts there is but one variety, and genuine imported seed is the best.

One word more. The proper way to appropriate the plant is to remove the sprouts from the stem as soon as they are fully grown, and before they begin to expand. Continue this practice all through the piece from first to last, and when it appears that no more good buttons are coming, take the top cabbages, and you will find them a delicious vegetable, if nicely cooked. But if you take the top cabbage first, you will have very few good sprouts, and indeed what can you expect from the plants after they have lost their heads, and their stems are exposed to the buffeting of wind, rain, frost, and snow?

SPROUTING BROCCOLI.—This may be grown in precisely the same way as recommended for Brussels sprouts. If not well grown, it is simply unprofitable, but when well done is a most valuable vegetable, because it comes into use at a time when greenmeat is scarce. There are several sorts in the market, but the best is the old *Purple Sprouting*. However, the new *White Sprouting* is worth having where there is plenty of room, and a variety of spring vegetables is required. It is altogether too unproductive for a small garden.

SCOTCH KALE and COTTAGER'S KALE must be sown early and planted out early, and liberally cultivated from first to last. But if the ground is poor and the practice not quite first-rate, these are the best of all the winter greens, for they make a fair return when badly treated.

BUDA KALE is of dwarf growth, and may be planted close. It is useless during winter, but of great value in the spring, and may be cut from later than any other plant of its class.

CHOU DE MILAN forms a small head, which should not be cut. In spring it produces a number of tender shoots that form a most delicious dish of greens at a time when vegetables are scarce.

SIBERIAN KALE is, as its name would imply, exceedingly hardy, and of great value for poor soils and bleak situations. It rises only six inches high, the leaves are green, coarsely serrated, and plaited on the margin. The spring shoots are tender and delicious. It is not sufficiently productive for strong lands in mild climates.

VARIEGATED KALE is grown for decorative purposes and garnishing. Its ornamental value depends on management. The seed should be sown rather late, on rather poor soil, and if the plants are intended to furnish flower beds during winter, they must be planted in them soon enough in autumn to become well rooted before severe frost occurs. If long legged, they should be planted deep to shorten them. As soon in spring as vegetation shows signs of renewed activity, carefully cut out the crowns of all the plants, but leave on them as many leaves as possible. They will at once produce rosette-like shoots of the most delicate colours, and for two or three weeks make a beautiful display. The crowns and sprouts of variegated kales are nearly, but not quite as good as those of the green kales when cooked. A row or so of this interesting vegetable should be sown every year even if there is no serious intention to employ them in the flower beds. They will come in usefully in various ways, if only as now and then affording a subject for conversation.

We plant Sprouting Broccoli, Scotch Kale, and Cottager's Kale, in rows four feet apart, alternately with potatoes, and the plants touch one another long before winter, and Become in a considerable degree self-protective.

BROCCOLI AND CAULIFLOWER.

IT is customary in gardening books to treat of the Broccoli and the Cauliflower as altogether distinct, and requiring different modes of cultivation. This is a mistake—they are not distinct—they differ in name chiefly; and as to cultivation, whatever rules apply to one, apply with equal force to the other. That we may be clearly understood, we are bound to say that the term "cauliflower" may be conveniently applied to the most perfect white curd-like varieties that are cut during summer and autumn, as they are at once the most handsome and the most delicate-flavoured. But there is no inherent impropriety in regarding broccolis and cauliflowers as members of one class of vegetables, and the well-known Walcheren variety may be instanced in illustration, for this is acknowledged to be either a broccoli or a cauliflower, at the discretion of the cultivator. If it be asked how the supposed distinction originated, it may be answered that the varieties of broccoli differ in degrees of hardiness, and the most tender of them require to be sheltered during winter; and as only such of the finest quality are worth the trouble of protecting, these form a group which it is convenient to separate from the rest as cauliflowers, although in every essential particular they are as truly broccolis as any of the more hardy and less elegant varieties.

THE BROCCOLI *(Brassica oleracea botrytis)* and CAULIFLOWER *(Brassica oleracea cauliflora)* are gross feeding plants, and therefore require a rich deep soil. The cultivator who seeks to obtain a supply from a poor soil will be disappointed unless he happens to be favoured with a hot summer, and gives the plant regular and copious supplies of liquid manure. Only on good living can handsome heads of broccoli be produced, and, therefore, the first step towards a good supply is deep digging and abundant manuring. In our heavy damp clay land, all the varieties attain to their highest possible quality, but a rather light, well-tilled loam is to be preferred for varieties that produce their heads during winter and spring. However, we have cut abundance of the finest broccoli during ten months out of the twelve, the times of scarcity being June and December; and though we have seen our plantations under water for days together, and at other times stiffened with fifteen degrees of frost, we have rarely suffered from the trials the plants are exposed to on our cold soil in the winter season. On those old garden soils that produce club, the seed-beds should be prepared by digging in lime or plaster, and the ground for planting on should be prepared by double digging, and putting a heavy layer of good manure between the two spits. By such management the club will be exterminated, and the land will be constantly increasing in cleanliness and strength.

BROCCOLI AS AN ORDINARY GARDEN CROP.—By good management broccolis may be cut during eight or nine months out of twelve, and entail but little more trouble than a crop of cabbage. It is best to make three sowings—the first as early in March as the state of the heavens and earth will permit, the other two in the first week of April, and about the middle of May. Sow in drills in the same way as cabbage, and on as good a seed-bed as can be prepared for them. From these three sowings a constant succession of plants will be obtained, and they should be planted out as fast as they become large enough, on land heavily manured and thoroughly well prepared by deep digging. The large growing sorts should be in rows three or four feet apart, and the plants three feet apart in the rows. Moderate growers, such as the Walcheren, may be two and a-half feet each way, and smaller sorts, such as the Cape, may be two feet apart each way. If the spring is late, the March sowing will be comparatively worthless, but the cost of seed is trifling, and it is always advisable to sow a pinch of broccoli with the other small seeds in March, for the chance of some strong plants to put out early. It is a great help to the supply if a sowing of *Walcheren* or *Hammond's Improved* be made in February in a seed-pan under glass, and the plants carefully handled for planting out in April. If at any stage the plants receive a check, or if allowed to grow to any considerable size in the seed-bed, they will fail at last, more or less. Therefore, showery weather should be chosen for planting out, but rather than delay too long waiting for showers, put out the plants when they are ready, and by shading and watering, help them to take hold of their new stations quickly, without, as we say, "feeling the move." The after culture consists in leaving them alone, for they will not even require water. However, if extra fine heads are desired, and the summer is hot and dry, or the soil too poor to do them justice, water must be given, and, in the case of a poor soil, the water must be flavoured with some nutritive material, such as guano, or drainings from the manure heap. In the hot dry summers of 1868, 1870, and 1876, we had fine crops of broccolis and cauliflowers, but not one had any artificial waterings except for a few days after being first planted out. But then ours is a very deep, heavy, and productive soil, and for broccolis we assist it by laying a coat of fat manure between the two spits, as the trenching proceeds. Supposing a good selection to have been made from the seed-list, you will begin to cut nice broccolis in August, and continue cutting until frosts stop the supply, which, perhaps, will not occur until January. Towards the end of February, if the weather is mild, the supply will be renewed, and will increase as the spring advances, and be at its height during April, and will come to an end during the latter days in May. Plants raised from seed sown under glass in February, and carefully managed afterwards, may give nice heads in July, which enlarges the scheme by one month in starting, and plants that have stood in a north aspect all winter may not flower until June, and this will enlarge the scheme by a month at winding up. Nevertheless, by what may be termed the rough and ready way of growing broccoli, there must be a break in the supply. To ensure continuous supplies, other and more troublesome methods of procedure must be resorted to. This brings us to another section of the subject, namely:—

BROCCOLIS AND CAULIFLOWERS ALL THE YEAR ROUND.—To ensure a continuous supply, there should be three sowings of broccolis, as above advised, and a dozen sorts, at least, should be grown. But cauliflowers must be grown also, and there should be three sowings of these, one at the end of August, another at the end of September, and another in February. In the far north, the August sowing will be most useful; in the far south, it is not advisable to sow until the beginning of October. It is impossible to advise for every climate, but this rule may be useful, that large plants are not to be desired before winter, and, therefore, a little judgment must be exercised in determining the dates of sowing. As soon as the plants are large enough to handle, they should be potted or planted in a bed in a frame in rather light soil, and be kept well aired all the winter to prevent spindling or rotting at the collar. As they will stand five, or even seven, degrees of frost without harm, it is not advisable to keep them closely muffled up at any time during winter; for, indeed, if they are weakened by coddling, they will in the end come to no good. The February sowing should be aided with a gentle heat, and the plants potted as soon as large enough, and after about ten days' enjoyment of a greenhouse temperature to assist them in filling the pots with roots, should be removed to a cold frame, and be gradually "hardened" preparatory to planting. Put out the autumn-sown plants first, and shelter them if the weather is bleak, but it is better to wait a week or two, and even to shift a lot into larger pots to keep them growing than to plant too early, for the check of exposure to cold, may cause them to "button," that is, produce heads the size of a florin, or crown-piece, of no use at all. From these several plantations you ought to cut fine heads from June onwards far into the autumn.

Now, let us suppose you have by some accident lost your autumn sown stock, and are speculating how to gain time, and keep up the supply by some other method. It would in this case be a good plan to sow in the first week of February and the first week of March a pinch each of *Walcheren*, *Purple Cape*, *Hammond's White Cape*, and *Beck's Early Dwarf*, and carefully nurse them, so as to be enabled to put out strong plants at the earliest moment the weather will permit. It may be worthy of notice, too, that all the foregoing sorts are worth trying for supplies in May and June, by sowing them in autumn, and planting them out in cheap protectors, such as Boulton's, or in ground vineries of wood or brick. In March they should be thinned to twenty inches apart; the thinnings planted out, and those remaining left to flower in the frames. It would be necessary to give plenty of air, and to take the glass off entirely at the end of April.

There yet remains the depth of winter to be provided for. It is important, therefore, to bear in mind that broccolis in flower may be kept a long time in perfect condition under cover during winter. If, therefore, in the latter days of December there is a good supply of nice heads of Walcheren, or any other good sort on the ground, take them up, with roots and all complete, and plant them close together in dry earth in a shed, or any other suitable place from which they can be obtained as wanted. The winter supply is a question of weather as regards outdoor cutting, and of prudence as regards cutting under cover. In a mild open winter there will be plenty of nice broccolis turning in during January and February, provided suitable sorts are on the ground to produce them.

Winter Culture demands a paragraph, because broccolis are considered tender things. It is customary in November to "lay them down." This process consists in heeling them over with their heads to the north without in any serious degree disturbing their roots. The practice may be needful in districts where the winters are usually more severe than in London, but on our cold wet clay in the valley of the Lea, five miles north of the metropolis, it is altogether unnecessary, for we grow broccolis largely, and never lay them down, and our losses in severe winters are really of no material consequence at all. Another practice preparatory to winter protection is to sprinkle the ground between the plants with salt, at the rate of ten or twelve bushels to the acre. This is done early in October, and is certainly not a waste of labour or of salt, for the result is a wholesale destruction of vermin, and a consequent protection of the plants from their ravages, during those mild winter and early spring days, when slugs and other such come forth in troops, and eat out the hearts of the best vegetables in the garden. It is worth remembering, too, that the salt is worth its cost as manure, and its presence in the soil will benefit the next crop.

WALCHEREN BROCCOLI demands a note, because of its distinctness and value. It may be sown at almost any season, and cut at almost any season. Indeed, we know not what a master of broccoli culture might do with it, if supplied with good seed, and denied a supply of any other. He could certainly, by good management, cut from it beautiful white heads of medium size very nearly all the year round, and we think the whole circle of the year might be compassed with it in a garden where all needful appliances were at hand. As it will not endure severe frost, it is rarely cut from open ground plantations after the end of the year, or before the end of July.

QUALITY.—Some of the sorts have "leafy heads,"—a considerable number of leaves appearing among the intersections of the flower. It is a fault certainly, but quite a small one. The largest sized broccolis are usually considered the best. But small heads are preferable to large ones; though great size is not a great defect, because a large broccoli may be cut from, and a portion cooked as required, provided the form and texture are what they ought to be. In the spring of the year 1872, we had a head of Cattell's Eclipse that weighed 21 lbs. It was remarkably handsome; a wonder to behold. It was carefully cut from as required, and made five dishes on five successive days, and, from first to last, as a table vegetable, was about as perfect as any broccoli ever eaten, and in every case the fifth part came to table as complete as an individual head. As to colour, it is impossible there should be two opinions. The whiter the head the better, and the texture should be fine, and firm, and close, not a gap anywhere, and the general outline hemispherical. The Purple Cape is invaluable for its earliness, and we cannot do without it; but its colour is faulty, and we should be well off if we had a white Cape to equal it; but we have not, though Hammond's White Cape is good. Indeed the old Purple Cape is the best flavoured broccoli in cultivation.

SELECTION OF VARIETIES.—The following are probably the

best broccolis in cultivation for general purposes; they are selected from a hundred sorts grown on our trial ground:—*Baskett's Late*, in use from March 27 to April 16. *Brimstone*, in use April 5 to April 20. *Brown's Incomparable Hardy*, in use April 2 to April 30. *Carter's Champion*, in use April 3 to May 18. *Cattell's Eclipse*, in use April 13 to May 20. *Early White*, in use April 6 to April 26. *Grainger's White*, in use February 28 to March 28. *Hammond's Improved*, in use September 4 to December 1. *Large Late White*, in use April 6 to April 26. *Lake's Fine Late*, in use April 20 to May 18. *Maber's Giant*, in use March 10 to April 15. *Penzance*, in use February 28 to April 2. *Reading Giant*, in use March 17 to April 10. *Snow's Winter White*, in use April 2 to April 15. *Sutton's Superb*, in use February 28 to April 12. *Walcheren*, in use from June 24 to the end of the year.

From the foregoing sixteen we will select six, and they shall be *Walcheren*, *Grainger's*, *Sutton's Superb*, *Lake's Late*, *Carter's Champion*, *Cattell's Eclipse*. The best cauliflowers are, *Frogmore Forcing*, *Early London*, and *Lenormands*.

For special purposes the following deserve attention as distinct and good: *Autumn Purple Cape*, and *Hammond's White Cape*, for planting close and insuring early supplies. *Beck's Early Dwarf*, *Hammond's White Cape*, and *Miller's Dwarf*, for frame culture. *Carter's Champion*, *Cattell's Eclipse*, *Dilcock's Bride*, *Hammond's Improved*, *Hampton Early White*, *Late Goschen*, *Maber's Giant*, *Malta*, *Reading Giant*, and *Sutton's Superb* are frequently remarked upon in our note-books as beautiful in form and colour, and usually attaining to a considerable size. We have dismissed *Dancer's Pink Cape* as "not wanted," but, as it makes extremely pretty heads, it may be turned to account for exhibition.

Enemies of Brassicas.—Club and caterpillar are the only enemies that seriously engage our attention. Aphis is destructive in dry weather, but rarely appears on plants that are doing well. It is commonly understood that club is peculiar to old garden soil, but it happens with us that in an old garden where we raise all our seeds, and have had for many years past seed-beds of hundreds of kinds of brassicas, we have never seen a club on a single root, while in another garden consisting of quite newly broken clay land, club occurs frequently. Deep digging and liberal manuring are the surest preventives of club, and indeed smart cultivation is death to vermin of all kinds, for if the spade, the fork, and the manure do them no direct harm, the frequent stirring of the earth exposes them to the keen eyes of the thrushes, and robins, and nightingales, and thus "their ranks are thinned by wasteful war." To operate against caterpillars, the first thing is to search for patches of eggs on the undersides of leaves, and destroy them; the next thing is to catch and kill caterpillars. A dusting with tobacco powder will settle them wholesale, and so will watering the plants with very weak salt and water. We must confess we do not trouble ourselves much about vermin, for life seems to be too short for such small things to interfere with our happiness. We mentally ignore their existence, and they probably sicken through loss of importance, for we so rarely suffer by their depredations, that we know of no better way than to persuade oneself that such things exist only in morbid imaginations

HIBBERD'S TRIANGULAR EDGING TILE.

CHAPTER VII.

SPINACH (*Spinacia oleracea.*)

"Our bodies are our gardens ; to the which, our wills are gardeners : so that if we will plant nettles, or sow lettuce ; set hyssop, and weed up thyme ; supply it with one gender of herbs, or distract it with many ; either to have it sterile with idleness, or manured with industry ; why, the power and corrigible authority of this lies in our wills."

Othello, I., 3.

THE simplicity of Spinach is the cause of its ruin in thousands of gardens. It is put upon the poorest ground, badly prepared, and to make amends for slovenly work, five times as much seed as is requisite is sown in the drill, and the crop is a mere shadow of what spinach ought to be. It is so accommodating and wants so little to make much of it, that it rarely occurs to amateur gardeners to grow it well and enjoy it thoroughly. The practice of sowing spinach between rows of peas is good, for it can be cleared off before the peas are ready, and in this sense may be regarded as a stolen crop. To grow a first-rate sample requires good ground, and the complete exposure of the plant to light and air from the first, and a very important part of the matter is to sow thinly, so that there will not be much thinning of the plants required, for spinach should spread almost flat upon the ground to make fat leaves and be thoroughly first-rate in every way.

SPRING SPINACH may be sown from February to the end of April, after which time it is waste of work to sow another grain of seed, for the heat of the summer will overtake it, and bolting will soon follow. If sown on a plot by itself (and not between peas), the distance from row to row should be not less than eighteen inches, and indeed, if the ground is strong, the rows may be two feet asunder with advantage, for if well done there will even then be scarcely space enough for one to go between to gather the crop. Where the demand is great there should be two or three sowings, but great things may be done with one sowing, and it will not bolt in haste. The first business will be to thin it by drawing out plants as soon as they are large enough for use. Draw out a tuft with the right hand, twist off the roots with the left, and thus fill the basket with spinach that will not require either to be picked or washed. Continue to thin in this way, and if the consumption does not use the thinnings fast enough, draw them and waste, so as to have the plants as soon as possible a foot apart. You will probably obtain an abundant supply by thinning only for about a month, and then the plants that remain will be giants in their way, and you may gather from them immense quantities of the finest spinach by nipping off their tops only. Begin at one end of the piece and go regularly through, and then begin as before, and go through again. You will probably not need to touch single leaves at all, for the topping process will enable you to gather a few bushels in about half-an-hour or so, and these will not need to be washed or even looked at by the cook, and being quite dry and clean, it will be necessary to use a little water to cook them, and that way of cooking produces a richer and greener dish than the customary one of cooking it in the water that drains from it after it is put over the fire. Again and again the plants may be topped, but at last the heat of the weather will compel them to make flower spikes, which is the signal for clearing the ground. *Round-seeded Spinach* is the best for the first supply.

ORACH *(Atriplex hortensis)* may be secured in abundance from June to November, by the same course of procedure as described above, but more space must be allowed, and as other vegetables abound in the summer, a few rows only will perhaps be needed. It will be well, however, to sow three times at least; say last week in May, first week in July, and first week in August. There are several plants available for the summer supply, but we have in mind now only such as produce a genuine spinach, requiring to be cooked the same way, and having when well served the same elegant appearance and very nearly the same delicious sooty flavour. The best of them is the *Golden Summer Spinach*, a selection from the *Common Orach*, which also is first-rate, but coarser than the other. The first of these two is when growing the same colour as the "golden feather" pyretheum, and in large places may be employed as a yellow-leaved bedding plant;

the common orach is more robust, of a bluish or grey-green colour, and not quite such a brilliant green when cooked as the yellow-leaved plant.

NEW ZEALAND SPINACH *(Tetragonia expansa)* is a close-growing plant that in some degree resembles the ice-plant. The seed is sown in heat in April, and the plants are put out in May, in the hottest and driest spot that can be found for them. The young tops are pinched for spinach, and are very nice, but lack the sooty flavour, and so perhaps will suit some people to whom the flavour of real spinach is objectionable. It is a common occurrence for New Zealand Spinach to become a weed by sowing its seed from year to year, but when a cold wet summer occurs it is likely to be swept off the ground, for drought and heat are the conditions that favour its growth and increase.

SUBSTITUTES FOR SPINACH abound, and the Tetragonia named above is one of them. The common Fathen, or Good King Harry *(Chenopodium Bonus Henricus)* is the best of them, and it will generally be found in plenty as a weed on the rubbish heap. The young tops, when the plant is growing freely, make a delicious spinach, but when the plant runs up to flower it is useless. *Chenopodium quinoa*, a native of Peru, promises to become a garden plant for the supply of summer spinach. The poke-weeds, and especially the *Phytolacca decandra*, may be used as spinach when young, but is scarcely wholesome when fully grown. Any of the amaranths may be used as spinach, and especially *Amaranthus blitum*, a native of Britain, and *A. oleraceous*, a frame or greenhouse plant. The tender tops of the gourd or pumpkin vines make a very elegant spinach, but their removal is calculated to lessen the production of fruit. Finally, the youngest leaves of mangold or white beet may be cooked as spinach, but the flavour is somewhat earthy, and the removal of the leaves does in some degree check the growth of the roots.

WINTER SPINACH is sown on rather dry ground, from the middle of July to the middle of August, in drills a foot apart, and the plants are by degrees thinned to six inches apart. It comes into use at the turn of spring, and if the weather is not forcing, lasts until the first supply of spring-sown spinach is ready. It sometimes happens that the crop is destroyed or seriously injured by the obnoxious black grub of the Daddy-long-legs *(Tipula oleracea)*. To prevent this, prepare the ground sometime before sowing, by digging it well and sprinkling lightly with salt. The process will expose the vermin to three dangers: some will be buried too deep to see daylight again; some will be killed by the salt; some will be eaten by birds, whose quick eyes will see them as they prowl about at daybreak, looking for a breakfast. If it is seen that a plant here or there drops over suddenly through being eaten across at the collar, you may be sure this pest is the cause of the mischief. Then take a piece of stick and scrape the soil slightly from every plant, and scratch between the rows with a hoe, and you may stop the mischief. There are two kinds of spinach available for Autumn sowing. The best is the *Prickly seeded*, which should always be preferred unless there are reasons for preferring the hardier plant, known as *Spinach Beet*, which suits better for bleak places and undrained soils.

DEATH'S-HEAD MOTH.

CHAPTER VIII.

SEAKALE AND ASPARAGUS.

Cas. Will you sup with me to-night, Casca?
Casca. No, I am promised forth.
Cas. Will you dine with me to-morrow?
Casca. Ay, if I be alive, and your mind hold, and your dinner worth the eating.
Cas. Good: I will expect you.

Julius Cæsar, *I.*, 2.

THESE two elegant vegetables agree pretty nearly in their requirements and their uses, and whoever can grow one satisfactorily will find it an easy matter to grow the other. To speak of their respective qualities is needless; it is a subject for a gastronomic essay, and a fine subject too. In a book intended to assist the work of the garden, it is more to the purpose to say that these vegetables come in at a time when there is usually nothing else in the way of vegetables obtainable except cabbage and spinach, and even these may run short if the winter has been exceptionally trying. As no home is complete without a stereoscope, so no garden is complete without at least one bed each of asparagus and seakale, and the question with the uninitiated perhaps will be "how much ground shall I devote to these estimable plants?" It must be understood then, at starting, that as regards the relative bulk of food produced, seakale is certainly the more profitable of the two. As to their relative gastronomic merits we have nothing to say. A general advice may, therefore, be hazarded, that a bed of seakale, twenty yards in length by two yards wide, may suffice for most families to begin with; and two beds, twenty yards in length and four feet wide (with two feet alley between), devoted to asparagus, may also be enough for a beginning. If pinched for space, begin with half these quantities, and take time to determine whether to do more or less in future. You need not think of forcing at the first start, because you can buy roots for that purpose;

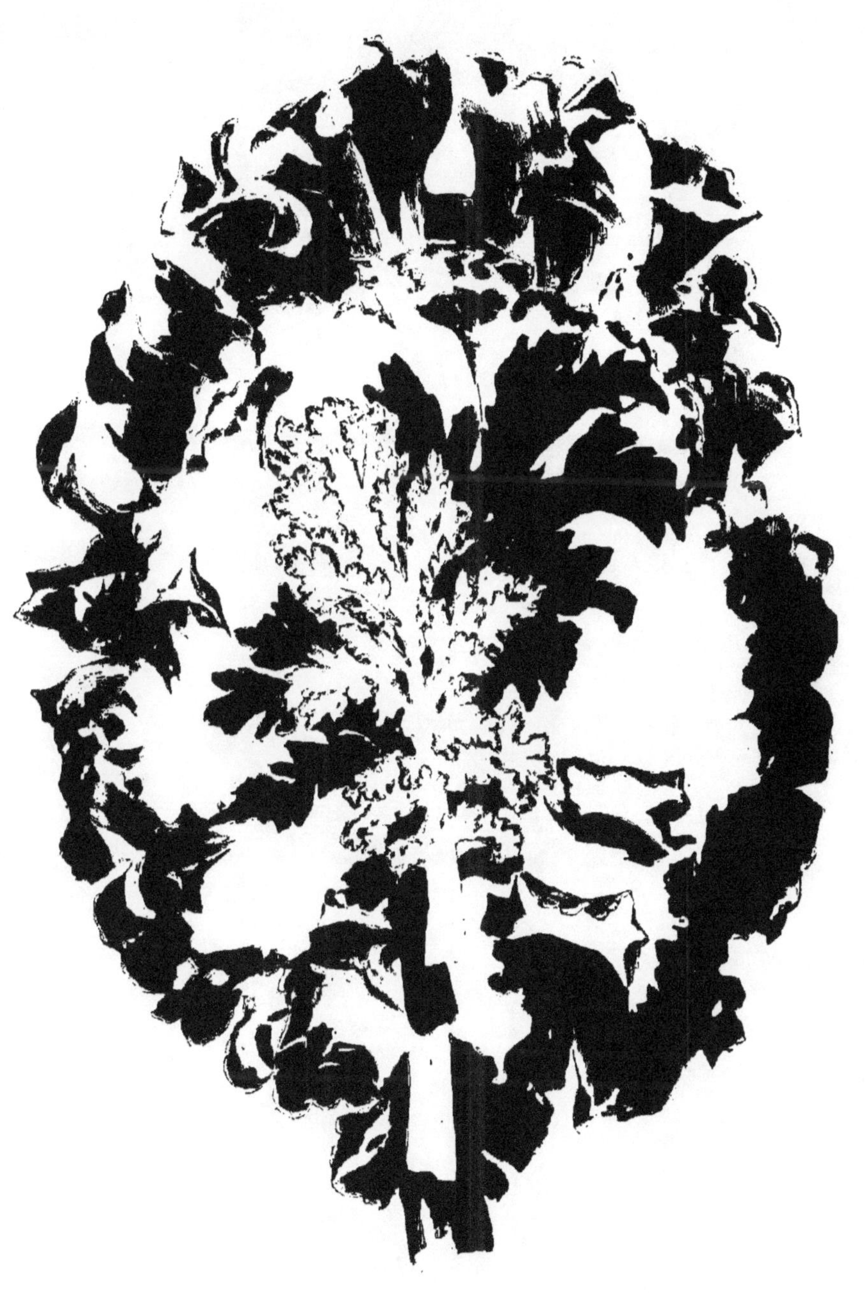

but when the forcing of asparagus and seakale becomes a matter of settled routine, there must be established a routine culture of roots for the purpose, and it will be found necessary to sow seed every spring, and carry on the culture nursery fashion.

It is generally represented that these plants require an extravagantly rich soil—that is to say, a soil loaded with stable manure—and that the cultivation is complicated and costly from first to last. This is an injurious mistake, for although these are certainly not to be regarded as vegetables suitable to the circumstances of a cottager, they may be produced in plenty, and of the finest quality, in any middle-class garden, and will make an ample return in money value for all reasonable expenditure incurred in their cultivation. Their one grand requirement is a *deep* soil. It should not be waterlogged, and it may with advantage be made fat with manure, and the better every way by the addition of sand, unless it is already sandy in the staple. But the main requirement is not fatness or sandiness, or anything else in respect of either chemical or mechanical peculiarity. The main requirement is *depth*, and it follows, of course, that on a soil naturally shallow, some kind of stuff must be added to make root room for these far-rooting plants. A rich deep sandy soil suits them both perfectly, but as fine samples as ever were seen may be grown on clay land, provided a little care is taken in the first instance to humour the plants in the preparation of the beds.

SEAKALE, *Crambe maritima* requires a deep good soil, a quite open situation, and sufficient space for the full development of its large handsome leaves. Prepare the bed by trenching and manuring, and sow seed in March and April, or plant roots in September. In strong lands the plants should be a yard apart every way, but the usual distance allowed is two feet. Our beds are six feet wide, with two-feet alleys between, and there are two rows of plants. In sowing seed, put in two or three seeds where a plant should be, and as soon as they have made a good start, thin them out, leaving ultimately only one at each station. The clump system is a bad system, for it groups together several plants where there is room only for one, and as one strong stool in its third year will supply as many handsome heads as will fill three market punnets, it is a pity to crowd the plants and diminish the production. All the rest is easy work. You will keep down weeds of course, and you will be wise to blanch the crop on the ground, and to abstain from forcing until you have had some experience, which you will find very easy and agreeable work. You may supply the plants while growing with any amount of water or clarified sewage; but if you cannot irrigate you need not be troubled, for this thrifty plant has a way of taking care of itself, provided only it can obtain a deep root hold in the heart of the world.

Forcing Seakale in the Open Ground is a very easy matter. In the course of the autumn the dead leaves should be cleared off and the ground strewed with a thick coat of salt between the stools. This will kill the vermin and nourish the roots. Some time during winter put on the seakale pots and cover the bed with leaves and other such clean litter. In this process the pots must be buried, to screen them from frost. It will depend upon the weather when you will begin to cut, but you will have a fine sample by this process if the roots are strong, and you may expect supplies from the middle of March to the end of April. It must be remembered that in any case seakale *must* be blanched when it is intended to be cut, and, as a rule, it is not desirable to blanch a bed raised from seeds until the third season, that is to say, when the plant has had two seasons of growth and is entering on the third. If we sow in the spring of 1876, we begin to cut in the spring of 1878, and thenceforward cut annually until the beds begin to decline.

Forcing in Frames is accomplished in a variety of ways, but the plant is so manageable that convenience is a matter for first consideration. For an early supply the following plan may be recommended: Make up a bed for a small two-light frame, using tree leaves with a little fermented manure just to form the outsides, to bring the bed into shape. For small families New Year's Day will be quite soon enough to commence. The leaves, etc., are well beaten with a fork as the work of making up is going on. A height of four feet at back, and three and a-half feet in front, will give out sufficient heat for the purpose, as not more than a bottom-heat of 60° is wanted; indeed, anything above 60° will induce a weak growth. This bed may be made in any out-of-the-way corner of the garden or frame-ground, and after it has been made a few days, put in about six inches of leaf-soil. This will keep down the steam, and will serve to plant the roots in. A convenient size for a frame is eight feet by four, and and it should be divided into three parts, as in the accompanying plan :—

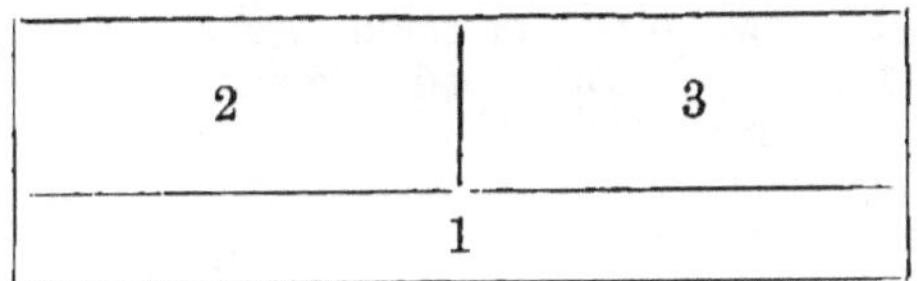

No. 1 compartment is planted first, and as six inches of soil will not admit of the roots being planted down, they may be laid in a little on the slant, so as to have the soil up just under the crown, and these ought to be three inches from each other, and gently watered with tepid water after the planting is finished. The frame should then be covered up, first with a mat, and over that a layer of short hay two inches thick, with another mat at top. This will effectually exclude all light, and if the heat is what it ought to be, some well-grown kale will be fit for table in about six weeks. Nos. 2 and 3 compartments are filled at an interval of about a fortnight, so that there are always plants in three different stages of growth; and in this manner, by filling up with fresh plants every time a part is all cut, a succession may be kept up either till the plants are exhausted or the season over.

But this cannot be done with the heat of the bed alone, for in the course of two months this will be exhausted, and linings will be required. This is done by simply putting a good thick layer of fresh stable manure round that part of the frame which has been last planted. This will want turning and well shaking up about every ten days, to renew the heat. It appears necessary to add that a very little air should be given every other day for about a couple of hours, to let out any steam that may arise from the heat of the bed. This will insure a sweet and pure atmosphere, which, if not attended to, might perhaps be detrimental to the flavour of the produce; but, on all occasions, or on whatever plan of forcing is adopted, it is important to remember that the admission of light or air for any length of time will discolour the growth, which must be avoided.

For very small gardens, the following plan will be found serviceable and convenient. Procure a good box, about four feet wide, and as much in depth. Take this to a warm, close cellar, and in it put six inches of moderately light dry soil. In this soil place the crowns, and give them a gentle watering, and in the course of six or seven weeks, if the place is a moderately warm one, some good kale may be expected.

SEAKALE UNBLANCHED.—Those who are obliged to have a large supply of early spring vegetables will find it a very useful plan to grow a breadth to cut from without forcing or blanching. Plant under a north wall say fifty strong plants a foot apart each way. Keep them clean, and fork between them once a year. Do not force them or cover them, but let them come on naturally, which they do just as the spring greens and broccolis are over, and it is just at this season that green vegetables are scarce, and consequently we very often have to commence cutting the spring cabbage at a sacrifice. Now, the fact that this method of growing seakale will serve to fill up a gap between these two crops is a very important one, for apart from the great advantage to be gained by giving the cabbage bed another ten days or a fortnight to grow larger, it is a good and delicious vegetable, little inferior to asparagus, but perhaps will not suit the taste of dainty epicures. It is never in better condition than when it has grown to the length of eight or nine inches. The flower-heads of seakale make a nice dish if cut before the flowers open.

SEAKALE RAISED FROM CUTTINGS is not so good in the end as that raised from the seed, but with good management cuttings will make plants fit for forcing in one season, and, therefore, this system of propagating has its merits. To raise stock from roots quickly, take stout thongs or tails of roots from plants that have been forced, and plant in a bed in a frame until they have formed a fair head of leaves, when they should be planted out in the open. If this is not convenient, prepare a thoroughly good bed, and in the month of March cut up a lot of roots into pieces a span long, and, as a rule, ranging in thickness from that of a man's middle finger to that of a common lead pencil. Plant these with their top ends one inch below the surface, and cover with fine soil and finish the bed fairly. They will soon push through and make fine plants. If to be lifted the next winter for forcing they may be eighteen inches apart; if to remain they must be two to three feet apart, according to the strength of the ground. As we recommend giving seakale plenty of room, it may be well to add that a crop of onions may be grown between the first year, and what little they take from the bed may be made good by a mulch of fat manure in the ensuing winter.

ASPARAGUS *(Asparagus officinalis)* may be grown in the same manner as advised for seakale, with a few very trifling modifications, as noted already. It has been remarked that these valuable vegetables may be produced in fine condition by modes more simple than are usually followed, and we will give here an illustration.

In the spring of 1870 we sowed two rows of asparagus seed in a piece of ground occupied with raspberries, in the fashion of what we call a "stolen crop." In the spring of 1871 we prepared two beds, each fifty feet in length by six feet wide. The ground was trenched two spits deep, and a heap of sweepings from the poultry-house, saved for the purpose, was spread over and slightly forked in. The earth was then taken out of the alleys adjoining and thrown on the beds, and they were thus roughly reduced to about five feet in width. The plants from the previous year's sowing were carefully lifted and planted in May, in rows one foot apart and the plants one foot asunder in the row, and the beds were then carefully cut to four and a-half feet in width, the crumbs from the alleys being spread over them. The beds were kept clear of weeds, and the asparagus stems were removed in the autumn, and a top-dressing put on of sweepings from the poultry-house, saved for the purpose. In March, 1872, the beds were slightly pricked over with a small fork to loosen the top crust and destroy rising weeds, and then a mixture of fifty-six pounds of salt and an equal bulk of dry earth was spread over their surface. The growth that followed was tremendous, not a weed appeared; in fact, not a weed could have lived with such a growth of asparagus to crush it. In the spring of 1873 another dressing of salt was given, and a still more vigorous growth followed. We began to cut early and left off cutting in the last week of June, taking from the beds an immense supply of fat, green asparagus of the most delicate texture and delicious flavour.

In the autumn of 1873 the plants stood six feet high,

making a dense mass of herbage over the bed, and saying, as plainly as they could speak, "We want more room." Therefore two more beds in another garden were prepared for them. For this purpose a piece of pasture on a heavy, clay-like loam, was broken up. The ground was first trenched two spits deep, and a great body of vegetable refuse of the nature of coarse hay—the result of trimming up with scythe and sickle amongst long grass, and such weeds as "fat hen," etc., etc.—was laid between the two spits. Then fifty barrow-loads of lime and plaster rubbish, mixed with an equal quantity of rotted grass mowings and grit from the rubbish-yard, was spread on the surface. The next thing was to lift and plant. When lifted they were cut back to about three feet, and carefully planted in rows eighteen inches apart, the plants the same distance in the rows, and so regularly opposite each other as to form rows *across* the bed, for convenience of hoeing, the beds now being six feet wide. They were then moulded up with half-rotted grass-mowings and grit from the rubbish-yard. This mode of growing asparagus, it will be seen, is scarcely more costly than the ordinary growing of parsnips and carrots. Seakale may be grown in the same manner.

Good old garden soil will grow asparagus well with very moderate manuring. Clay is the worst soil for the plant, and rich, well-drained sandy loam the best. It loves sand, and stones, and salt, and alkaline manures; but if the beds be of good texture, deep, well-drained, and somewhat sandy, there is no occasion at all for extravagant manuring; therefore, a poor man who loves asparagus may grow it to his heart's content, in spite of the elaborate directions of the books. It is a wild weed on the sandy and rocky shores of these islands, and therefore can "pick up a crust" in a comparatively poor country.

To Raise a Stock of Plants, sow in March in drills one foot apart, and one inch deep. In the following spring transplant them to the beds, when they are growing freely, taking advantage of showery weather for the operation. Put them out a foot apart every way, unless the ground is particularly well adapted for asparagus, in which case put them eighteen inches asunder every way. In common with all other plants, asparagus will pay for manure and water where these can be provided in plenty, but if either of them are costly articles, the cultivator is advised to make his mind easy and leave his asparagus-beds to take care of themselves to a very great extent. A thin sprinkling of salt may be put on the beds once a month from February to July; but we prefer to use a heavy dressing in March, to kill the weeds and feed the plant for the season. As a rule, the best time to transplant is March and April, and seed-beds that are to stand for a crop should, at that season, be thinned to a foot apart every way in poor or middling ground, and to eighteen inches apart in ground known to produce strong growth. If, however, the time for spring-planting be lost, the plants may be moved with safety from the middle of July to the end of September, and dull, showery weather should be waited for; and the job, when once commenced, should be completed as carefully and quickly as possible.

THE ROUTINE CULTURE is very simple. The soil should be deeply trenched and made as light and gritty as the materials available permit. If the situation is damp raise the beds above the level, and always select an open position exposed to the full sunshine, for shade is deadly to asparagus, although shelter not producing shade is beneficial, promoting, what is always desired, an early growth to compete in value with forced asparagus. Never allow the roots to be exposed to the air for any length of time, for they are succulent and thin-skinned, and soon suffer if their juices are drawn from them by evaporation. Hence it is not well to buy shop roots, for the length of time they are necessarily exposed seriously impairs their vigour to the injury of the purchaser. As the plantation is expected to stand for several years, never a foot should go on it except through sheer necessity, for if the ground becomes much consolidated the plant ceases to thrive; hence the importance of deep digging in the first instance, and the need for stony and gritty substances in the staple. We have gathered the grandest asparagus ever seen from beds twenty years old; therefore it may be concluded that it will pay to do the work well in the first instance. As to cutting, the rule is to begin in the third year, and that is a good rule for a poor soil; but cutting may begin the second year on a good soil, and it should cease at the end of May in early districts, and at the end of June in late districts. The plants then have time to make up for losses, but it would seriously impair their vigour if we were to cut until the middle of

July. Besides, asparagus becomes a drug in the market when peas and cauliflowers are plentiful, and if the writer may hazard his own private opinion, asparagus is but a lollipop, whereas peas and cauliflowers are like marrow and muscle to repair the waste of the frame in the activities of life.

WHITE *versus* GREEN ASPARAGUS.—It is easy enough to produce either. If you want tough white asparagus, put an extra six to twelve inches depth of fine gritty soil over the crowns, and cut with a proper saw below the surface. If you want tender, juicy, tasty, come-again flavoured green sticks, do not mould the beds more than enough to fairly cover the crowns, let the shoots rise six inches or so above ground, and then cut with a knife level with the surface, or snap off the shoots at the surface with finger and thumb.

FORCING.—The simplest way to force asparagus is by bringing the heat to them, for then the roots are undisturbed, and will gain in time and size. For this practice the beds should be four feet wide, with two feet alleys between, and the beds selected for forcing should be left uncut in the *preceding* summer, that they may accumulate the strength needed to enable them to endure the trial. The first business is to determine when the first cutting is required, and the later it is wanted the better for the plants and the gardener. If you wish to cut in January, you must commence operations six weeks in advance; if in February, five weeks in advance; if early in March, four weeks in advance. The forcing consists in covering the bed with litter, and then taking a shallow spit from the alleys and throwing it equally over the litter. The alleys are then filled with hot dung, which must be raised to at least one foot above the level of the beds, and when slightly trodden must be covered with boards to shut in the heat and keep out the cold and wet. Finally, the beds should be covered with six inches depth of the same hot dung. In a mild winter the routine may be modified with a view to economy; and, as the season advances, the amount of heating material required to start a bed will become less and less.

A better quality of forced asparagus, less fat, but green, and therefore tender, and with the welcome flavour of a good sample, may be obtained by taking up the plants and forcing them in pits and frames. It is a very simple business. The plants should be taken from beds three or four years old, and planted in light soil on well-made hotbeds, or beds heated by hot-water pipes. A gentle heat suffices, and indeed the slower the forcing the better the produce. As the glass protects the plant from frost, it may enjoy light and air, except when the weather is severe, and therefore need not be much moulded up, the object being to obtain short, plump, dark-green shoots of the most tender and richly-flavoured kind, fit to "set before a king." A large, deep bed of leaves, with a sufficiency of old lights and walls of turf, or loose bricks, or stout boards set on edge with pegs to hold them, afford machinery enough for the production of the finest forced asparagus, provided only there is a strong plantation of some years' standing to begin with for the supply of stools for the purpose. As a matter of course, the gardener who has to provide largely for a family will take measures to insure a succession, and this book is not intended to teach him his business.

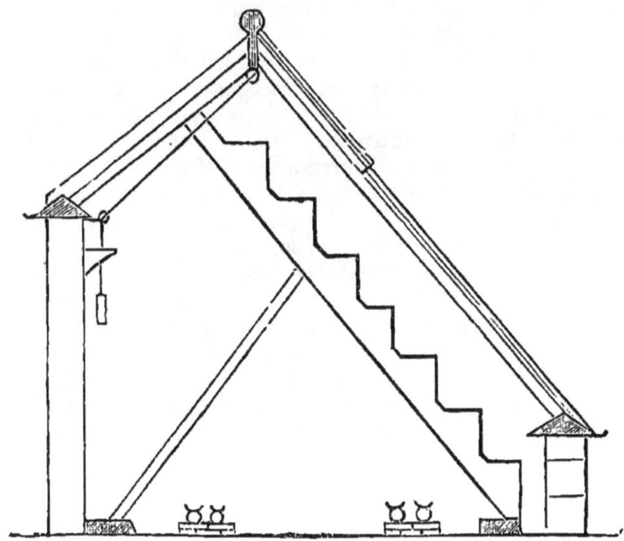

COMBINED GRAPE AND STRAWBERRY HOUSE.

CHAPTER IX.

ARTICHOKES, CARDOONS, AND MAIZE.

"These may prove food to my displeasure."
Much Ado, I. 3.

THESE three vegetables are scarcely worth growing, and it will, therefore, be proper to dispose of them briefly. It must be confessed, however, that the first two are admired by many, and there are a few to be found who value the green cobs of the maize as a quite delicious vegetable. We can find no good reason for eating any one of the three, and very many are of our mind, so it may be at least agreed that these are not "popular" vegetables. They make some amends for their poverty on the table by their grandeur in the garden. They are remarkably handsome plants, and the cardoon is certainly the handsomest of the three, and quite worthy of a place in what is called the "sub-tropical" garden.

THE ARTICHOKE *(Cynara scolymus)* is a fast-growing grey-green plant, producing large flower heads in the fashion of a thistle ; the varieties with very sharp-pointed scales on the flower-heads being the most conspicuously ornamental. Any ordinary good garden soil will grow good artichokes, and there is indeed only one difficulty to be recognised, and that is, to carry the plants through a severe winter safely, for they are somewhat tender in constitution.

Having trenched and manured a piece of ground, mark it off in lines three feet apart, and sow seed or put out suckers from old plants in the month of April. It is much the best plan to sow a row or so every year and destroy the old plants when they cease to be profitable, which is pretty sure to happen when they are five years old. In a hot season much of the seed will lie dormant and come up strong the next season, and the plants may be transplanted during showery weather to make permanent plantations. They should be in rows a yard apart, and the plants two or three feet apart in the row. We have on many occasions cut nice heads from plants the first year, but, as a rule, they do not produce until the second year, and in the third year they are immensely productive and the heads are extra fine. In taking offsets for planting, carefully cut them away from the stools with a few roots attached, and plant at once and cover with empty flower-pots until they begin to grow, giving them as little water as they can do with, for if much watered they are apt to rot.

To protect in winter is a troublesome job, but the best plan appears to be to pack a lot of waste straw around the plants, and then throw some earth on to keep the straw in its place. Towards the end of April the protective material should be cleared away, and the ground should be forked over and a coat of manure pricked in.

We have always some fine plantations that cost but little trouble. We sow a row or two in April or May and thin to a yard apart, and *that is all we do.* We never protect in winter, and about once in five years or so we lose a lot of plants, but it always happens that enough survive to supply ten times more heads than are wanted, and in the course of the summer a new lot rises to make all right.

THE CARDOON *(Cynara cardunculus)* is grown for its tender leaf stalks, which are blanched for use in stews, soups, salads, and in the manner of seakale. There are several modes of raising a crop, but the best is to sow on rich deep soil in rows four feet apart, in the last week of April, and thin to a foot apart as soon as the plants are growing freely. From the thinnings a plantation may be made, and in this case they may be put at six inches apart, but the rows must be four feet asunder, to allow of necessary work between. This consists in loosely tieing them together and earthing up to blanch the stems, which should be commenced in August. More earth should be added from time to time until they are banked up two feet high. If extra fine growth is required, treat precisely the same as celery. Our practice, however, has always been to grow on the flat, for we have on several occasions lost many plants when they have been in trenches, owing to their dislike of moisture. When the stems are cut up for cooking they should be thrown into a bowl of clean water, into which a little juice of a lemon has been squeezed; if this is not done they are apt to have a blackish appearance when placed on the table.

It is always worth considering how the beauty and interest of the kitchen garden may be maintained, and therefore it is often advisable to grow a few rows of such interesting plants as the cardoon, maize, salsify, and scorzonera, and allow them to run their whole course naturally. A plantation of artichokes and cardoons, displaying their magnificent blue flowers, is a sight not to be forgotten in haste, and one that may persuade their owner to have a daily walk round amongst the seakale, cauliflowers, scarlet runners, and gourds, which are also in their way attractive, while suggestive of enjoyments of another kind. A certain few of such decidedly ornamental plants do serve a place in the shrubbery, and in many instances, where a proper kitchen garden is scarcely obtainable, a dish of asparagus, vegetable marrows, and some few other things might be secured without disturbing the place or diminishing the beauty of an ornamental garden—indeed, a stout cardoon in flower is as noble a border plant as can be provided for the front of a shrubbery.

MAIZE or INDIAN CORN *(Zea Mays)* may be sown in April where it is to stand, or may be sown in heat in March and be planted out in May. The best way to sow is to select a piece of deep ground that has been well prepared, and dib the seed in about six inches deep in clumps of three to five seeds; the clumps to be a full yard apart. When well up thin to three plants each, and if the weather is dry, water frequently and liberally. The cobs are cut when quite young, and are boiled and served in the same way as asparagus.

CHAPTER X.

SALADINGS.

"These five days have I hid me in these woods; and durst not peep out, for all the country is lay'd for me; but now I am so hungry, that if I might have a lease of my life for a thousand years, I could stay no longer. Wherefore, on a brick-wall have I climbed into this garden; to see if I can eat grass, or pick a sallet another while, which is not amiss to cool a man's stomach this hot weather. And, I think, this word sallet was born to do me good: for, many a time, but for a sallet, my brain-pan had been cleft with a brown bill; and, many a time when I have been dry and bravely marching, it hath served me instead of a quart-pot to drink in; and now the word sallet must serve me to feed on."

2 Henry VI., IV. 10.

SO many things are used in salads that we claim the right to begin where we please and stop where we please in selecting subjects for this chapter. A potato, a cauliflower, an egg, a tuft of mint, a stick of celery, a pumpkin, a tomato, and a lobster, may all in turn be designated "saladings." So to avoid having to travel round the world we shall restrict this chapter to a series of notes on the vegetables that take the lead in the preparation of salads as commonly understood.

THE LETTUCE *(Lactuca viridis)* is the most important of all salad plants, and one that may be enjoyed the whole year round in plenty with comparatively little labour. Lettuces of some kind, moreover, may be grown in any soil with little more trouble than once digging and sowing the seed; but in common with most other things, a first-rate sample demands something of the cultivator. The close-hearted and delicate-flavoured cos varieties require a rich soil to insure a fine growth, but the smaller varieties of the cabbage section do well on poor soil, endure drought and heat well, and make the most acceptable of lettuces for salads. The two points of importance in the cultivation are to sow frequently, and never to transplant if it can be avoided.

SUMMER LETTUCES are usually raised from spring-sown

H

seeds, and it is desirable to begin in February, by sowing a pan or two of *Paris White Cos* and *Berlin White Cabbage.* If placed in a gentle heat these will soon start and grow freely. As soon as it is possible to place them out-of-doors, if only for an hour in the middle of the day, let them have the advantage of sunshine and air. It is desirable to prick out a few on to a bed of light rich earth in a frame, and give them attention to promote growth without keeping so close as to make them long-legged. These will come in early and will be good, provided the lights are removed at every opportunity to expose the plants fully, and in warm weather left off altogether. The remainder must be carefully hardened by frequent exposure, and be planted out on a piece of nice mellow ground that has been well manured, as soon as the weather is favourable in the month of April; and during bright sunshine, or in case of frost at night, cover with empty flower-pots for the first ten days or so. When enjoying sufficient warmth, lettuces should have abundance of water.

Another sowing should be made in March, in pans, and this sowing will not want heat, but should be placed in a frame or greenhouse; such varieties as *Paris White Cos, All the Year Round, Neapolitan,* and *Wheeler's Tom Thumb* are the most useful. These must be hardened with care and planted out at the end of April, and will pretty well take care of themselves. The cos varieties should have the richest ground and a situation where it will be handy to water them, but the Tom Thumbs will do on comparatively poor soil and will want but little water, but will supply charming little round hearts, very close and dry, and of the best possible texture to mingle with oil and vinegar in the salad bowl.

Early in March, and thenceforward every two or three weeks until the end of June, small sowings should be made in the open ground where the plants are to stand. Hence the sowing should be done with care to put in the least amount of seed possible, for these are *not to be transplanted.* As crops come off it is easy to find room for a row here and a row there in the open quarters, and it is advisable to open a trench and put in a lot of rough manure, and then fill in over the manure with part of the earth taken out, leaving the remainder in a ridge on the south side, and then to sow thinly, the ridge serving to shade the seed a little. In any case lettuces should be in the open, for the shade of trees causes them to run up, but a slightly-shaded spot may be selected for seed sown in May and June. As to distances, the cos varieties must be a foot apart at least, the Neapolitan two feet apart, Tom Thumb six to nine inches, and so on, according to the relative vigour of the variety.

WINTER AND SPRING LETTUCES are obtained from sowings made in July, August, and September. In the seed catalogues will be found the names of many varieties that are described as hardy; but we have found only two that we could thoroughly trust, and they are *Hammersmith Green Cabbage* and *Black-seeded Brown Cos.* Sow twice at least, say about the 20th of July and the 20th of August. In each case the seed should be sown in rows a foot apart on a raised bed in a position well drained. If the work is well done there will soon be a nice plant. The profitable way to manage is to begin in October to transplant to dry sheltered borders, and to frames and pits, and to leave enough in the beds to make a good plantation to stand the winter. What you can do in the utilization of these sowings will depend on the nature of your appliances, and you will sow accordingly; but you cannot ensure a supply of lettuces in February and March, when they are very much wanted, without the aid of pits and frames or some similar kind of protectors. In these they should be planted with care and kept as hardy as possible by being close to the glass and having abundant ventilation at all times, except when severe frosts prevails. They may be planted pretty close in the frames, and as they are drawn for use, those remaining will have room to swell. Early in March get ready a piece of good ground in a sheltered, sunny spot, and on it plant with care a lot of the Brown Cos that have been protected, and give them a litttle extra attention, and you may expect delicious lettuces in May. As for the Hammersmith, they must not be planted out in March, for they will bolt, that is, run to seed, almost immediately.

If the work is well managed, there will be a regular plant on the seed beds, for the plantations under frames and on sheltered borders will be made with the thinnings, leaving those in the seed beds in rows a foot apart and four inches apart in the row. In a mild winter all will survive, and the spring supply may be largely assisted by thinning from the beds, for the smallest of lettuces is useful in the salad bowl. Those left to swell off will be fine lettuces from April to June, and if any then remain they will run up to seed and finish their career. The Hammersmith is useful for its hardiness alone; it has no flavour, and it soon bolts; but the Brown Cos stands well and should keep the supply going until lettuces from spring sowings are ready.

It is usual to tie lettuces to blanch them. It should not be done until they are nearly full grown, and are to be used in about a week afterwards. We have for many years abandoned the tieing as troublesome. But we always give the preference to varieties that fold in their leaves neatly, and may be said to tie themselves, for the very large loose-growing kinds are certainly all the better for tieing.

Endive *(Chicorium endivia)* is hardier than lettuce, and often takes its place in winter and early spring. It requires nearly the same course of cultivation, and in its final stages rather more care. The soil for endive should be rich and light, and on a dry foundation. Generally speaking, very fairly good garden soil will produce good endive. The first sowings are made in April and May for a small early supply, and the main crop and the only important crop, generally speaking, is sown about the third week in June; but it is advisable to make another sowing in the latter part of July. Sow in rows a foot apart and thin to four inches apart, and from these transplant, leaving the original sowing a foot apart every way, with the exception of the Batavian, which should be fifteen to eighteen inches. Those that stand where sown will make the finest plants. Endive does not require much water, but must have a little help when planted out and also during protracted drought.

In the course of the autumn and through the winter the plants must be blanched, and only a few should be done at a time. We usually begin to blanch those of the June sowing where they stand, by simply laying tiles over them, and in about a fortnight they are ready. But in November a number of the July and August sowings should be transplanted to a dry border under a wall looking south, where, if needful, they can be protected with frames, litter, and mats during severe winter weather. They should, however, be kept as hardy as possible by giving them air whenever the weather will permit. To blanch in winter requires a little skill, and it will take fully three weeks; there is a probability of the plants rotting if they are not well taken care of. The surest mode of operating is to fold the leaves round the heart and tie with bast, and then to put a seakale pot over. A less sure, but not a bad way, is to heap coal ashes over each plant to form a cone, but sand or common mould will answer nearly as well if more convenient. The plants should be quite dry when tied up.

DANDELION, CHICORY, and WHITLOOF.—A good supply of dandelion salad may be obtained by digging up a lot of roots in the autumn, and packing them in boxes with fine earth, and putting the boxes in any warm dark place. A little water will be necessary, and the salad must be cut when ready, for it soon becomes discoloured and decays if left too long. But a better way is to sow seed of *Thick-leaved Dandelion* in April, and give the plant good cultivation. In November take up the roots and pack in earth in a shed until wanted for forcing. *Chicory* is to be treated in precisely the same manner; but *Whitloof* should not be sown until the end of May, and should be thinned to six inches apart every way as soon as fairly up. As a rule, the mushroom-house is the best place for forcing these salads, but a warm cellar answers very well, and they may be easily managed in the same way as forced rhubarb and seakale, which can be well done even in a cottage garden, for a slight warmth, a little moisture, and perfect darkness are the only requisite conditions.

SMALL SALADS comprise *Mustard, Rape,* and several sorts of *Cress.* They should never be mixed, but sowed separately, and in very small quantities at a time, so as to be cut fresh and young, for when the rough leaves appear they become worthless. The only nice point in the cultivation of these useful adjuncts to the salad bowl is to keep up a regular supply all through the winter. After trying several plans we have settled down to a routine that answers perfectly. We reserve a few old boxes for the purpose, cutting them down so as to be only two inches deep, and they are mostly two feet or so square. An inch of fine earth is put in, then a sprinkling of water, then a sprinkling of seed, and the work is done. The seed is not covered. The boxes are put in a geranium-house, where the seed soon sprouts, and when the plant is wanted we draw out a tuft with the left hand, cut off the roots with a pair of scissors held in the right hand, and the pretty stuff goes to the kitchen so clean that it might be eaten without washing it. We only grow *White Mustard* during winter, and of course regulate the sowing by the probable demand, which for our small household is rather heavy and constant.

WATERCRESS is not usually regarded as a plant that an amateur can grow advantageously, but the real truth is that if only one edible plant could be grown for home use, it should be the watercress, provided of course that the watercress is required, and that whatever else is wanted can be conveniently purchased. It is not necessary to enlarge on the risks incurred in the consumption of watercresses that are obtained in the usual way; nor if we send to the beds for them are we safe, for the natural waters everywhere are more or less polluted, and the watercress is more than any other edible plant exposed to agencies detrimental to its wholesomeness. When you grow your own cresses you know what they are made of, provided of course you do not gather from a stream that comes from you know not where.

For a nice supply of cresses in winter make up a frame with a bed of very rich loam, with which, if possible, mix some broken chalk or lime rubbish—say light turfy loam three parts, and fat manure, and lime rubbish or plaster, of the size of walnuts, one part each; the bed to be one foot deep of this mixture. In August or September sow seed very thinly and keep the frame close shut, and when the plant appears give air, and indeed keep the light off altogether, except when it is really needed for protection. Give water freely, but do not burden your mind with the idea that watercress should swim, for you will be able to gather most delicate cresses with only a moderate amount of watering, and the supply will last far into the winter. To keep up a succession, make up a smallish hotbed and on that sow again, and thus you will carry on the supply far into the spring, and then you will be enabled to gather from pots and pans, for these come in to help in a most important manner in the garden culture of watercresses.

PAN-CULTURE.—Cresses may be grown in pots or pans of any size, but the size that has proved the best in our practice is fifteen inches wide and nine inches deep. Every pan has perforations at the bottom, and is fitted with a larger pan to hold water, as shown in the accompanying figures. If it be asked whether a running stream is required, the answer is that the pan culture, as now recommended, if carried out with reasonable care, produces the most elegant and delicious watercresses ever seen, and that is sufficient proof that run-

WATERCRESS IN DEEP PAN.

ning water is not needed. You may begin with seed or cuttings, and any kind of watercress will serve the purpose;

but if you enter into the business with enthusiasm you may be recommended to obtain seed of the *Erfurt Sweet Cress*, for that is the best variety known.

In preparing a pan it is first half filled with lumps of

WATERCRESS IN SHALLOW PAN.

chalk, old mortar, and broken bricks of the size of one's fist, then a little moss is laid on, and finally a good body of rich soil is heaped up, and made firm by pressure, so as to have a convex shape. Very small cuttings of the cress are then dibbled in all over the soil, about three inches apart, and the pot is then stood in a pan of water, two or three inches depth of water being sufficient. In case such suitable pans are not available, common fifteen-inch seed pans answer admirably. These should have a layer of broken chalk or old mortar, and a good body of rich soil heaped up to a convex surface, and when planted be placed in pans of water. In hot weather it is desirable to put the newly-planted pots and pans in a cool shady place for a few days, but as soon as growth commences they should be removed into a place where they will be fully exposed to the sunshine, for a first-class sample cannot be grown in the shade.

It may occur to you that the rough lumps of chalk and old mortar may be dispensed with, but they are really essential to first-class production. So, again, it may be suggested that to plunge the pans to the rim, or even deeper, will be for the advantage of the plant; but a better growth is obtained by a depth of two or three inches than by complete immersion. The deep pot is better than the shallow pan, and the soil should be good enough for fuschias or pot roses; say, cucumber bed, or something of that sort. It matters not how rough it is, and to mix sand with it is to waste time and material.

A fifteen-inch pot will supply at one cutting half-a-peck of first-rate cresses in the height of the growing season. Three full gatherings are the utmost that can be taken from the pan in the summer, and as soon as the growth becomes wiry it should be knocked out and replanted. The same hard stuff may be used again and again, but the soil must be fresh, and the smallest cuttings usually make the best growth. The managenent will of course vary somewhat with the seasons. In the summer the growth is so rapid that you may gather in a fortnight from the time the pots are started, but as the heat declines the growth, of course, is less rapid. The latest date to plant for frame culture during the winter is the last week of October.

RADISHES are sown in almost every month of the year, and the routine culture depends entirely on the requirements of the family. The elegant early spring radishes that are so much prized are grown on gentle hotbeds in frames, and are succeeded by sowings made on warm dry slopes, and these again by sowings in open quarters and odd stolen bits of ground "anywhere." The matters of importance are to sow very thin; to thin them where crowded; to sow very small pieces, so as to avoid a glut at anytime; and to sow frequently, so as to ensure a constant supply of tender radishes, for when they stand long on the ground they become as hard as wooden nutmegs, and as hot as unmixed mustard. Quick growth is of the greatest importance, and a rich light soil will produce the best radishes.

For frame culture, *Wood's Early Frame* and *White-tipped Olive* are the best sorts. In the open quarters these with the *Long Scarlet* may be sown in March and April, but not later, for as summer radishes they are no use. The good old-fashioned *Turnip Radish*, white and red, cannot be surpassed for successional summer growing. The *Long White Naples* is a worthless curiosity.

Those who indulge in winter salads will find it advantageous to sow in July, August, and September, small pieces of *Black Spanish*, *China Rose*, and the *Giant Californian*.

CORN SALAD or LAMB'S LETTUCE *(Valeriana olitoria)* is valued as a winter and spring salad. Any soil will suit it, but an open situation is required. Sow in August in drills six inches apart, and thin to three inches apart in the row. Gather the leaves as required, taking care not to take many from any one plant at a time. It may be sown in February and March for summer supply, and then the plant may be cut over, but it is of no value as a summer salad.

AMERICAN and AUSTRALIAN CRESSES are useful as substitutes for watercress, and are to be valued both for summer and winter use. They may be sown at almost any time, but the most important sowings are made in March and August. In summer the plants are cut over, but in winter the leaves must be gathered, and the plants injured as little as possible.

BUCKWHEAT sown in pans and gently forced makes an agreeable winter salad.

CHAPTER XI.

THE ONION AND ITS ALLIES.

"Most dear actors, eat no onions nor garlic, for we are to utter sweet breath."

Midsummer Night's Dream, IV., 2.

THE ONION *(Allium cepa)* is too generally valued to need explanation of its uses or eulogy of its merits. It is not generally understood that the year of the onion begins in July, although it is everywhere known that the year of the spring bulb ends in August. The established rule for onion growing is to sow in March, and take up the crop when ripe; and the time of ripening so much depends upon the season, that the storing of onions begins in some years in the middle of July, and in others is deferred until far into September, or even October. What we have to say on this part of the subject may be new to many of our readers, but is not, in the proper sense of the term, new at all. We intend to insist on the policy of sowing in summer, and that is why we lead off with the remark that "the year of the onion begins in July, or at latest in August."

The onion is a profitable plant, in every sense of the word, and therefore should be generously dealt with. Many of us might endure, without any excruciating pang, the loss of a crop of asparagus, delicious as it is; or of carrots or parsnips, undeniably useful; but to lose the onion crop would be a heavy blow, and it would be especially felt, for our sakes, by the sweet salads on sunny spring days, and on hot summer nights, and by the ducklings that had been fattened near the herb garden, and had known the smell of sage from their earliest days upwards. The three graces of the kitchen garden are the potato, the cabbage, and the onion; and they are also qualified to play the parts of the three strong men, for which performance the potato should be regarded as Atlas, the cabbage as Hercules, and the onion as Milo of Crotona.

Soil for Onions.—There is much too much said in the books on this subject. Opinions are less valuable than facts. The onion obtains a very large proportion of its sustenance from the atmosphere, and hence onions may be grown for several years in succession on the same soil, with little or no help from manure. A collection of some thirty varieties was grown in our trial-ground on the same plot for fifteen years in succession, without one failure, except in 1860, when the excessive rain made them gross and thick-necked, and we had to dry off the crop in an oven in the month of October, and they kept very badly. On this plot, spring and summer sowing have been systematically practised, the plots devoted to spring-sown onions being occupied all winter with collards or winter greens, planted immediately after the removal of the onions, and the ground prepared for each crop by being well dug, one spit deep, and a thin sprinkling of phospho guano put in at the bottom of the trench as the work proceeded. We have long been convinced that the diseases to which onions are subject are more frequently caused by excessive manuring than by any inherent tendency of the plant to disease, or any extravagant *penchant* for it by the insects that occasionally decimate the crop.

There is no soil so good for the onion as that of an old, well-cultivated garden. A newly-broken pasture, on which potatoes or brassicas would do well, should not be selected for onions. The ground having been long cultivated should be thoroughly well dug, and as a rule, it is sufficient to dig one spit deep; but if the second spit is good, double digging may be useful; and whenever double digging may be safely practised, it should be resorted to, for it pays well to provide a deep-rooting plant with a deep, well-pulverized seed-bed. In a rotation system, onions should follow celery, the land being previously heavily manured for the celery, and not manured at all for the onions. But if a heavy crop of onions is desired, and the ground on which they are to be sown was not heavily manured for the previous crop, a sprinkling of guano or bone-dust will be required, or a good layer of rotten stable-dung must be put in between the two spits as the ground is trenched. We repeat that we take heavy crops of the finest possible bulk by digging one spit deep, and refreshing the soil with a thin sprinkling of phospho-guano, and know nothing of grub or any other impediment to success, save and except the weather, and we generally have the crop ripened early and perfectly. All carbonaceous manures are particularly good for onions; hence, it is well to save for them the sweepings of chimneys, the finer stuff from a smother, in which, of course, there is much fine charcoal; and the finer parts of lime and plaster rubbish that may result from building operations. Any of these substances may be dug in as the ground is prepared, and it will be an additional advantage to the crop if some of them, more especially the soot, is spread over the surface *after* the seed is sown. In the books the use of soot as a top-dressing is advised; but the writers all agree in recommending that it be spread before sowing, which is a mistake, for it is more effectual if put on afterwards thick enough to make the ground quite black.

SOWING AND SUMMER CULTURE.—Prepare the bed by breaking up the soil well, for the onion will not thrive amongst clods, or on a very wet or very dry staple. The beds should be in an open sunny situation, four and a-half feet wide, and the seed should be sown in drills across, so as to facilitate the action of the hoe between them. We never mark off beds, in the proper sense of the word, but sow lengthwise of the piece in drills six to twelve inches asunder, and walk between the rows when the hoe is used. The drills should be drawn carefully to the line, and be fully one inch deep. Sow the seed as thinly as possible, cover with the back of the rake, and tread the rows firmly. The times for sowing are from February to May, and from the last week in July to the first week in October. We find that two sowings are sufficient for all ordinary purposes, the most important sowings being made in July and early in August, comprising *Tripoli*, *Lisbon*, and *Rocca;* and the others in the latter days of March, or as early as possible in the month of April, when *White Spanish*, *James's*, *Blood-Red*, and other keeping sorts are sown.

As soon as the plant is well above ground, thinning should commence, and the spring-sown onions should be thinned earlier and more severely than those sown in autumn. A little judgment is needed in this work, and it may be exercised to the advantage of those who love young onions, for by successive careful thinnings, supplies of tender, sweet, small salad onions may be obtained nearly the whole year round from two sowings only, for just as the last thinning of the autumn-sown takes place, the spring-sown will be ready for use. The final distance for a good useful crop is three or four inches, but on a rich soil they should be left at six inches apart, for they ripen better when they jostle each other, and to do onions well the ground towards the end of the season should be literally paved with them. Ply the hoe between whenever weeds appear; be careful always not to break the necks of the plants, or loosen their roots. Give them frequent heavy waterings with sewage, if you can, while they are green and growing, but not a drop after they show a tendency to ripen. When the ripening season approaches, say the middle of July in a hot season, and the end of the month or later in a cold season, pass the handle of the hoe over the plants carefully, to bend the stems down on the bed; this helps to swell the bulbs and promotes perfect ripening.

Exhibition Onions are grown in two ways: the one occasioning much trouble, the other little; and the last-named always very nearly, and sometimes quite, as good as the first. The seed is sown on well-pulverized, unmanured ground, about the middle or last week in May, in rows six inches apart. The crop is only moderately thinned, and of course is kept very clean with the hoe. In October the crop, consisting of bulbs the size of walnuts, is taken up, dried, and stored. Early in March the little bulbs are planted in rows a foot asunder, and six inches apart in the rows, on ground heavily manured; and when the planting is finished, a coat of fine charrings is spread on the surface between the rows. In the process of planting, the bulbs are placed on the surface, and a handful of rich soil is put around each to hold it in position, this plan being preferable to inserting them in the soil, for the onion does not thrive when the neck is covered. The easier method is to prepare the ground by laying a good coat of fat manure at the bottom of the trench in digging the ground, and then to prepare the seed-bed in the usual way, and sow in rows, nine inches apart, the last week of August or first week of September. They are to be thinned several times, and to have a final thinning to nine inches apart in the month of April, after which they should be systematically watered with liquid manure until they begin to show an inclination to ripen, when the blade should be bent down, and not another drop of water given. This method of cultivation will pay in any garden, without reference to exhibiting or the possible profit of praises and prizes. By either of these two methods onions may be grown in English gardens equal to the best of those that are imported from Lisbon and Madrid. *White Lisbon* and *Giant Tripoli* are the best for this system.

PICKLING ONIONS should be small, and perfectly ripe. Sow in April, on well-dug soil, without manure, and do not draw a single blade; let the whole crop ripen as it stands, and the starving system will insure beautiful bulbs for pickling. The *White Nocera* is the best pickling onion save one, to which we shall presently refer, but *White Spanish* or *White Globe* may be sown instead, and they will answer nearly as well, though nothing can equal in appearance the silver-skin race, of which the *Nocera* is the best variety.

HARVESTING AND STORING.—It is usual to wait until the whole crop is ripe, and then to draw the roots and lay them in the sun to finish. This is bad practice, for some roots ripen earlier than others, and if rainy weather sets in, they make fresh roots after having had a rest, and are then deteriorated beyond recovery. Amongst a bulk of onions treated in this off-hand way, many will begin to sprout before the winter is half gone; whereas, by better management, the whole may be kept nearly the same length of time, this, of course, depending in a great measure on the keeping properties of the variety. The proper way to harvest the crop is to draw the roots as fast as they ripen, and lay them on mats or boards in the sun, and take them under cover at night and during wet weather. By this treatment every separate plant is humoured, and the trouble is no greater; at all events, the more uniform and perfect ripening secured will more than compensate for any little extra labour occasioned. As they become thoroughly well dry and shrivelled at the neck, they may be put in nets, or bags, or wicker baskets, and temporarily stored in a dry shed *in the full light*, and on wet days they may be roped and hung to the rafters to supply the kitchen or market as required. A capital off-hand way of disposing of them is to tie them in convenient bunches and hang them in a shed, or even against a wall in the open air, under the eaves. By this rough method they keep well until April.

It may happen that just as the crop is ripening, and should be lifted, dull rainy weather will set in. As to what is to be done in such case, each one must judge for himself, but a general advice may be given to this effect—that, as the crop is too valuable to be lost without a struggle, it would in such a case be prudent to take it up, and cut off the blades four inches above the neck, and put the whole of the bulbs in a cooling oven, with the door open, and repeat the process three or four times, at intervals of a day or two, to compel them to ripen. If it be asked what should be the temperature of the oven, we can safely give a wide range, for it must be above 60° and it may be below 100°, but an average of 80° may be considered the proper temperature. When onions are stored in dark houses, they should be on ropes, or very thinly spread on shelves. If the household demands large onions late in the spring, a sufficient number of large bulbs of late keeping sorts should be seared at the neck and the base with a hot iron, but it must not be so hot as to scorch the place it touches.

Diseases and Insect Enemies.—We have never had on our ground any serious disaster with the onion crop, and therefore, perhaps, cannot properly advise on the prevention or cure of diseases, or the extermination of insects that attack the onion. Some years ago we prepared some seed-beds for onions on a plot of old garden ground we had just taken, and in respect of which we were informed that it abounded with every possible grub, worm, and fly that wages war with the gardener. When the beds were ready for sowing, we gave them a heavy watering with sulphuric acid diluted with thirty times its bulk of water, and sowed the seed the next day. The result was a wonderful crop of onions, but whether the acid killed the vermin or simply enriched the ground by acting on its stony constituents we never took pains to inquire. We have sometimes seen a grub or two, or rather have noticed the blade fall over here and there as though there was something wrong, and have at once watered the crop with a solution of nitrate of soda, half-a-pound to the gallon, and that appeared to stop the plague. There is not a more certain or healthy plant grown than the onion, that is, of course, when it is grown properly.

Seed may be raised easily, but the cottagers' rule is the worst possible. He selects soft and half-spent bulbs, that are not good enough for roasting, and if they produce seed it is of poor quality, and will not produce handsome bulbs. At the end of February the finest bulbs obtainable should be planted in poor soil, a foot apart each way, and so deep that the necks are just covered. Keep them clear of weeds, and before they come into flower provide them with rails attached to posts, to which tie them to prevent their destruction by storms. Stout tarred string will answer, but rails are better if the heads are large. Cut the heads as soon as they become brownish, and lay them on cloths in the sun to finish. Our mode of saving onion seed is to lay some large bell-glasses hollow side upwards on a stage of a sunny greenhouse, and as the heads are cut they are thrown in. In the course of a few days the seed is found clean and ripe at the bottom, having shelled itself out without giving a moment's trouble. Nine-tenths of all the small seeds grown may be saved in this simple manner. The books say, "it is of the utmost consequence to employ seed of not more than one year old, otherwise scarcely one in fifty will vegetate." This is nonsense, for we have oftentimes obtained as fine crops from seed four years old as from that of the previous year. However, we do not recommend old seed, for it is generally agreed that onion seed should not be kept any great length of time, and things commonly agreed on are usually founded on observation and experience.

THE SELECTION OF VARIETIES must be determined by the requirements of the cultivator. For a good crop of spring sown onions any of the race of *White Spanish*, such as *Reading*, or *Nuneham Park*, will answer every purpose, and as they keep well and look well, they are among the best of market onions. For autumn sowing, the *Tripoli* or *Strasburgh* sections are the best; and, perhaps, the very best two sorts amongst them are *White Tripoli* and *Giant Rocca*. If particularly large onions are required, sow *Giant Lisbon*, both in the open ground and in a frame in August or September, and plant out in March, in a bed of rotten stable manure six inches deep, made on a bottom of hard soil. None of the Madeira or Portugal race keep long, and therefore there should be no more grown than are likely to be required for autumn and early winter use. Amongst the late-keeping sorts, *James's Pear-shaped* is considered the best. A true sample of this variety should be tall, and broader at the shoulders than at the base, somewhat of the shape of the great oil-jars which figure in the story of "Ali Baba; or the Forty Thieves." A fine onion for main crop is *Trebons*, which may be known by its appearing as if pinched by finger and thumb near the root. The *Welsh*

Onion, or "scallion," ranks high with many who require salad onions in winter; but we could never find any use for it, always having plenty of silvery little onions from autumn sowings, which are certainly preferable to the rather puffy green blades of this variety, which does not produce bulbs. However, the Welsh onion is very hardy, and may be very useful in cold climates, where the Tripoli or Spanish onions refuse to stand the winter. Moreover, if the green blades are desired in early spring for salads, as in many houses they are, there will always be found plenty rising from old bulbs in the store; and while these are fresh and crisp, they are excellent, both for soups and salads.

The Potato Onion is a serviceable cottage garden root, but of comparatively small importance to those who cultivate a kitchen-garden in a systematic manner. It is the rule in the West of England to plant the bulbs on the shortest day, and take them up on the longest. They may, however, be planted as late as March, but as they keep badly, the earlier they are in the ground the better. They require the ground to be well dug and in good heart. The rows should be one foot asunder, and the bulbs six inches apart in the row, and the best way to plant is to lay down the line and insert the bulbs with the aid of a dibber, every bulb being planted deep enough to have a firm grip in the soil without being quite covered. The hoe should be plied frequently between the rows, but in such a manner as not to inflict any injury on the roots, and a mere skin of earth may be drawn to the base of the green blade once or twice during the summer.

The Tree Onion produces a double crop, one consisting of small bulbs at the top of the tall stem, the other of large bulbs similar to those of the potato onion, at the root. Both root and top bulbs may be planted for a crop, but the root bulbs are the best. Treat in precisely the same way as the potato onion, but do not plant before the end of February, for if a severe frost occurs the roots may be destroyed. As soon as the stems rise, provide laths or tarred rope, or some other cheap and rough support for them, for if they lay on the ground slugs and snails will eat through the stem, and the development of the top bulbs will be arrested. When the stems begin to turn yellow, cut them close over the ground, and lay them with their crowns untouched on boards or cloths in the sun to dry, and after a few days tie them in bundles, and suspend them in a dry loft or store-room ; or rub off the little bulbs and store in nets or chip boxes. The root bulbs are excellent for stews and other purposes for which onions are employed in the kitchen, and the top bulbs make a better pickle than any other kind of onion, their flavour being peculiarly sweet and mild. The tree onion is but little known, yet it is at once good and profitable, provided it obtains the few small attentions it requires at the proper time. If the crowns are allowed to lie on the ground, as they will do if unsupported, there is a likelihood of a considerable proportion of the crop being lost through the assaults of vermin; snails, slugs, and woodlice having a peculiar liking for this particular sort, owing, no doubt, to its delicate flavour.

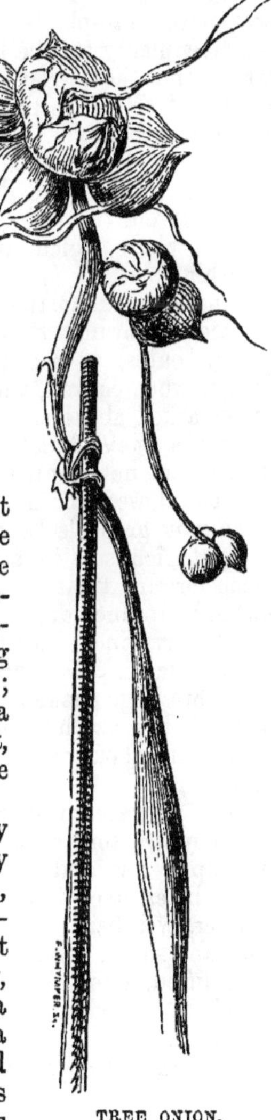

TREE ONION.

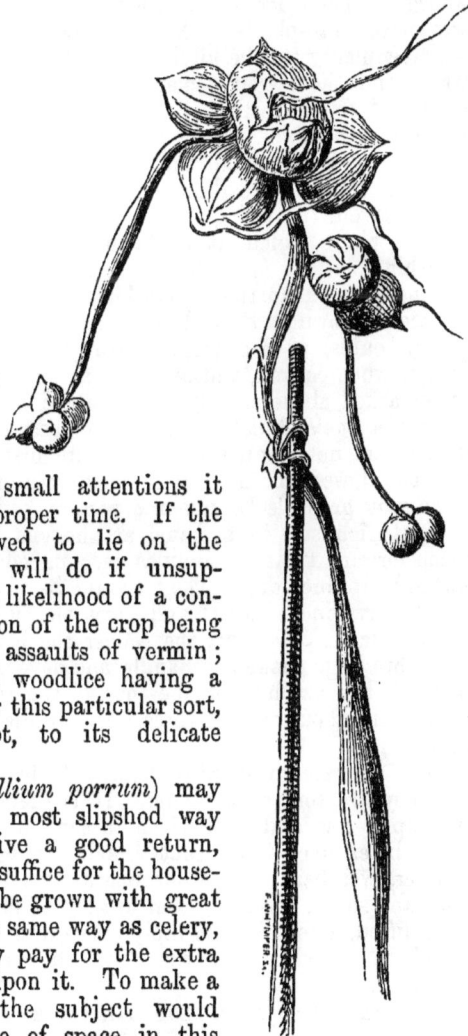

THE LEEK (*Allium porrum*) may be grown in the most slipshod way and will then give a good return, and in most cases suffice for the household, and it may be grown with great care in nearly the same way as celery, and will certainly pay for the extra labour bestowed upon it. To make a long article on the subject would really be a waste of space in this volume of concentrations. There stands in our garden now (July 29, 1876) a long row of leeks, to which we resort occasionally for a few bulbs to stew in gravy, and those and the like of them are things "not generally known." These leeks were sown in the spring of 1875, and were never transplanted. Yet in the autumn of the same year, we drew plenty for the kitchen that were as thick as a child's wrist, and those that remained were not disturbed. As a matter of course, in the following spring they threw up flower heads innumerable, and one day we went along the row, knife in hand, and cut off all the heads, save half a dozen of the strongest, which were allowed to stand for seed; and as for those cut off, the tall green stem was left unhurt, as a part of the plant which it could not spare, for every green breathing surface is useful to a plant, but flowering and seeding are exhausting operations. In the course of the summer following, these leeks produced at the root pretty silvery bulbs, of the most marrowy texture and delicious flavour when cooked, and available as onions if need be, but, as remarked above, chiefly to be valued for stewing in gravy to form a *bonne bouche*. It will be observed, therefore, that if leeks are not wanted when they are first fit for use, they may be allowed to remain until they are wanted.

To grow grand leeks, sow in a pan, or, better still, in a bed of light rich soil in a frame, at the end of February, and thenceforward treat precisely as recommended for celery, the earthing up included. They should be planted out in the trenches six inches apart and have plenty of water, and as to the time of planting, the sooner the better provided the plants are large enough to handle, and have nice tufts of roots. It helps the swelling of the root if the tops of the leaves are cut off about once in three weeks, while they are growing freely.

Leeks are rarely injured by frost, but when grown to a great size they are somewhat tender. It is therefore advisable to take up a few and pack them in sand in a dry place, and throw litter over those that remain during the prevalence of severe weather. When the weather changes take up a few more, and so on, observing that as they do not keep long after being lifted, a fortnight's supply is the utmost allowance that should be stored at one time, and the drier they are the better.

THE SHALLOT OR ESCHALLOT *(Allium Ascalonicum)* may be

grown on any good soil, but as it is desirable to have them large, the cultivation should be liberal. Make up a bed for the purpose, digging in plenty of rotten manure, and putting a coat of ashes from the burning of garden rubbish on the top. The bed should be four feet wide, rising from the sides and nicely finished. The offsets may be planted in October, or from February to April, the spring being the best time in cold or damp localities. In planting, press the offset firmly into the soil, and the work is done. Keep clean from weeds, and take up and store when the leaves die down in June or July.

Some years ago the rats pulled out the shallots from a bed we had just planted, and dragged them about the place. We planted again, but in shallow trenches, quite covering the bulbs and treading them in firmly. In the ensuing season they produced an abundance of seed, and since then we have found it quite an easy matter to obtain seed. It is not much needed, however, seeing how largely they increase from divided bulbs. The *Common Red* is the best, but there is a nice *yellow* variety in cultivation, which is considered in some respects superior.

Garlic *(Allium sativum)* is grown in the same way as the shallot, but should not be planted before March, as it is rather tender in constitution. The cloves should be put into holes dibbed with a stick, or by the quicker mode of making a hole with the finger and thumb, and leaving the clove in it. The proper distance is six inches apart each way. In June tie the leaves in knots to prevent seeding, and take up the roots when the leaves die down. For all culinary purposes English grown garlic is as good as any, but it is never so silvery and finished in growth as that imported from the continent.

Chives *(Allium schœnoprasum)* are useful to cut from at any time for soups or salads. The bulbs are sometimes used, but they are never wanted if onions or shallots are at hand. The tender green tops in spring impart an agreeable flavour to a salad, and may be used in place of young onions. Half-a-dozen tufts of chives are enough in most places, and it is desirable to lift, divide, and re-plant every four or five years.

CHAPTER XII.

CELERY AND CELERAIC.

"There's pippins and cheese to come."
Merry Wives, I, 2.

THERE should be some very peculiar and forceful reason for growing celery in any quantity in a small garden. It is one of the few good things that most people can do without if restricted in their gardening operations, or that, at least, they may trust the greengrocer for when it is wanted. Market celery is generally of the finest quality, and none the worse for having gone to market, for it carries well, keeps well, and if you take the tender centres out of a few heads, you may save enough of the less tender sticks for flavouring soups and gravies.

But though the owner of a small garden cannot be recommended to grow many rows of celery, if he gives his mind to the thing at all, he may secure as fine a sample as ever was seen; for he can do what is often impossible in a large garden —that is, give the plant plenty of water, for that is one great point in the cultivation of celery.

THE SEED BED.—To raise a small quantity of first-rate celery, one of the most important matters at starting is not to be in a hurry about it. Do not begin until the season is so far advanced that the plant will not be likely to suffer a check, for if it starves in the seed pan, or is pricked out too soon, and is several times pinched by frost or shrivelled by the east wind, it will never acquire the fine quality you aim at, for you are bound to do your best for celery, or leave it alone altogether. For the main crop in a large garden, the seed is usually sown in February and March, and the plant is nicely nursed on half-exhausted hotbeds until the time comes for planting out. But when only a few rows are required, and the conveniences are not of the best, it is advisable to wait until the first or second week in April, and get the seed sown before the 15th. Prepare for the sowing a large pan or a few pots, by putting in a good body of potsherds and filling up with light rich compost, such as you would use for potting young fuchsias or balsams in. Give the soil a good wetting from the fine rose of a watering pot, and an hour or so afterwards sprinkle the seed thinly and cover with a mere dusting of fine dry earth. Lay over the pan or pots squares of glass or tiles or sheets of paper, and put them in a warm place. A mild hotbed will answer admirably; wanting that, a sunny corner of a frame or greenhouse will serve pretty well. If kept moist and warm, the seed will sprout very quickly, and as soon as the little seed-leaves begin to rise remove the covering from the pots, and take care that while the young plants have light and air and a very careful supply of moisture, they must not be roasted in the sun, nor be blown away by a keen east wind. If they rise rather too tall, dust some fine earth amongst them, and take the hint that a little more light and air will be good for them. They will soon be large enough to handle, when the important business of pricking out must be attended to.

First Planting.—If you have a nearly-exhausted hotbed you can spare, you may refresh the top by spreading on it about three inches depth of quite rotten hotbed manure. On this dib the plants tenderly three inches apart; keep them a little close and shaded for two or three days, then give light and air carefully, and in the course of a week ventilate more freely, and keep regularly watered. Your object must be to ensure a vigorous growth from the first without the slightest check, but at the same time you must keep your plants hardy by allowing plenty of light and air.

In the absence of a hotbed, a small frame or a few hand-lights will be found of great service. First spread on hard ground in a sunny spot four inches depth of rotten manure. Over this put the frame or hand-light, and shut close. A few hours' sun will make the bed quite warm. In the after part of the day, plant on this warm bed, water well with tepid water, and shut up close. Next morning screen off the sun with a mat, or two or three thicknesses of newspaper. About three days' nursing will give the plants a good start, after which give light and air, and regular supplies of water. As soon as they begin to grow vigorously, remove all the shelter, that they may become quite hardy for planting out.

Final Planting.—The next business is to prepare the trenches. There must be no stint of manure in this business. Take out the soil to a depth of twelve inches, and throw in a good body of half-rotten manure, and dig it into the bottom of the trench, mixing it well with the soil to form a rich substratum. Then put into the trench about four inches depth of fat manure about half rotten, and throw on it a little of the earth that was taken out, and the trench is ready for planting.

The plants will lift from the bed on which they were pricked out with fine roots, which must not be injured; therefore do not take up many at a time. Plant them six inches apart, pressing them in carefully, and finish with a good watering. Dull cloudy warm weather with a promise of rain is the best for this work; but if you must do it in sunny weather, take care to plant late in the day, and next morning shade the plants by some means, and in this way give them a little extra help to prevent exhaustion, remembering at this stage of the business the advice already given, that the plant should never suffer a check of any kind. As you cannot possibly use too much manure for celery, and as the crop will not exhaust all its goodness, you are bound to be liberal; and, as a matter of fact, you will not obtain good celery by any stinting process.

Earthing up.—As by sowing late you shorten your season, you must make amends by sharp action at every stage; and, now that you have got the plants out, you must give them plenty of water, and occasionally chop the surface of the soil with a hoe to prevent the caking that always follows watering. The earthing up must not be commenced until you have a fine plant, for when earthing begins growth stops. You may reckon that from the final earthing up six weeks must elapse ere any of the celery will be fit for eating. It will be well if you can wait to begin earthing until the growing season is pretty well over, for you really must not expect an early supply by the method of culture now placed before you as especially adapted for a small garden. When you begin to earth up choose dry weather. Tie a few plants roughly to keep them together, then chop the earth down and pack it against them to a depth of about three inches. Tie a few more and proceed in the same manner. In the course of a week add another inch or two of earth, and a week afterwards a little more. When you have earthed up the plants so that the tips of the inmost sticks are covered, finish off the work nicely to a neat slope, and the cultivation may be considered completed.

In about five weeks from the time you finished earthing up

you may take out a few plants at the end you began with, and we trust you will find them all you could wish—white, wax-like, and of the most delicious flavour. If they are a little green inside, you will know they wanted a few days' more darkness; but once well blanched they may remain undisturbed until threatened by frost, when something must be done to save them. A few degrees of frost will not hurt celery, but a downright severe frost will kill it to the roots. Our rows are saved by the A frames described in Chapter III. These are put over the rows betimes, and the frost never touches the celery so protected. You must find some means of protecting, or you must lift a lot and store it in moist earth in a shed. Fortunately celery can be kept in good condition for some time, if carefully packed in moist earth in any snug outhouse.

SELECTION OF SORTS.—The white varieties are most in favour, but the pink are the best, both for flavour and beauty. If you want large celery, take *Hooley's Conqueror* and *Ramsey's Giant White.* If you care more for quality than size, take *Leicester Red* and *Sulham Prize Pink.* If one sort suffices, as in most cases it will, the last-named should have the preference over all others.

CELERAIC, OR TURNIP-ROOTED CELERY is not thought much of in this country, but is much cultivated on the Continent, and is, indeed, imported to this country, and may be seen for sale at shops where German and Italian goods are sold. It is well worth a trial in any garden, for its nutty root is agreeable, and of a similar flavour to the solid root portion of the common celery, which by many is regarded as a *bonne bouche.* One of the advantages of growing this esculent is, that it can be taken up and stored in the same way as carrots or beets, whereas celery must be kept in the ground to some extent, for if stored for any great length of time it deteriorates.

Celeraic seed should be sown in March and April on a mild hotbed or on a warm sheltered border, under a hand-glass. It will require to be pricked out as advised for celery, and in the third week of June should be planted out on well-manured land in rows two feet asunder, and the plants one foot apart in the rows. The plants must be put out on the level, not in trenches, and in the process of planting lateral shoots and lateral fibres on the roots should be removed. Give plenty of water, and occasionally scrape away a little of the soil with a pointed stick from around the bulb, for it is like the onion in this respect, that it swells faster above than below ground. When full grown earth up the roots slightly to blanch them. Before winter take up and store, but leave them in the ground as long as it seems safe to do so. In storing, remove all the leaves except the centre, and pack in earth with the centre leaves just peeping out. Celeraic is hardier than celery, and may generally be left out all the winter; the taking up is merely a precautionary measure in case the winter should prove unusually severe.

The Celery Fly is not usually a terrible pest, but, in common with other insects, it comes out in force occasionally—it has its season, like everything else. Dustings of dry soot will mitigae the attack, but the only course of procedure to be trusted is the tedious one of pinching every blistered leaf to kill the maggot, and removing and burning any leaves that are very much blistered. It must be borne in mind that removal of leaves weakens the plant; therefore, do not remove any if the pest can be kept in check by pinching.

Compound Celery Culture, as practised by Mr. Duncan, formerly gardener at Basing Park, answers admirably when large quantities are required. The routine is as follows:—

In the month of June the broccolis and cauliflowers are planted, and so arranged that the celery trenches for the next season's crop may be formed as soon as the cauliflowers have perfected their growth, and in this operation the mould is placed among the stems of the broccoli, which, with after covering, effectually protects them from the severity of the winter; and when the ground is in a condition to require draining, these trenches afford a ready means for the performance of the operation. The manure is placed in the trenches during winter, whereby an advantage is gained in having this kind of work performed at a less busy season than early spring or summer. But the plan also affords space for the production of early esculents. For the kinds that require a rich medium for perfect development, or such as sea-kale or rhubarb, which need, in addition to a slight bottom-heat, an extra accumulation of matter as a means by which to blanch the stalks of the leaves, the situation is equally appropriate. The trenches form, too, a ready receptacle for such plants as are required for the summer decoration of the *parterre*. Cuttings struck in hotbeds in early spring, or plants which have been kept in crowded places during the

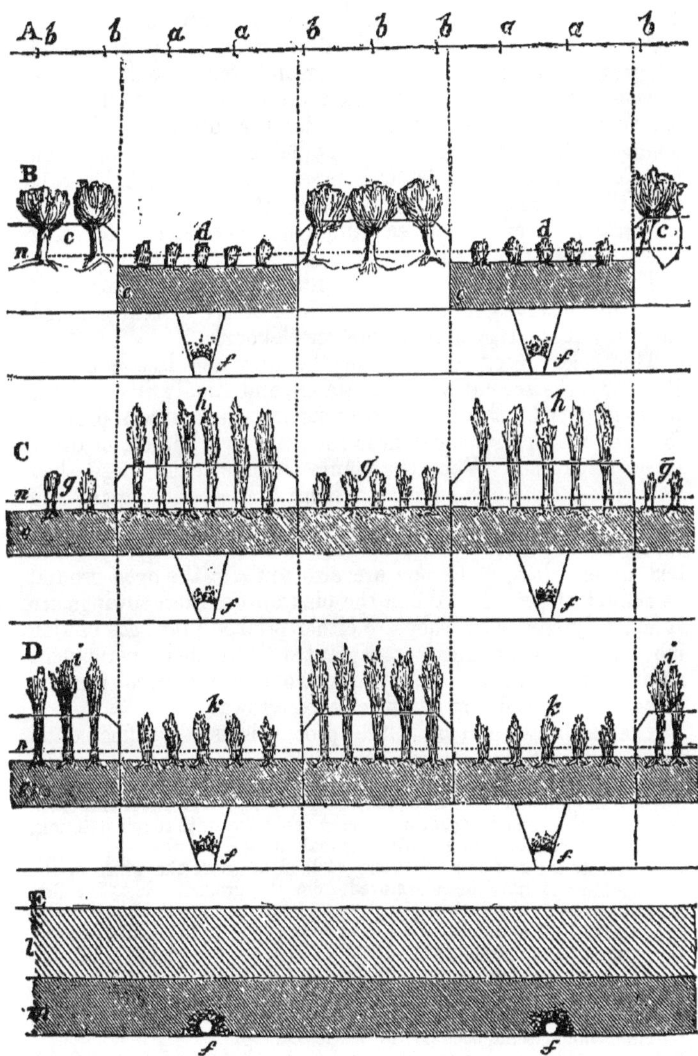

A represents a section of ground planted with Broccoli and Cauliflower.—*b b*, Broccoli ; *a a*, Cauliflower.

B represents the ground after the Cauliflower has been removed and the Celery trenches prepared for under-cropping, the Broccoli stems being earthed up as a protection from frost.—*c c c*, protected Broccoli ;

depth of winter, planted on these gently warm beds towards the end of March, and protected from frosts by glass and other covering, soon become strong and well rooted, and are moved with much facility to their proper situations when the planting season has arrived. After the broccoli has been removed the ridges are also available for crops of such vegetables as spinach, lettuce, peas, radishes, &c., the only conditions necessary being that they should be cleared from the ground previous to earthing the successional crops of celery as they require it.

The diagram, representing a course of celery-culture, will probably convey a more accurate idea of the system pursued than any mere description, however elaborate.

The celery seed is sown in the first and last weeks of February, the second week in March, and finally in the first week in April; the first two crops are raised in well-drained fourteen-inch pots, placed near the glass in a hotbed, or other warm situation. When the plants are sufficiently large, they are pricked out on a somewhat spent hotbed under glass, and well inured to the weather before being planted out in the trenches. The last two crops are sown on a slightly warm bed under glass, and some are also sown in the open ground at the latter period. When the plants from these sowings are sufficiently advanced, they are either pricked into beds of rich mould, or are at once transplanted into their permanent situations, provided the early crops have been cleared from the trenches previously prepared for their growth.

The earthing-up or blanching process is usually effected by three different operations: the first takes place when the

n n n, ground level; *d d*, trenches for Celery and under-cropping; *e e e*, manure-bed; *f f*, drain-pipes covered over with rough materials, and forming a connexion with the main drains.

C represents the first crop of Celery earthed up after the whole of the under-crops have been removed from the ground.—*h h*, the first Celery crop; *g g g*, the second crop, planted on a bed of manure in the trenches formed by the operation of earthing up the first crop.

D represents the second crop, earthed up from the material on which the first crop had been grown, and the third succession planted on a new bed formed on the space formerly occupied by the first crop.—*i i i*, the second crop; *k k*, the third crop, which will ultimately be earthed from the material occupied by the second crop.

E represents the ground trenched and thoroughly mixed with the rich material so abundantly used in the cultivation of the Celery crop, the subsoil being broken up as low as the drainage, but not mixed with the top soil.—*l*, top soil; *m*, subsoil.

plants have grown nine or ten inches in height; the small leaves immediately above the roots, and all embryo suckers are very carefully removed. After that the bed is completely saturated with rich liquid manure, but subsequently to this period no artificial watering should take place; the beds are then covered with about four inches of mould from the ridges, which helps to keep the plants in an erect position, and acts like a mulching on the roots, thereby preventing in some measure the evaporation of moisture from the bed. Some three weeks before the early crop is required for use, the second earthing takes place, and is performed in the following manner by two operators: two boards some eight or nine inches in depth, and equal in length to the width of the bed, are placed edgeways between the rows, each board resting against the plants in either row, so as to form at once space for the reception of the mould and a protection to the leaves whilst the operation of earthing is being performed. When the required quantity of soil has been deposited, the boards are carefully withdrawn and placed between the next two rows, and so the work proceeds until all has been completed. When the soil is of a very wet, tenacious, or repugnant character, dry ashes, fine mould, or other material can readily be introduced next the plants, for which purpose double boards properly adjusted and fixed to each other form a ready medium by which to introduce the material thus.

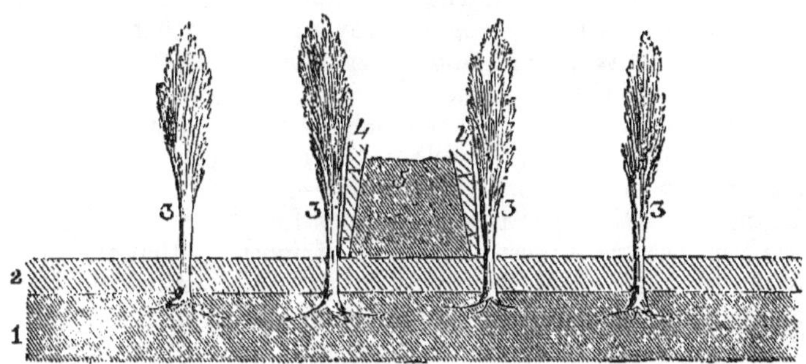

SECTION ACROSS THE BED, SHOWING THE MODE OF EARTHING CELERY WITH DOUBLE BOARDS.

1, Manure-bed; 2, First earthing; 3, Celery Plants; 4, Vacuum between the adjusted boards to receive fine blanching material; 5, Common earth from the ridges.

When sufficient blanching material has been deposited, the boards are carefully withdrawn and placed in the opposite row; and it will be readily understood that the fine mould which had passed through the vacuum formed between the boards will be in immediate connexion with the leaves of the plants, the common earth placed in the centre of the row enabling it to maintain that position. These boards can, of course, be readily set at any required distance apart, that distance being determined by the quantity of blanching material at command.

The third and final earthing of the early crops is accomplished at intervals of ten or twelve days before the celery is required for use—placing the mould high and close about the leaves. A different system is adopted with celery intended for winter use. Some time towards the latter part of October, when the weather is dry and favourable, the plants are fully earthed up, but the soil is neither put so high nor is so closely packed to the leaves as is recommended for the earlier crops. After the winter has fairly set in, a sufficient quantity for a fortnight's consumption is covered over with leaves which had previously been heated, and from which cause they will readily remain in flakes of some six inches in thickness, and resist alike the action of frost or moisture. The covering over a day's consumption is merely removed with a fork so much farther on to the bed, and this takes place from day to day. When, however, severe frosts set in, the whole of the ridges are covered over in the same manner, but the protection is removed on the recurrence of favourable weather, in order that the plants should not suffer from being too closely excluded from the atmosphere.

It will be perceived from the system here recommended that an enormous mass of vegetable matter can readily be obtained from a very limited portion of ground—that from the mode of arrangement the operations necessary for the cultivation of one crop become subservient to that of another—that the soil, from being so very frequently turned and aerated in fine weather, becomes fully disintegrated, and, finally mixed with so large a proportion of rich material, it is in a very favourable condition for the succeeding crop—and that such a system carried through any part of a garden must inevitably change its condition, however obdurate or sterile the nature of the soil may be. Moreover, this concentrated mode of cultivation economizes not only labour, but manure and water also; the plants, too, being in close proximity, afford a mutual shelter, and consequently a quicker growth ensues than under circumstances of greater exposure, and on this altogether depend that crispness and solidity so desirable in this esculent.

A root-crop is that which usually follows in the routine, being not only of a totally different character to the crops of the previous seasons, but, from the circumstance of the ground having been cultivated so deeply, and so frequently and thoroughly aerated, it might be considered to be in a state well adapted for their growth, and more especially the tap-rooted sections of that class.

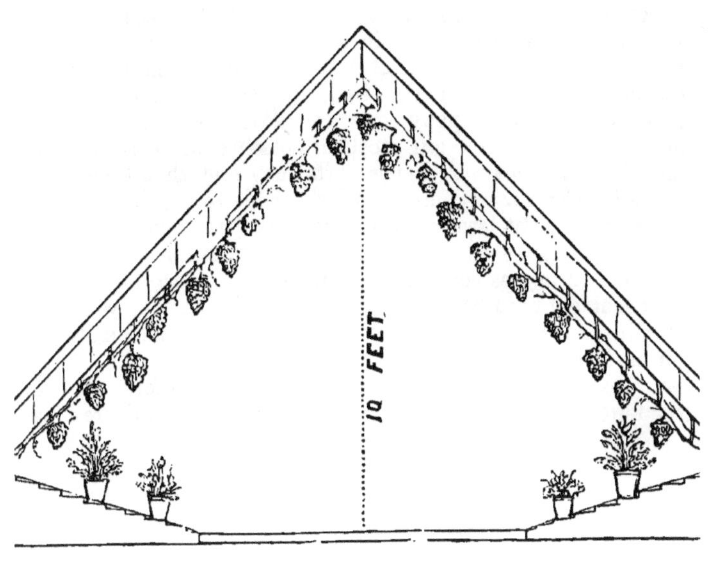

VINERY AND PLANTHOUSE COMBINED.

CHAPTER XIII.

THE POTATO.

"Let the sky rain potatoes."
Merry Wives, V., 5.

THE POTATO (*Solanum tuberosum*) is one of the most important of kitchen garden crops, considered as to its utility, and it ranks higher than any other as a subject for exhibition and fancy cultivation. About 500 varieties have passed through our hands as subjects of trial culture, and the proportion of really inferior kinds amongst so many is remarkably small. On the other hand, very many are so nearly alike that their names are a burden to the catalogue and of no use whatever to the cultivator. To find 100 distinct and useful sorts, however, is by no means difficult, and the earnest potato-fancier would not be content to plant less than that number as comprising a fair collection. The grower who aims at supplying the table only should not be afraid to grow twenty or thirty sorts, if it can be accomplished without inconvenience, for in seasons when disease prevails it is most capricious in its attacks; so that while some sorts escape wholly or in part, others are entirely swept away, and those who have many sorts are most likely to come out of the conflict with a fair stock of potatoes, while those who have been content with a few sorts may find that they have lost all. Certain sorts are peculiarly liable to the disease, and these comprise at least a few of the very best, but some very inferior kinds are equally liable, and there is not one variety known that enjoys complete immunity.

It scarcely need be said that to treat the subject with the amplitude befitting its importance, and the abundant material for an exhaustive treatise that exists, would be quite beside our present purpose, which is to convey useful information in the fewest possible words, to the end that potato-culture may be rendered as certain and profitable as sorts, soils, and seasons will allow. As a rule, the potato is a profitable plant. By good culture on a good soil, aided by a good season, we may expect to lift ten to twelve tons from an acre of ground, and we have known the crop to amount to over twenty tons. As a rule, eight tons may be reckoned on from a good deep well-drained loam by the roughest method of procedure; the value of the crop at £5 per ton will be £40, which will generally afford a liberal margin of profit after rent, labour, and manure have been paid for. In the American potato trial of 1874, the produce of a quarter of an acre of *Compton's Surprise* was reported to be 7,350 lbs., which is equivalent to 490 bushels, or over 10 tons, per acre; and of *Brownell's Beauty*, 8,899 lbs., equivalent to 594 bushels, or 14½ tons, per acre. But these were not the highest yields known to the committee by whom the prizes were awarded, and they expressed their regret that those who obtained these larger yields refrained from entering into the competition.

The Soil for potatoes should in any case be open to the sun, thoroughly well dug, and in good heart. Drainage is not of great consequence, because the crop occupies the ground only during those months when water in the soil is rather beneficial than otherwise; but, as a well-drained soil is warmer than one water-logged, drainage must be voted for as at least desirable. As to the kinds of soil, a sandy fertile loam is certainly to be preferred, but the potato will make a fair return in any soil, whether loam, or clay, or peat, or dusty shale, or starving limestone, or roasting chalk. The plant is the product for the most part of the sunshine, and as a rule, the measure of the sunshine is the measure of the crop. But, as no one can live on love, so the potato needs something in the shape of food in addition to sunshine. It takes a large amount of mineral matter from the soil, for in one ton of tubers there are 11 lbs. of potash, 1 lb. of soda, 1 lb. of lime, 1 lb. of magnesia, 4 lbs. of sulphuric acid, and 2½ lbs. phosphoric acid. It is evident that alkaline and phosphatic manures will suit the potato if the ground is poor, and, of all minerals,, it stands most in need of potash. As a rule, the best possible manure for this crop is good farmyard dung, which may be dug in when the ground is made ready, or may be laid at the bottom of the trench when the sets are planted. It is very commonly believed that the use of manure is in-

K

jurious to the potato, but that is a fallacy. Judicious manuring, by strengthening the plant, enables it to some extent to resist disease, but if the ground is very heavily manured and a wet season follows, the crop will be likely to suffer in consequence of the retention of moisture by the manure, for the potato loves dryness, and generally pays best in a droughty season. Extravagant manuring that would suit the cauliflower might prove injurious to the potato, but it does not follow that because excess of food is bad, starvation is to be practised in its stead.

If good stable manure is not obtainable, the manures known as artificials must be resorted to. The best manure of this class for general purposes are phospho-guano and Amies's patent manure. These are rich in phosphates, and promote high quality in the produce. Poor sandy and shaly soils may be greatly aided by kainit and superphosphate, or better still, perhaps, by muriate of potash and superphosphate in equal proportions, applied at the rate of 5 cwt. per acre. Charred vegetable rubbish is of great service, especially on a clay soil, and if any quantity can be obtained by burning hedge clippings and weeds and such-like refuse, it should be stored in a dry place for the potatoes; or, if that is not convenient, should, as soon as made, be spread upon the ground it is intended to crop with potatoes.

Dry deep soils should be trenched for potatoes, and the manure laid between the two spits, but it is not desirable to trench heavy damp soils, for on these it is desirable to grow the crop on the surface, as will be described presently. The digging, whether one or two spits deep, should, if possible, be done in autumn, and the land left in rough ridges to be well mellowed by the frost. The work can be so managed that the planting may be done by laying the line in the furrow, putting the sets to it, and knocking down the earth of the ridge to cover them. When a heavy crop costing but little labour is aimed at, it is a quite easy matter for the workmen to lay up the ridges at a suitable distance apart, so that there will be no more digging needed until the crop is lifted. The distance will range from two to four feet according to the sort, and whether they are to ripen or be dug as new potatoes.

The Sets should be prepared in good time, for it often happens that fickle weather compels us to plant and sow and do other spring work in a hurry, and everything that can be forwarded beforehand should be ready for the rush. The very best way to prepare potato sets is to select tubers of the right shape, that is to say, a good sample, averaging four to six ounces each, and spread them out only one or two deep in shallow baskets or boxes in full daylight in the month of January. A corn loft is a good place for the business, being cool and airy and light. Should severe frost occur, they must be covered with sacks and the place kept shut, for potatoes that have been frozen are thenceforth useless, and must be thrown away. They will soon push out short stout purplish or green sprouts, and when these are an inch long the sets are ready for planting. A little damp is beneficial, and it is the practice of some cultivators to sprinkle the sets with water; but we have found the inconvenience of the proceeding to outweigh its benefits, and so make our sets ready without sprinkling.

It must be understood that a good crop of potatoes may be grown without any preparation of the sets whatever. It is by no means essential, though it is certainly desirable. Sets that have formed long, thread-like, blanched shoots in the dark are certainly not to be desired; but we must own that from such we have obtained as fine crops as ever were lifted. The fact is, a good soil and a hot summer will do anything for the potato up to twenty tons an acre; while a poor soil and a cold season will make mere rottenness of the crop on which the most painstaking care has been bestowed. We are dealing with facts well established, and while we admit that the roughest ways may end remarkably well, we are bound to say that nine times in ten good management from first to last will have its reward.

The selection of proper-shaped and equal-sized sets is not always possible. If the variety is scarce, you may be compelled to plant mere marbles, and even these may give a good crop; or you may have to cut large potatoes, and here again you may indulge in cheerful expectations. If the sets are to be cut, it should be done only a few days before planting. It is good practice to separate the eyes that come in a cluster on the crown or nose end from those on the side of the tuber, for they will differ slightly in time of ripening and in style of crop. If you want a few large potatoes, cut large sets with one plump side-eye to each, and when these have fairly sprouted plant them, allowing somewhat more space between the sets and between the rows than you would for an ordinary crop.

PLANTING may be done at any time from October to the end of May. We have planted on the 24th of June and taken up a good crop the first week in October. But that is bad practice, and requires a peculiarly favourable season to bring it through. Autumn planting is recommended where it suits the labour market, for the pressure of work in spring renders it desirable in many cases to get all heavy work out of hand before the spring comes, so far as that can be done to advantage. Now, potato-planting is a case in point, and ought to be much more practised than it is, to fill up a season when work is scarce, to the relief of a later season when there is more work than can be properly done to catch the season. Only on well-drained land should potatoes be planted in autumn. The ground being double dug and well manured, open trenches with the spade three to four feet apart, sprinkle the trenches with lime, and put down the sets and cover. They must be nine inches deep to be safe from frost, and to prevent too early a growth in spring. They will not start particularly early; but if the haulm appears too soon and is in danger of frost, cover it with crumbs drawn up by the hoe. Autumn planting should be completed before October is out, for there is risk of frost interrupting and damaging the work later in the season.

Potatoes may be planted in January and February if the weather is favourable for the work, but having missed October, it is best to wait until March, and in any and every case the planting should be finished before the end of April, because, as the root is peculiarly the product of sunshine, it ought to have as long a spell of the radiance as possible; and as disease does not usually break out until towards the end of the growing season, it is well if we can lift and store the crop before the disease has time to catch it.

And here we must make two remarks that we consider of importance. In the first place, the plant requires plenty of air and light, and therefore close planting is apt to prove unprofitable. It is better to put the rows, in the case of strong growers, four feet apart at least; and, to economize the ground, plant winter greens or broccolis or some other upright-growing plant between, than to put the rows so close that the haulm will intermix, and the plant be thereby deprived of the full influence upon it of air and light. Many a field of potatoes goes to ruin through the plant being over-crowded, so that if disease appears, it runs through the whole mass like wild-fire; whereas if the plant had been well exposed to light and air, it would to some extent have resisted the fungus, and a profitable crop might have been lifted. As the varieties differ in growth, so must the distances differ; but the *maximum* distance required will pay better than the *minimum;* so the proper way to conclude this remark is to advise the fullest possible exposure of the plant to the life-giving air and sunshine.

The second remark on planting that should come in here is to the effect that when the object of the cultivator is simply to obtain store potatoes of the finest quality, he should plant the late potatoes early, and the early potatoes late. The philosophy of the remark will be understood without the aid of argument. The early sorts begin to grow so soon after planting that they are in danger of injury from frost; but the late sorts move slowly, and early planting does not usually expose them to frost. So far as to the beginning of the business; now let us look to the end. When lifting time comes, the early sorts planted late will be ripe and ready before there is much risk of disease, and the late ones planted early will, in all probability be ready also, and the sooner they are out of the ground the better. On dry lands potatoes may be advantageously planted in trenches opened by the spade or, as above described, in trenches made for the purpose in getting the land ready. They should be four to six inches deep at least, and have two hoeings up in the course of the season, to keep down weeds, to aërate and fertilize the soil, and to ensure the tubers being well covered; for if they grow out and become green, they will be only fit for seed, for green potatoes are poisonous to man and beast. It must be admitted, however, that if the sets are planted six to nine inches deep nothing more need be done in the way of cultivation, for in a good season there will be a good crop, and a small proportion of greened tubers will not materially deteriorate its value. If a casting vote be required, we vote for earthing up: it is a tidy way, and good for the ground as well as the growing crop, for every time the soil is knocked about something is added to its fertility.

PLANTING ON TILES is a plan followed here as a means of

averting disease, and it has proved sufficiently successful to be well spoken of. The tile we use is made for the purpose, but

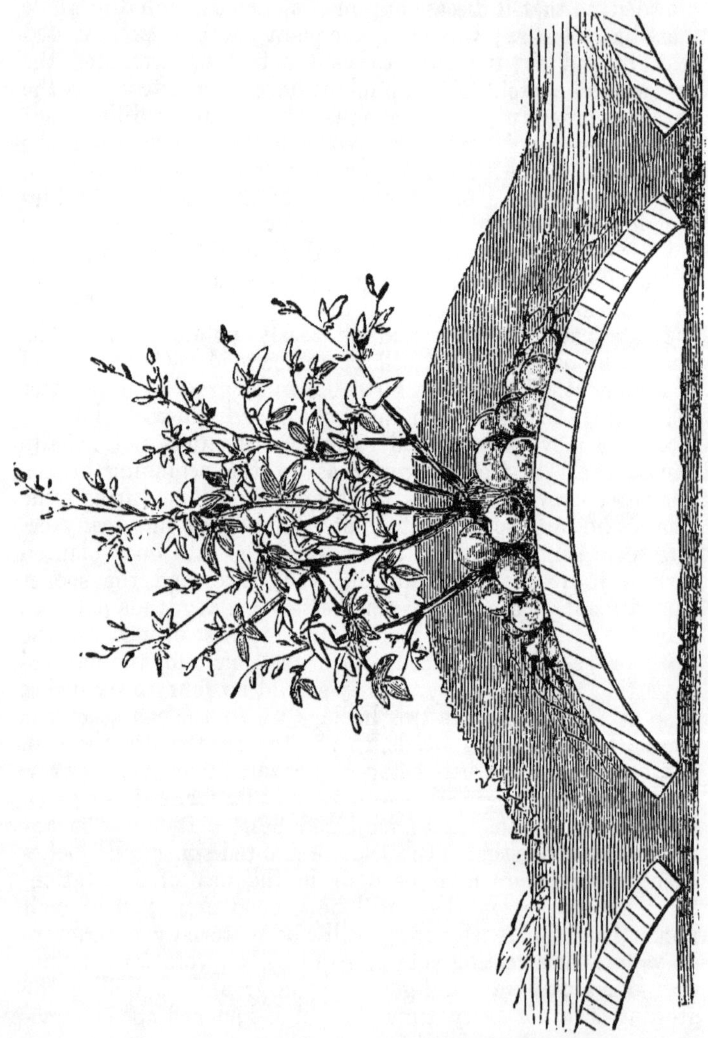

any cheap hollow tile—say, a roofing tile—will answer. The tiles are laid hollow side downwards in rows three to four or more feet apart, the sets are laid on them, and covered with earth from between. Twice during the growing season the plant is moulded up with more earth from between, and the result is that the whole of its growth is made in a ridge above the general level, and a body of air is enclosed by the tile beneath its roots. In a wet cold season, when disease rages, potatoes grown on tiles are scarcely touched, and the quality of the tubers is above the average. On the other hand, in a very hot dry season the tile system does not pay so well, as the plant is apt to be starved through lack of moisture. Our tile potatoes are always planted in January or February, that the plant may make a good root-hold as soon as the ground is warm enough, to be the better enabled to withstand a drought. On light dry lands tiles are not to be thought of; on heavy lands they will make a good return for a reasonable outlay.

Planting Above Ground is a compromise, and a capital compromise, between the expense of tiles and the risk of ruin by disease. It is especially adapted to heavy soils. The lines are marked out four feet apart, and slightly trodden, and the sets are laid down on the surface to the line, and covered with stuff taken from between. In the first instance, an inch or two of soil is enough to cover them with. The soil between the rows is now well dug, and, if needful, a good body of stable manure or suitable artificials is mixed with it, and the top crumbs are drawn to the potatoes to add an inch or two more of soil to them. They are several times moulded up until the haulm is seated on ridges a foot high. The spaces between are planted with winter greens or broccolis, and when the potatoes come off there remains on the ground a profitable crop of brassicas. Potatoes grown in this way on strong land are remarkably fine: in fact, it is the right way, for they obtain a maximum of sun-heat, are not distressed by drought, and, in the event of disease occurring, lie so high and dry that it has no fair chance of decimating them.

Potato Disease has been so largely discoursed upon, that in this practical treatise it will be advisable to say the least possible. It is certainly associated with the growth of a fungus *(Peronospora infestans)*, on the haulm first and in the tuber afterwards. Whether the fungus is the cause or the consequence or the mere accompaniment of the disease, is of little consequence. In a season characterised by dry weather and continuous sunshine but little is heard of disease; but if when the crop is nearly matured cold wet weather should set in, the disease appears and spreads quickly, unless arrested by the return of hot dry weather, for the sunshine the plant loves is a deadly foe to its enemies. The practical lessons of the facts known in relation to disease comprise early planting, planting above ground or on tiles, early lifting, and the selection, so far as may be convenient, of early sorts. As we must have late as well as early sorts, the selection in reference to earliness cannot be carried beyond a certain point. Nevertheless, early sorts might be much more extensively used than they are at present for autumn and early winter supply.

EARLY POTATOES may be raised with very rough appliances in the shape of old frames, thatched hurdles, and other means of protection. In any and every case the protective agency should also serve as a trap to catch a sunbeam. To grow potatoes well in frames is rather a troublesome business. In first-class frame culture, operations commence in November, but in a majority of gardens it will suffice to begin in January or February. In either case the routine is the same. A pit or frame is the most suitable structure, because the haulm can be kept near the glass, and be fully exposed to the light, and enjoy a free circulation of air. A heated pit is not absolutely required, although, in the case of the crop planted in November, the hot-water pipes will be useful in assisting to keep out the frost, but too much artificial heat at any stage will be injurious, as it will promote the too rapid production of haulm. Good crops may be obtained from unheated pits, as, with the assistance of mats and dry litter, there will not be much difficulty in keeping out the frost. In any case, the best results will be obtained by making up a bed of leaves in the pit or frame, and then covering it with a layer of soil in which to plant the sets. The leaves should be moderately dry, and be trodden firm, to prevent their sinking very much after the soil is put on. Where leaves cannot be obtained, stable manure may be employed instead, but it is apt to heat too violently at first, and then become cold. With leaves there is no danger of overheating, and they may, therefore, be covered with soil immediately after they are made up into a bed. With reference to the preparation of the soil, it may be said that it should be rather light and rather rich. Any good light soil will do very well after it has been incorporated with a liberal proportion of well-decayed manure. A depth of twelve inches will suffice for the soil, and in planting, open out trenches twelve inches apart, and four inches in depth. In these lay the sets, already well sprouted, from nine to twelve inches apart, and then cover them with the soil drawn from the trenches. The frame may then be shut up until the tops begin to make their appearance above the soil. After this stage a little air must be admitted whenever the weather is favourable to air-giving, to ensure a stocky growth. The weather alone must regulate the admission of air to the frame. In December and January very little air will suffice, but from the beginning of February onwards the frames will require ventilating more freely. The earliest crop should have a little soil drawn over the tops of the shoots when they first make their appearance above the surface, as an additional protection from frost, and in all cases, when six or seven inches in height, they will require earthing up in the usual manner. After the crop is in full growth, rather liberal supplies of water and abundant ventilation will be required. When nearly full-grown, the lights may in mild weather be drawn off altogether during the day, and, as far as practicable, advantage should be taken of these opportunities for watering.

For the earliest crop the *Old Walnut Leaf* is the most suitable, as it turns in quickly, and it is so dwarf in growth that it takes up very little space. But for the best crop *Veitch's Royal Ashleaf* will be found preferable, as it is a much heavier cropper than the Walnut Leaf, and is of the most excellent quality.

Modifications of this plan will occur to those who are anxious to raise new potatoes, and the rough Lancashire method will no doubt prove the most profitable. This method, however, taxes the energies of the cultivator so severely, and needs such constant watching, almost night and day for months together, that it cannot be recommended as generally useful.

To grow early crops in the open ground requires only a little more care and trouble than the rough-and-ready modes by which store potatoes are obtained. Sloping borders under warm south walls, beds in old brick pits, with thatched hurdles or old lights and mats for occasional covering, and open plots of ground well screened by hedges and plantations on the north and east, and nicely sloping to the sunny south, may be turned to account for early crops of *Ashleaf Champion, Myatts*, and the old *Walnut Leaf*. The soil must be light and dry and well prepared. There should be in readiness plenty of charcoal and burnt earth from a garden smother, and, if possible, also plenty of rough lime rubbish. Plant well-sprouted sets as early in February as weather will permit. In planting, open trenches one foot deep and eighteen inches apart; put into the trenches six inches of hot dung, and over that lay two inches of earth. Then put down the sets six to nine inches apart, and cover with two or three inches of soil. In the course of a fortnight or so spread over the rows two or three inches of a mixture of the charrings and lime rubbish from which bits of lath and brickbats have been removed. When the shoots begin to push through, give them a final moulding up, first drawing an inch or two of fine earth to the haulm to comfort it. As soon as you have cauliflower or broccoli or collard plants large enough to put out, dib them in between the rows. You will be able to dig new potatoes in June, and, to do justice to the cauliflower or cabbage crop, the potatoes must be cleared off as soon as possible.

THE SELECTION OF SORTS must be regulated by the requirements of the planter and also by the taste of the household. A working man taught us a lesson in selecting that we might never have learnt otherwise. He asked us to start him in potato-growing with half a dozen good sorts. So we looked him out about a peck of each of Late Rose, Paterson's Victoria, King of Potatoes, Scotch Blue, Dunbar Regent, and Model. At the end of the season we asked him how the potatoes turned out. He said he had lifted splendid crops, but he was obliged to sell them, for they were all floury potatoes, and he and his family could only eat waxy ones. It must be a puzzle to potato-fanciers to observe how sorts regarded by them as objectionable obtain and maintain extensive popularity, especially in the country. The reason must be in part because the inferior sorts are preferred; but another reason comes into force, for many cottagers will grow any potato that is likely to yield a large crop, without any regard whatever to quality,

All the *Ashleaf* and *Lapstone* types are more or less yellow-fleshed and extremely rich in flavour, especially towards the close of the winter. The *Regent* type are mostly white and mealy, and the true old *Yorkshire Regent* is so exceedingly sensitive in texture of flesh that it should always be steamed, because when cooked in water it melts, and some amount of waste is inevitable. Most purple-skinned potatoes are exceedingly white inside, but whiteness, though a good quality, is deceptive, for the finest flavoured and most nourishing potatoes are more or less yellowish, and some few are almost a golden yellow. The *King of Potatoes* is an example, but there is nothing finer in respect of quality to be found. As yellow potatoes appear white by gaslight, they may be served at late dinners with more satisfaction than by daylight. The *Fluke* and *Daw's Matchless* are the most perfect in appearance of any potatoes known, and, though by no means rich, they are fine in quality, but unfortunately very subject to disease. The American potatoes are mostly white-fleshed and mealy—in fact, too mealy, for they may be described as frothy, and they are of necessity innutritious. There are, however, exceptions amongst them, and a certain few, such as *Climax* and *Early Goodrich*, are as good as any English varieties of their class. In the following selection all the kinds named are suitable for garden culture and first-rate of their kind.

A SELECTION OF VARIETIES.—A few of the best potatoes for special purposes having been named, we have now to consider the interest of the potato fancier, who, as a matter of course, must have a collection. The following are handsome varieties, of good quality in their several classes, and have been prominent in successful competitions at exhibitions the last few years. They are arranged according to habit of growth, the distances apart being determined by the length of the haulm.

Varieties to be planted 14 *inches from set to set, and* 30 *inches from row to row.*—Alpha, Blue Ashleaf, Early Market, Early White Kidney, Early Union, English Rose, Pioneer, and Sextus.

16 *inches from set to set, and* 36 *inches from row to row.*—Blanchard, Bountiful, Cottager's Blush, and The Schoolmaster.

16 *inches from set to set, and* 36 *inches from row to row.*—Ashtop Fluke, Barron's Perfection, Beckenham Kidney, Biddles' Seedling, Breadfruit, Bresee's No. 6, China Orange, Devonshire Kidney, Early Goodrich, Early Hammersmith, Eclipse Kidney, Garibaldi, Golden Eagle, Harry Kidney, King of Potatoes, King of the Earlies, Lady Webster, Lady Abbiss, Lapstone

(Cobbler's), Prince of Teck, President, Salmon Kidney, Table King, The Favourite, Trout Kidney, and White Perfection.

17 *inches from set to set, and* 42 *inches from row to row.*—Early Gem, Extra Early Vermont, Early Dimmisk, Early Oneida, Early Rose, Emperor, Excelsior (round), Gloucestershire Kidney, Headly's Nonpareil, Hayes's Superb Kidney, Idaho, Jackson's Improved Kidney, Late Rose, Model, Prince of Wales Kidney, Peerless, Prolific, Peach Blossom, Premier Kidney, Rector of Woodstock, Royal Ashleaf, Ruby, Snowflake, Scotch Blue, Shiner, Sedilla, Schoolmaster, Waterloo Kidney, Willard, Wonderful, Red Kidney, and White Rose.

18 *inches from set to set, and* 48 *inches from row to row.*—Campbell's Late Rose, Carpenter, Compton's Surprise, American Pink Eye, Dalmahoy, Early Paragon, Excelsior Kidney, Gleeson's Late, Garnet Chili, Henderson's Prolific, Johnson's Seedling, Keystone, Late Vermont, Marchioness of Lorne, Nonsuch, New Hundredfold Fluke, Ohio Beauty, Orono, Pink-eyed Regent, Pink-eyed Rusty-coat, Porter's Excelsior, Porter's Hero, Porter's Sunflower, Prince Arthur, Queen, Red Emperor, Rintoul's Striped Don, Rose Blush, Victoria (Paterson's), Vermont Beauty, Walker's Regent, Webb's Surprise, and Yorkshire Hero.

18 *inches from set to set, and* 54 *inches from row to row.*—Eureka, International Kidney, and Magnum Bonum.

20 *inches from set to set, and* 60 *inches from row to row.*—Red Fluke, Red Regent, and Red-skin Flourball.

CHAPTER XIV.

THE JERUSALEM ARTICHOKE.

"That's a good root."
Merry Wives, IV., 1.

THE JERUSALEM ARTICHOKE *(Helianthus tuberosus)* is so well known that to describe it would be waste of time, and imply lack of respect for the reader. It is, however, a fact of some importance that it is not often well grown, and that it is rarely seen on good tables. There is, we think, room for a little reform in respect of this useful plant, first, for the suppression of a prevailing prejudice against it; and secondly, for the ordering of its cultivation in a more profitable manner. When well grown and sufficiently cooked, it is a most acceptable vegetable, but a little training of the palate is requisite to the full enjoyment of its flavour. It is usually served with white sauce; but this is by no means necessary, for any good gravy may take its place advantageously. It often happens that when brought to table these roots are of a bad colour and too crisp to be agreeable. These are the common results of unskilful cooking. They require to be washed and pared as potatoes are; but as this is done, they should be thrown into a bowl of clear water, into which a few drops of juice have been squeezed from a lemon. If this is not done, the roots are apt to become slightly discoloured in the process of cooking; but a very little lemon-juice suffices to preserve the colour. When all are ready, put them into a pot containing sufficient boiling water to just cover them, with a rather large allowance of salt, and keep them boiling twenty to forty minutes. They should be quite tender, and, indeed, almost pulpy when sent to table. They are then delicious, and thoroughly wholesome.

The Jerusalem Artichoke is rarely well cultivated, and consequently the roots are often so small as to be scarcely worth the trouble of cooking. This plant, like many others, pays best in good ground. Ours are grown on strong clay land, that has been well trenched during winter. On a poor soil we should use manure liberally; but our heavy clay does not need any such aid, and we find our artichoke roots average in weight 1lb. each, which is considerably above the weight of fair samples in the market. The small roots are set aside for planting, and are generally planted in the later days of March, April, or early in May. They are put in rows two feet asunder, and the sets fifteen inches apart in the row. This is a more liberal allowance of space than they usually obtain: but they pay well for it, for while the aggregate crop is heavy, a majority of the roots are large, and it is a fact of some importance that Jerusalem Artichokes cannot be too large, owing to the inevitable waste that occurs in preparing them for cooking. We measured some of our stems in the year 1875, and found the shortest to be eight feet, and the tallest fifteen feet, and nine-tenths of them flowered.

RENDLE'S FRUIT WALL PROTECTOR.

CHAPTER XV.

THE TURNIP.

"I had rather be set quick i' the earth
And bowl'd to death with turnips."
Merry Wives, III., 4.

THE TURNIP *(Brassica rapa)* must be regarded as of quite secondary importance to the gardener, and in a small garden it will be found by many a prudent course to throw it out of the list, and to purchase turnips as the demands of the kitchen may render necessary. In large gardens, where regular successions of all kinds of vegetables are grown, tender and juicy turnips are produced the whole year round; but in such as we may call middle-class gardens they are expected only in the autumn and winter, and to produce them for those seasons is a comparatively easy matter. Before describing the various methods adopted for obtaining turnips at different seasons of the year, it may be proper to remark that the turnip is fully as precarious in the garden as in the field, being more directly influenced for weal or woe by peculiarities of the seasons and the weather than any other garden crop, the potato alone excepted. A cold wet season will not produce good turnips, for the bulbs grow too fast and soon burst and rot in the ground, emitting a most offensive odour. A hot dry season causes them to become tap-rooted and misshapen, owing to their eager search for moisture, and in the end they may be compared with wooden nutmegs of a large size or very badly-diseased potatoes. Another point of some importance is that turnips do not long keep in good condition after they have completed their growth; so that, unless the gardener's management ensures a constant succession, the turnips come in a glut at one time, and very soon afterwards there are none at all. It is true they keep pretty well in the winter, and are then in greatest request; but in spring and summer they must be used as fast as they become large enough to draw, or they will become fibrous and rank in flavour. As a rule a glut of turnips is not so welcome as a glut of peas in a private garden, but in the market garden it is a good thing to secure a heavy crop which can be cleared off all at once, or nearly so, to make the ground ready for other purposes. The market grower can draw his turnips when they are perfect, but the private gardener draws a few this week and a few next, and keeps them going as long as possible; so that, although he may begin with a sample equal to any ever seen in market, it soon deteriorates, and he makes an end of his crop by sending in turnips tough as fiddle-strings. Hence, if we compare the turnips offered by greengrocers with those from the home garden every day throughout the year, we shall find that the vendor has the best of it; and hence, in some cases, it may be better to depend upon the market for turnips than to trust entirely on the production of the garden. Let everyone judge for himself on this point, but let none who employ gardeners be in haste to find fault with their intermittent and defective supplies of turnips. If the market beats them in this matter, they can beat the market in almost everything else grown in the kitchen garden, and especially in peas, beans, cauliflowers, and all kinds of green vegetables.

SUCCESSIONAL SORTS.—We shall first speak of the simplest mode of growing turnips and the practice that is adapted for a majority of middle-class gardens. When March winds have made the seed beds ready, and a general sowing is made of what we call "small seeds"—*i. e.*, cabbage, winter greens, etc.—a few rows of any of the quick-growing white turnips should be sown with them. There can be nothing better for this purpose than *Early Dutch* and *Early Snowball.* These will afford a supply of nice juicy turnips in May and June, and perhaps until the middle of July. The times of coming in and going out are, however, dependent on the weather. It will be well if small successive sowings of quick growing white sorts can be made in April, May, and June, and in the early part of July the main crop for winter and spring use must be sown. The July sowing is the most important of all in a small garden, for it not only ensures plenty of turnips when they are much in request, but there is usually no difficulty in finding ground for it, as the early peas are then cleared off, and a general disposal of the ground for winter crops is in progress. The July sowing should comprise at least three or four sorts, one of them being a quick grower, such as *Mouse-tail* or *Six Weeks*, and the others slow-growing kinds for late autumn and winter use, such as *Red American*, *Veitch's Red Globe*, *Orange Jelly*, and *Chirk Castle Black Stone*. If ground can be spared, and there is any probability of turnips being in great demand, sow again in August, and this time give the preference to *Jersey Navet*, a very hardy conical-rooted turnip, and *Orange Jelly*, which endures hard winter weather equally well. In favoured districts turnips may be sown in September, and then the sorts should be about two in number—say, one of the earliest, such as *Six Weeks*, and one of the latest, such as *Jersey Navet*. During a quarter of a century's experience in kitchen practice we have never obtained turnips worth having by sowing so late as September, and therefore we advise all who have no better climate than that of Stoke Newington to be in time with their sowings of winter turnips, and make sure of a plant ere the dark days come and growth is arrested by fog and frost.

Where a regular succession is required, the first sowing should be made at the end of January on a gentle hotbed covered with six inches of light rich soil. Thenceforward every month a bed should be sown, first on warm sheltered borders, and afterwards in the open ground. For hotbed culture brick pits are well adapted, but whatever the structure it must be one from which the lights can be easily removed, for it is impossible to grow turnips wholly under glass.

SOIL.—The turnip will grow in any good garden soil, but the best for the purpose is a deep, rich, mellow loam. An abundance of manure may be dug in when the ground is prepared, for not only is the turnip a hungry plant, but the sweet tender bulbs required for the table are only to be obtained by growing them as quickly as circumstances will allow, and a rich soil is essential to promote rapid development; hence also irrigation, whether by means of pure water or sewage, is a grand aid to the turnip crop, whether in the garden or the field; but the cultivator must take care to proportion the sewage to the amount of sunshine, for mere saturation of the ground is an injury, but plenty of moisture with a warm soil and a strong light will assist the development of the plant immensely. The best of all artificials for a turnip crop is phospho-guano.

TURNIP-SEED SHOULD BE SOWN in rows at least a foot apart,

and in good soil; the large-growing sorts may be allowed eighteen inches—indeed, we have found it to pay to allow two feet between the drills when sowing in June and July, so rapidly do the coarse leaves meet and cover the ground. We can think of no more appropriate designation for the thinning that should take place as the crop advances than to say that it must be terrific. We have, indeed, many times sent the people in to hoe field turnips with instructions to this effect: "Hoe them *all* out," the result being that after "all" had been hoed out enough were left to make a grand crop. We frequently see turnips in gardens so crowded that they are only fit to pull to throw into the poultry-yard or the cow-byre. To economise seed, sow as thinly as possible, and as soon as the plants are large enough to handle thin them in a merciless manner to at least a foot apart each way. The thinning, however, should not be done all at once—say, at the first thinning, when they are just large enough to handle, thin them to about six inches, and a week afterwards thin again to a foot or more, always leaving, if possible, the most vigorous plants, and being none too particular to keep the rows precise, for in weeding them out a lot will be found a little out of the line, and these generally bulb first of all, through having had plenty of room from the first.

Enemies of the Turnip.—The turnip-fly, or flea *(Haltica nemorum)*, is the chief enemy of the crop, and, though a mite of a mite of a jumping thing, is not to be despised, for so terrible are its ravages in some seasons that it may be regarded as an emblem of one of the plagues of Egypt. This insect is a beetle, and a very pretty one, too, as the microscopist, who knows it, will readily declare. It attacks the plant in the seed-leaf instantly upon its emergence from the ground, and if the plant survives the attack it quits it, and is seen no more. In fine and rather dry seasons it is not at all uncommon for several sowings of turnips to be destroyed by this little jumper; but if the plant grows quickly from the moment of its emergence, it survives the attack and soon appears none the worse for it. There are several modes of procedure for the protection of the crop against this enemy, and we will first consider those of a preventive nature. By digging the ground deeply, and adding at the same time a good dressing of manure, the chrysalids are in part buried and in part poisoned, and the plant grows so fast in consequence of the good preparation made for it, that the few jumpers left are comparatively powerless to injure it. Dressing the ground with fresh soot, or fresh lime or gas-lime, three days after sowing the seed, is a good practice, as it renders the soil and plant alike offensive to the insect, and at the same time promotes growth by the nourishment afforded. Another very important preventive is to destroy all charlock and bird-turnip that appear in the form of weeds: for these sustain the insect and keep the race in force, so that there is always a brood of Haltica where weeding is neglected, and especially near railway banks, where charlock is plentiful. There is yet another and apparently suicidal, yet not so foolish as it appears, system, and that is, to provide the rascal with food of another sort to decoy him away from the young turnips, on the plan of outwitting garden plagues by openly encouraging them. When sowing turnips sow also common rape in rows between them, and when the proper crop is advanced enough, hoe out the rape and let it perish.

Another pest of the plant is "Ambury" or "Finger and toe," the result of the puncture of the roots by a weevil. There is no cure for this, but it may be in great part prevented by deep digging and liberal manuring, and by the employment of soot, when the seed-beds are made ready for sowing, just "pricking it in" a few inches deep. It is generally on badly-cultivated old garden ground that ambury occurs, and it may be accepted as a proof that the ground has been dug, not with a spade or digging fork, but with a tooth-pick or a spoon. We have had to face the pest many times on land rented for garden purposes away from home; but it never troubled us beyond one season, for at every opportunity deep trenching was practised, and the whole generation of weevils were thereby consigned to deep graves beyond the reach of vegetation and the enjoyment of life.

Storing.—It is advisable to store turnips before they suffer in any material degree by the frosts of early winter. Take up only the finest bulbs and pack them away in dry earth or sand in a cool dry shed or outhouse, leaving the inferior roots to weather the storm, and if they survive they will be useful to supply turnip-greens in spring, when vegetables are scarce. They may also be clamped in the same way as potatoes, and a week's supply may be taken out at a time, as in winter exposure to the air for a week or so does them no harm, and it is a saving of time to fill a basket and send it to the kitchen for the cook to dip into as demands arise. Before storing cut off the tops and tails, but never wash the bulbs.

SUBSTITUTES FOR TURNIPS.—There are two good substitutes for turnips which must be noticed here. If the winter store is exhausted, and there is no prospect of securing a crop in time to keep up the succession, a brisk hotbed should be made up with six inches of rich light soil for a seed bed, and a sowing made of common *White Turnip Radish.* These will "turn in" quickly, and may be served as turnips. Though small, they will be elegant, and, if carefully cooked, as delicate as the most perfect crop of frame-grown turnips. The other substitute will answer for autumn and winter use on heavy soils where turnips do not thrive. It is the *Kohl-rabi,* or *Knol-kohl,* a plant intermediate between a turnip and a cabbage. This must be sown in March, April, and May, and planted out when large enough to handle, in just the same way as winter greens. The bulb is formed above ground, and is strikingly marked with the point of attachment (hilum) of every separate leaf stalk, in precisely the same way as we see the old stump of a cabbage marked, and those frail "walking-sticks" that are made of the stems of Jersey cabbages. When cooked (without peeling off the rind), in the same manner as the turnip, this is a first class root, the flavour similar to that of the turnip, but richer, and somewhat nutty and buttery, and the flesh is as soft as marrow. We have always obtained our best supplies of Kohl-rabi from the later sowings, preferring small to large roots for the table, but those who want large roots must sow early. The best sorts are the *Purple* and the *Green,* and of the two we prefer the latter.

CHEMICAL CONSTITUTION.—The nutritive value of the turnip is of little consequence, while we are regarding it as a table vegetable only. As a matter of course, in common with all foods that are prepared by *boiling,* the nutritive properties of the turnip are in great part washed away and lost. The only practical advices that can be given on that point are that they should be cooked whole, and that they should be dished the instant they become sufficiently tender ; for, although we may be careless as to their powers of nourishing, the more they are cooked the more completely is their fresh and relishing flavour destroyed. But the chemical constituents of the turnip should be taken note of by the cultivator, as affording a key to the proper system of manuring to ensure a paying crop. The ashes of the fully-developed turnip-bulb consist for the most part of potash, soda, lime, phosphoric-acid, sulphuric-acid, and common salt. In a ton of turnips there are about 7½ lbs. of potash, 1½ lbs. of soda, 6 lbs. of lime, ¾ lbs. of magnesia, 2½ lbs. of phosphoric acid, 3¼ lbs. of sulphuric acid, 5 lbs. of common table salt, or chloride of sodium. Now, if the bulbs abstract these substances from the soil, the system of manuring must be such as to restore them, or such of them, at least, as the soil is naturally deficient of. For a sandy soil kainit and superposphate will be suitable refreshers; guano and phospho-guano will suit any old garden soil; and good fat stable manure will answer in the very best manner to prepare any soil for turnips, whether loam, clay, or sand.

SELECTION OF SORTS.—As to sorts there is not much choice, and nobody goes mad about turnips, as they do about peas and potatoes. A few have been already mentioned, but here is a list of such as we consider sufficient, having tried again and again *ad nauseam* in the experimental garden at Stoke Newington all the sorts we could obtain by worrying the trade and scouring the country.

TURNIPS FOR EARLY SOWING.—*Early White Dutch, Six Weeks, Early Snowball.*

FOR SUCCESSION.—*Red American* stands well after the growth is finished; *Yellow Malta.*

FOR MAIN CROP.—*Red American, Six Weeks, Veitch's Red Globe.*

FOR LATE SOWING TO STAND THE WINTER.—*Orange Jelly, Jersey Navet, Chirk Castle.*

Where turnips are grown in any quantity it is of the utmost importance to shift them about from place to place, so as to put them on soil that has not seen turnips for a year or two, in other words, to observe the first principles of "rotation."

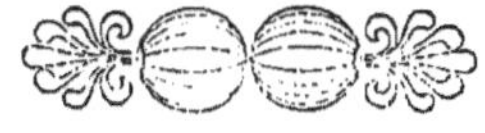

CHAPTER XVI.

TAP ROOTED VEGETABLES.

"Your greatest want is, you want much of meat.
Why should you want? Behold the earth hath roots?
Within this mile break forth a hundred springs:
The oaks bear mast, the briars scarlet hips;
The bounteous housewife, nature, on each bush
Lays her full mess before you. Want? Why want?"

Timon of Athens, IV., 3.

THE tap-rooted plants grown in the kitchen garden cannot usually be sown with advantage until the month of April, although in forward seasons parsnips may be sown with safety in the month of March. Important as these crops are, there is really not much to be said about them, though what little should be said is as important as the roots themselves; for good crops of roots make a great return for the labour bestowed upon them, and to secure good crops we must practise good cultivation.

THE CARROT *(Daucus carota)* is the most important of all the garden roots, the potato alone excepted. Two supplies of carrots should be arranged for in every garden. A dish of small, tender carrots constitutes one of the elegances of the table during the summer and autumn, and large carrots are in demand all the winter, and, indeed, as long as they can be obtained throughout the year. Fortunately, both sorts can be grown in any garden that will produce a cabbage; but first-class winter carrots fit for exhibition can only be grown in a deep, well-pulverized loam, or nourishing sandy soil that has been long in cultivation. In common with all other crops, deep digging some time in advance of sowing is necessary to insure a heavy production of handsome roots; and the best plot of ground that can be selected for sowing carrot-seed on is one that was heavily manured last season, and well trenched up before winter. To incorporate fresh manure with the soil in making preparations for the cultivation of the carrot, is bad practice; but in the case of a worn-out plot being required for this crop, it may be trenched two spits deep, and a good bed of manure may be laid in the trench as the work proceeds. It is of the utmost importance to have the surface soil dry and pulverulent, and it is better to wait for fine weather and a good seed bed than sow when the ground is cold and pasty. Carrot-seed is light, chaffy stuff, requiring careful handling to distribute it regularly in the drill. It is the custom of some cultivators to mix it with sand, to render it more tangible, but the practised hand needs no such aid. The drills should be drawn very shallow, at a distance of six to nine inches apart for the smaller kinds, and a foot apart for the larger. It is usual to sow rather thick, and to thin severely; and as the seed is cheap, we need not find fault with the common practice; but, with good seed, thin sowing is certainly better than thick, because seed is saved, and there is less thinning to do afterwards. The thinning of the crop should commence as soon as the plants are large enough to handle, and, at the same time, if weeds are rising with them, the scuffle-hoe should be employed between the rows, to keep the ground clean. A few very nice dishes of tender summer carrots may be obtained by careful thinning of the beds sown for winter use. But the proper carrot for summer is the *French Horn*, a small, elegant root, which may be stored for winter, but is most useful to draw when young for immediate cooking, when it is peculiarly tender and delicate. This small carrot is sown for an early crop on beds of light rich soil, made up with foundations of half-exhausted fermenting material, such as stable manure or leaves, and covered with frames. A proper hotbed would force them too rapidly, but a gentle warmth of soil and judicious sheltering, with plenty of air as weather may permit, are the conditions under which an early supply may be most surely secured. The first sowings are made in this way in January and February, and these are succeeded by sowings on open borders, in warm and sheltered spots, in March and April, and on any piece of ground that may be vacant in July. As a rule, the Horn carrot should be sown in very small breadths, or there will be a superabundant supply; but as the requirements of families differ immensely, a general caution against "overdoing it" is all that can be offered here. In our garden we always grow more than suffices for the kitchen, and so the cattle come in for a pleasant variation of their daily food.

The best of all the sorts for use in winter and spring is the *Long Surrey,* which is the handsomest and best flavoured. A more profitable, but a thoroughly coarse variety, is the *Altringham,* which has an objectionable green crown. In gross weight of crop this will always surpass the Long Surrey, and, though coarse and ugly, it is a good carrot. A most valuable variety for shallow soils is *James's Intermediate,* which has every good quality that can be desired except beauty, for it is short and club-like, but in colour and flavour excellent. The *Belgian White* carrot is one of the most valuable of agricultural roots, and especially for feeding horses. It is admissible to the table and makes a useful dish, and therefore may be recognized as a garden crop.

THE PARSNIP *(Pastinaca sativa)* thrives in any soil, with or without manure, provided it is fairly prepared for by deep digging some time in advance of sowing the seed. It is, perhaps, the most profitable of all the roots grown in the kitchen garden, but it is less generally esteemed, and is therefore less generally useful, than the potato. No one who cares to eat this sugary root need be deterred from growing it by untoward circumstances. We have grown a crop in a field of stones, in a sterile district, where we had to carry sand in to cover the seed, and the roots at harvesting time were only a little thicker than a big man's thumb, yet, when slowly cooked in a small quantity of water, they were as marrowy and sweet as the finest of the Jersey parsnips; indeed, we are inclined to believe they were a few degrees better. However, though small roots are not to be despised, large ones are most valued, and a rich, deep soil will produce them with just no more trouble than deep digging and sowing the seed, for they scarcely want weeding, and the thinning may be performed in almost no time. If, however, extra large roots are required, the way to secure them is to trench two spits deep, and put a good bed of fat manure in the bottom of the trench—the roots will find it in good time, and the result will be satisfactory. But manure dug in with surface-digging is more harm than good, for the roots, instead of going straight down, make all sorts of ugly forks and fibres, and a very large proportion of the whole bulk is wasted in preparing them for cooking. Therefore, if the labour of trenching and putting manure at the bottom of the trenches is too great, do not employ manure, and be content with smaller, but more usable roots. In any case, however, deep and earnest stirring of the soil is a proper preparation for this crop. Hard work, more than "fine words," tends to the buttering of parsnips.

Sow fresh seed in March, or early in April. The seed bed should be fine and dry. If large roots are desired, sow in drills, fifteen to eighteen inches apart, and thin to a foot; if the ground is poor, sow twelve inches asunder, and thin to nine or six inches. Distances depend on conditions, but a mistake will not ruin the plantation: for if parsnips are rather crowded, it does not much matter; but the size of the roots will of necessity depend upon the space allowed them. During showery weather in July and August, a final thinning may be made of roots that elbow each other, and they will be found exceedingly marrowy and delicate when cooked.

BEETROOT *(Beta vulgaris)* should be available every day throughout the year; but like other roots it can be grown only during summer. Where the demand is unremitting, the cultivator must secure early crops for use in autumn, and must store well and plentifully for supply in spring and summer. We have found it tolerably easy work to do this until July, and then the old beets were becoming fibrous, and the young ones were too small to pull, and there was the shadow of a hitch sometimes. But it can be done, and wherever salads are in request all the year round, beetroot must be provided for them. Our practice is to sow a few rows on half-fermenting beds in frames in February, as advised for the early production of Horn carrots, and this plan enables us to supply the kitchen with fine roots at the end of June and throughout July, when the roots in the store are acquiring an undesirable toughness. As the subject of storing comes before us properly here, we may as well dispose of it. A bed of earth in a shed of any kind, safe from frost, answers the purpose well. Better is it, however, to store the roots in dry sand in a place where neither moisture, nor frost, nor the warmth of spring, can reach them. Our best store is a shed built of brick in a north aspect; it is safe from frost, and the spring sunshine has but little effect on its temperature. Some time in March the whole stock should be taken out, and the new roots and shoots rubbed off and the stock pitted again. The roots should be laid horizontally, as that position affords a slight check to growth. But once a month at least—if late keeping is important—they should all be looked over, and every sign of growth removed, for if allowed to make roots and leaves they soon become worthless.

As for the cultivation, it is the simplest matter in the world. Sow in shallow drills, putting the seed as nearly as possible singly six inches apart. As nearly as possible, mind, and do not waste valuable time about it, because if you sow too thick, it is no great task to thin the rows to nine inches or a foot apart, when the plants are large enough to handle. It is not desirable to grow large beets as a rule, but if they are required, proceed in the same way as recommended for the production of large parsnips. For open ground crops, where especial earliness of production is of no consequence, sow in April and May, and take up in November. When storing them, cut off the tails and some portion of the crowns, but be careful not to wound any part of the usable fleshy root, for there should never be a puncture in a beet until it is cooked and cold—in fact, the cook who would put a fork into a beet to try if it is "done," ought to be disarmed without the honours of war. But careful topping and tailing is to be advised, as it promotes close storing, and prevents growth in spring. All the varieties of beets have been grown again and again in the Experimental Garden at Stoke Newington, and, as a matter of course, we find that very few are needed in any ordinary garden. The three best are *Sutton's Dark Red*, *Nutting's Dwarf Red*, and *Henderson's Pine Apple.* If large and handsome roots are desired, grow *Dewar's Short Top*, and *Whyte's Black.* For particularly small and delicate roots of fine flavour, grow *Carter's St. Osyth.* If the soil is shallow, and the production of handsome roots doubtful, sow *Egyptian Turnip Rooted*, which is too coarse for a good soil. Beet is occasionally grown in the flower garden for the sake of the deep colour of its leaves. In this case, a green-leaved variety will not do; the best for decorative purposes is *Dewar's Crimson*, the roots of which are second-rate in quality, but will be found useful in the kitchen.

SALSIFY *(Tragopogon porrifolium)* is sometimes called the "Vegetable Oyster," because, when properly dressed, its flavour reminds lovers of that favourite mollusk of the joys that belong to months in which the letter R occurs. This root has a natural tendency to forkedness, which it is the duty of the cultivator to correct, by treating it precisely as recommended for the production of extra large parsnips—that is by trenching, and putting a good bed of manure in the bottom of the trench. It would be vain to talk of growing salsify extra large, for the fact is, it is never large enough, and is, therefore, seldom worth having unless grown with especial attention to its fullest possible development. Be liberal with it, therefore, or do not grow it at all. Prepare the ground in autumn, manuring as advised, and sow in April, in rows a foot apart at least. If the ground is extra strong and liberally manured at the bottom of the trench, sow in rows fifteen inches apart, always remembering that you cannot grow the root too large. Thin to nine inches or a foot when large enough. Take up in November, and store in dry earth or sand; one row may be left in the ground to furnish a dish of spring vegetable. This is obtained from the rising flower-stems, which are to be cut early or they will be stringy, and cooked in the way of sea-kale. The proper way to cook salsify roots is to boil them until tender in a very small quantity of milk, and then mash them and fry them in butter with salt and pepper. But it may be cooked in the same way as parsnips, which should be boiled slowly in the smallest possible quantity of water, until they are almost in a melting condition. If boiled fast in plenty of water, the flavour of parsnips and salsify is in great part washed away, and lost for ever.

SCORZONERA *(Scorzonera Hispanica)* is cultivated as salsify, but, being a stronger grower, needs rather more room.

SCOLYMUS *(Scolymus Hispanica)*, the Golden Thistle, forms a root like salsify, and is cultivated in the same manner. When skilfully dressed, this root makes a better imitation of the buttery bivalve than any other of its class, and may therefore be regarded as the true "Vegetable Oyster."

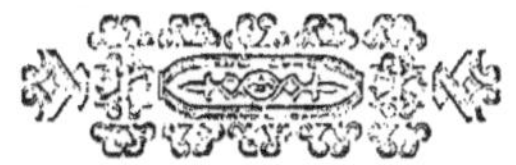

CHAPTER XVII.

RHUBARB.

"What rhubarb, cyme, or purgative drug,
Would scour these English hence?"
Macbeth, *V.*, *3.*

RHUBARB *(Rheum Rhaponticum)* is one of the many good things that ordinarily take such good care of themselves that it really obtains, in many gardens, less attention than it requires and deserves. In many instances, of course, it is a mere weed of the garden, that may prosper or perish for all the owner cares; for some good folks care but little for it in any shape or at any time, while not far off, perhaps, we may find those who esteem it highly, and would be glad to secure the best sorts and grow them in the best way to secure a full enjoyment of the various uses to which the plant may be put. Our own collection of rhubarbs comprises twenty sorts, and they differ considerably in relative value, and especially in the one important point of early growth; for those that grow earliest are the most to be desired, and as a rule they are the smallest, most highly coloured, and most delicately flavoured, and are of great service in the household in the early spring days, when the store of preserves is running low, and the largest of gooseberries are still too small to make insipid tarts. But the later and more robust growing varieties have their uses, for, to begin with, some people use rhubarb as a substitute for fruit in tarts all the summer long, while for preserving and wine making, the late kinds are much to be preferred, for they afford large supplies, while the early and very delicately flavoured kinds do not.

RAISING FROM SEED is a very simple business, but it will never pay the amateur unless he has some special object in view, such as the improvement of the varieties in flavour, earliness, productiveness, or some other desirable quality. In the month of July the seed may be obtained in plenty where the plants have been allowed to flower, and it should be gathered as early as possible, to insure ripeness, for if it is scattered about amongst the plants many seedlings will come up and injure the plantation. Cut off the whole of the seed-bearing stems close down to the heart of the plant, and lay them on cloths in a sunny greenhouse or wherever else they may be ripened in the full sun without risk of being blown away by the wind. As soon as it falls freely from the stalks it must be sown in drills two feet apart and an inch and a half deep. The ground must be kept clear of weeds, and in spring the rhubarb plants will appear in plenty, varying greatly in size and shape of leaf.

If you have practised cross breeding with a view to obtain plants of a particular style and quality, it will be well to let the whole remain until they become crowded in the rows, and then carefully transplant them in showery weather into rows three feet apart, putting the plants two feet apart in the row. The soil should be rich, deep, and moist, but not cold, and a sheltered spot should be selected to give the most precious of the seedlings a fair chance for an early start in spring.

If the object of seed sowing is simply to obtain stock for market, or to fill a plantation, thin the seed bed to six inches asunder, taking care to remove the weakest plants, and especially those that appear to differ from the type required. In the spring look over the plantation two or three times, and carefully lift every plant that pushes early and promises to be suitable for forcing. Plant these on rich, deep soil, with plenty of manure, putting them at least two feet apart in rows a yard asunder. Let them grow for a year, and then force them. Those that remain should be carefully rogued to remove unpromising plants and give more room to the best.

A Permanent Plantation of Named Sorts will be more useful in a small garden than seedlings, because a few plants of the very finest quality can be secured for a trifle, and may be multiplied to any extent required by the simple process of cutting up the roots. The soil best adapted for rhubarb culture is a deep, rich, moist loam, but the plant will thrive more or less, and at least usefully, on almost any kind of soil, but good living and plenty of moisture it will always appreciate. Our collection of twenty sorts forms a row of about a hundred feet in length, on a border of deep, damp loam, the stools being four and a half feet apart, and a trifle too close even at that, for the growth is tremendous. The border is well sheltered, and we secure usually a very early growth, so that really we do not need to force rhubarb. As soon as the leaves die down in the autumn we take cuttings of such as we require stock of. This is accomplished easily by cutting down by the side of the stools with the spade, and then carefully slicing off pieces of the root with incipient crowns. If the variety operated on is one of the scarce and valuable kinds, we pot the pieces and put them in a cold pit and plant them out when growing freely in spring. If they are sorts easily obtained, and too cheap to justify the trouble of potting, we plant them at once where they are to remain, for it is of very great importance to have rhubarb plants established as quickly as possible, and in all ordinary cases autumn planting is always to be preferred. Any amount of manure may be used in preparing the ground for rhubarb, and yet in a deep, damp, strong soil, it is scarcely necessary to use manure at all; certainly, on our oak and wheat growing clay we can do wonders with rhubarb without help of manure.

Forcing.—The simplest and, generally speaking, most useful mode of forcing is to proceed as follows:—When a frost has occurred in October (and not before), clean up the plantation, and put a barrowful of half-rotten stable or stye manure over every plant, taking care not to cover the crown more than three inches at the very utmost. On this point mistakes are often made, and the tender early stalks are unable to push through the hard cake of stuff above them at the time when they are most wanted and valued. The two or three inches of manure should be spread around the stool to insure some benefit to the roots of the plant, for, as a matter of fact, the crown does not want it; for the crown, indeed, we have next to provide. At the turn of the year, put on the crown of every plant that should give an early supply about a barrow-load of light dry litter. If you employ half-rotten manure, it may answer perfectly, but the comparatively weak and very early growing varieties cannot always push through stuff that has dried in flinty flakes, and it will be found in practice that our plan of operations is preferable to that commonly in use, because it insures a plentiful supply of early sticks that can be easily drawn, whereas stable manure put on after the turn of the year will prevent many of the sticks rising, and really should be used only for the assistance of the more robust and later varieties. Very well, remembering that complete success depends ofttimes on the observance of trifles, the next business is to find a lot of old boxes, or any kind of cover that can be put over them to keep in the warmth and exclude the cold.

At the risk of appearing prolix, we shall invite attention to a few facts of a representative kind. On the 11th of January, 1861, the temperature of the earth at a depth of two feet at Chiswick was 36½°, and the minimum temperature of the air the same day was 19°. On the 11th of January, 1862, the temperature of the earth at a depth of two feet was 43°, and the minimum temperature of the air on the same day was 30°. On the 11th of January, 1863, the temperature of the earth at a depth of two feet was 43½°, and the minimum temperature of the air on the same day was 28°. On the 11th of January, 1864, the temperature of the earth at a depth of two feet was 40½°, and the minimum temperature of the air on the same day was 29°. On the 11th of January, 1865, the temperature of the earth at a depth of two feet was 44°, and the minimum temperature of the air on the same day was 40°. On the 11th of January, 1866, the temperature of the earth at a depth of two feet was 43°, and the minimum temperature of the air on the same day was 17°. On the 11th of January, 1867, the temperature of the earth at a depth of two feet was 42°, and the minimum temperature of the air on the same day was 16°. On the 11th of January, 1868, the temperature of the earth at a depth of two feet was 39°, and the minimum temperature of the air on the same day was 29°. If we go on for ever the same kind of story will be told, and the facts cited will suffice to indicate that when early growth of outdoor plants is desired, we must shut them up from the variable atmosphere, and conserve for their use as much as possible the natural heat of the earth. In the course of the eight years to which the foregoing particulars refer, the mean difference between the temperature of the earth at two feet depth and the minimum of the air above the same spot on the 11th of January was 16°, the mean of the ground heat being 41½°, and the mean of minimum of air heat 25½°. The value of any kind of cover that prevents escape of earth heat without oppressing the plants must, on the face of the facts, be obvious.

It pays well to force rhubarb in sheds and outhouses where the demand is considerable, and there are plants at command for the purpose. The roughest machinery and materials will suffice, and the roots may be packed in any rough stuff that will hold moisture, and as for temperature, it should never rise higher than 60° if supplies are wanted quickly, and a better sample may be grown at an average of ten degrees less. If grown in the dark it will be more delicately flavoured than if exposed to light, while the colour will be scarcely less bright. In systematic forcing for the market, it is a good plan to plant in a well-made bed a lot of the best early sorts, putting the plants a yard apart, and cover with chimney-pots or large drain pipes, and surround these with hot dung, with a slate or some other rough cover on the top. Rough cradles made in the fashion of crates may be employed for the same purpose, and having been turned over to cover the stools, must be buried in hot dung, with rather loose and light litter on the top. The plant is so manageable and so profitable that whoever desires a supply of delicate rhubarb from Christmas to May will, after having read this chapter, find it quite easy to devise the means for the realization of the wish.

The rhubarb supplied to the London markets is in great part forced in tan. The first lot of roots are lifted in October, and are exposed to the weather for about ten days, and they are then packed in tan in a brick pit and very slowly forced. In the course of December they yield a nice supply of most elegant shoots. The second lot is lifted a fortnight after the first, and is also exposed to the weather for a short time, and is then packed in tan to give a succession. When the supplies from these roots are exhausted, the covered stools in the open ground will begin to be productive, and there will be no need for lifting any more roots. It is not necessary to destroy the roots that have been forced, but they must have one year's culture in rich soil to restore their vigour.

Finally, to maintain the health and strength of the plant, be careful not to remove the stalks extravagantly, for if you pull, pull, pull, with immoderate eagerness, the plant will be seriously injured, and will be very likely to die outright. A short anecdote will illustrate this point. An amateur who had a fine plantation of rhubarb gave permission to a friend to take as much as he liked while the owner was away for a summer jaunt. The friend was suddenly fired with an ambition to make some wonderful rhubarb wine, and for several weeks in the height of the season, he pulled every stalk he could get, so that when the growing season was over, the stools were stripped bare. The next spring showed the result of the greedy procedure, for two-thirds of the stools had died, and the remainder quite failed in respect of giving an early supply, but recovered by being left untouched the whole season.

Selection of Varieties.—The sorts best adapted for early supplies in a small garden are Maclean's *Red Currant*, *Johnston's St. Martin's*, and *Royal Albert*; for summer supply, *Victoria* and *Baldry's Defiance*. The noblest of the rhubarbs for ornamental purposes is *Stott's Monarch*, which is so grand in its proportions as to be fit for a place on the lawn. It has the flavour of an apple, but is a very poor imitation of that fruit, and, generally speaking, is too coarse for culinary purposes.

CHAPTER XVIII.

THE CUCUMBER.

"Before thee stands this fair Hesperides,
With golden fruit, but dangerous to be touched;
For death-like dragons here affright thee hard."
Pericles, I., 1.

IT is no part of our duty to make an apology for the cucumber. The human race might perhaps be divided into those who believe in it, and those who do not; and to reconcile the two great factions would be a triumph for the hypothetical peacemaker who, with the coolness of the cucumber, could set about the task, and accomplish it so completely that for ever after the world should be of one mind on the subject, the cucumber thenceforth becoming the favourite of all men. As a "golden fruit" it is in all probability poisonous, but that is of no consequence, for when ripe it is so bitter that no one can eat it. But between the tender sweetness and refreshing coolness of a quite young fruit in a perfectly fresh state, and the ill-looking yellow fruit full of ripening seeds, there are many intermediate stages, and all are more or less representative of danger, for the tender fruit becomes tough before it shows signs of ripening, and instantly on this stage being entered on, the poisonous bitter principle is developed and the "death-like dragons" dwell therein. Well-grown cucumbers cut at a proper age, and eaten fresh, are in all probability as wholesome as anything the garden produces, and beyond question those who have the courage to eat them would consider the deprivation grievous were the cucumber to be authoritatively proscribed. For the present they are free.

THE CUCUMBER *(Cucumis sativus)* represents an important group of plants characterized by rapid growth, love of warmth and moisture, unisexual flowers, and large fleshy fruits that usually attain to perfection in a space of time which is very small as compared with their weight. In common with other fast-growing plants, they abound in watery juices, and it is a commonly employed argument in defence of the cucumber against its many adversaries, that as it contains about 90 per cent. of water, the remaining 10 per cent. of substance cannot be pernicious—a *reductio ad absurdum.* The constitution of the plant does in part suggest the routine of cultivation it requires. Its rapid extension, and early and abundant fruitfulness, suggest that it requires generous treatment, and is equally unfitted to cope with starvation or with the arresting action of an occasionally too low a temperature. Any serious check will ruin the plant right off; and as regards food, it must have abundance near at hand, and in a state to be quickly assimilated, for it cannot, like a pine tree fast anchored in the rocks, employ its roots for centuries in searching in every direction for infinitesimal supplies of nutriment. What is true of the cucumber in these respects is true also of its kindred, the melons, gourds, and marrows, the principal difference in the requirements of these being in temperature.

RAISING CUCUMBER PLANTS FROM SEEDS AND CUTTINGS is an extremely simple business, and for all general purposes seedling plants are the best. When to sow is of more importance than how to sow, for by whatever system cucumbers are to be grown, it is a great advantage to begin with strong plants raised from seed for the purpose. When the month of May has come, and the amateur has cleared out the frames in which bedding plants have been wintered, and proposes to employ the frames for summer cucumbers, it is a serious matter to have to begin *de novo* by sowing seed. It would be better to buy plants than to wait for seeds sown so late; but it would be still better to have ready to hand a nice lot of plants raised at home from seed sown in February or March. The usual mode of procedure is to sow half-a-dozen seeds in a five-inch pot, and to place the pots on a warm dung-bed or in a propagating-house. It is better, however, to sow in large shallow pans, as the young plants can be more easily lifted out and potted separately without injury to their tender roots; but the best way of all is to sow the seeds singly in three-inch pots. Any rich light soil, with a rather large admixture of sand, will serve the purpose, and the seeds should be inserted sharp end downwards about an inch deep. A heat of 70° to 80° will bring the young plants to light in the course of a week or so, and they must have a warm moist atmosphere, and be kept as near the glass as convenient to promote a steady growth. In the case of several plants in a pot, they must be shaken out and potted separately in five-inch pots as soon as they begin to crowd one another; but when raised singly in pots they may be allowed to attain some size before shifting, but it will be advisable to shift them into six-inch or eight-inch pots before they acquire that yellowish colour which indicates that they are entering upon a stage of starvation. If there is no hotbed at work for raising plants, a supply may be reared by another method. About the middle of March sow singly in three-inch pots, and put these pots on a shelf at the end of a greenhouse where they will have the full power of the sun upon them daily. Keep the soil in the pots fairly moist, and take the best care possible that the cool breeze from the ventilators does not blow over them. In about a fortnight the plants will appear, and may remain on the same shelf until they have made some progress, and perhaps until the time arrives for planting them out. These will not want a shift, as they will not grow so fast as on a dung-bed; but they will be thoroughly useful, even if planted out somewhat small, and it will be an advantage to them to keep them in the pots until the season is well advanced and they may be put out with perfect safety.

In the height of summer plants may be raised from layers and cuttings with the greatest ease. A young shoot pegged down on the surface of a pot filled with light rich soil, with a few crumbs of soil put over it, will make roots in the course of a week, and may be separated in about fourteen days from the time of layering. It is of course advisable to defer the separation until the pot is pretty well filled with roots, and then the plant should be left undisturbed for a week to obtain firm hold of its independent existence. Cuttings should be taken from the extreme points of healthy growing shoots, and may be three or four inches long. They must be put into small pots singly, and be kept moist and warm, and close and shaded. In a propagating-house they make roots instantly; but makeshift methods do not answer well except in the height of summer, when cuttings may be inserted in the bed the plants are in, and if covered with a bell-glass will do very well.

THE PROPER SOIL FOR CUCUMBERS is suggested by their rapid growth. It must be mellow and nutritive. The staple should be turfy loam full of fibre, such as the top spit of an old pasture; but an unkind soil may be greatly improved by the admixture with it of rotten stable dung and leaf mould. A harsh gravelly soil or an untempered clay are equally unfit, but the top crumbs of clay that the winter has pulverised may be employed in a proportion of about one-fourth with the aid of rotted turves and other mellowing materials. The drainage must always be perfect, for stagnant moisture will soon destroy cucumber plants; and on the other hand, if the body of soil becomes dust dry below, the plants will soon become infested with vermin, and it is then a question whether it will be more economical to burn or to cleanse them.

CUCUMBERS IN FRAMES give the least trouble and make the best return. A good hotbed should be made up in February or March, and when quite sweet, the heat being about 80°, a small hillock of soil should be put under the centre of each light, and two or three seeds sown in each hillock. The soil should consist as nearly as possible of two parts turfy loam, and one part each of leaf mould and nearly rotten stable dung mixed together. When the plants are well up, give air with caution to keep them sturdy, but be careful no withering blast sweeps through; and do not shade at any time, unless there should occur strong sunshine, with a keen east wind. In this case it will be dangerous to ventilate, and therefore a little shade must be given for an hour or two at mid-day, by laying a newspaper over the plants or a mat on the glass. When the plants have made their first rough leaf remove all but the strongest, for one to a light is enough in any case. A few of the surplus plants may be nursed on in the frame for use elsewhere, to plant on beds a month or so later. It is usual to pinch out the centre of the plant as soon as it has two or three rough leaves, to cause it to branch and spread; but really the "stopping," as it is termed, is a matter of comparatively small consequence, and if neglected, will make but little difference in the end. However, it is orthodox to pinch out the point at an early date, and thus promote a spreading growth to cover the bed. Keep the heat at about 70° as nearly as possible; give air as often as possible, by slightly tilting the light on the leeward side; and always keep in the frame a can of water, that it may be warmed for use, and give the plants a sprinkle from the syringe daily from this can, as soon as they begin to grow freely. The general management will consist in occasionally adding more fresh soil to the hillocks as the plants require it; in occasionally ascertaining the state of the roots as to moisture, for they should be always fairly moist; and as soon as fruit appears, the shoot bearing it should have the point pinched out. The growth should be regulated so as to cover the bed equally without crowding anywhere; and if a paying crop is wanted, every fruit should be cut as soon as it is large enough to eat, for if one or two be left to attain a great size, there will be a comparative cessation of production. Large cucumbers are very well in their way, but small ones are more useful in every way; and the amateur may be properly advised to study, first, how to obtain a sufficiency of fruit nine to twelve inches long, before laying himself out for the production of exhibition specimens.

This simple mode of cultivation may be varied in a multitude of ways. We will suppose the making of a hotbed to be too great a task. In this case it will be a waste of labour to do anything until about the middle of May, and then perhaps the pits and frames in which bedding plants have been kept may be turned to account for cucumbers. From mid-May to mid-September, cucumbers do not need bottom-heat, therefore but little preparation is needed for growing a few in a rough and ready way. If the frames are on a hard surface, two or three large seed pans should be placed under each light to form a foundation for the bed. Place the pans bottom upwards, strew over them a layer of broken bricks and tiles, and then put on a barrowful of suitable soil as the beginning of each hillock. This mode of procedure will prevent injury from accumulation of water, for cucumbers are often killed by beginners, who permit them to become water-logged. Shut up close, and in two or three days these hillocks will be nicely warmed. Then put a strong plant on each, planting it with great care, that the roots are not injured: shut up close, and shade when the sun shines. In about a week new growth will begin, and thenceforward a little regulating and stopping must be done, and the treatment generally must be the same as already advised. It is not good economy to sow seed so late in the season, but it may be done for a late supply of fruit, and it is certain that no cucumber plant, *ceteris paribus,* thrives so thoroughly as the one that was grown from the first in a good body of earth, and has never been disturbed at the root.

One of the important points in management is to store up sun heat as much as possible, without injuring the plants. Give air as soon as the day is sufficiently advanced, and shut up early, so as to shut in warmth enough to keep things right until the morning. It never hurts cucumber plants to have a temperature of 90° with sunshine and air, but 70° is a good average, and 60° is not unsafe. It is good practice to avoid shading as much as possible, but weak plants must be shaded for some time after they are first put out, and there will occur in the summer roasting times when the most robust of established plants will need to be partially screened from the sun's rays. Syringe regularly, water regularly; but modify watering and ventilation to suit the changes of the weather. During a dull cold time in July give no water for a few days, and give very little air; remembering always that the cucumber is a delicate plant, and a certain degree of warmth is one of its first requisites.

As the plants acquire age, it is proper to consider whether they shall be removed and replaced by young plants, or whether an attempt shall be made to rejuvenate them. Generally speaking, the season will be too far gone for young plants to have a fair chance, but something may be done with the old ones. Cover the hillocks with about four or even six inches of fat dung, into which the roots will rise very quickly. At the same time cut out one or two of the oldest shoots, and about a week afterwards cut out one or two more. By this treatment a lot of new growth will be secured, and this in time will bear good fruit. It is of the utmost importance to remove only one or two of the old shoots at a time, for if the plants are much cut about, they will die, and there is an end of the matter.

SUMMER CUCUMBERS IN HOUSES are both ornamental and useful, as will be seen by reference to page 237 of the "*Amateur's Greenhouse and Conservatory,*" where will be found a figure and description of the manner in which we grow cucumbers in a span-roofed geranium-house during the summer. The house now used for this purpose is a span-roofed Paxtonian, put up by Messrs. Heremann and Morton. It is fitted on each side of the walks with the usual uprights, and a moveable flat stage under, in lengths, and consisting of open bars only. A few inches below this stage are large slates resting on stout cross pieces, and forming a continuous pavement five feet in width, raised about three feet from the floor, and running the whole length of the house on both sides. Close under the slates are the hot-water pipes, and therefore in the event of bad water the cucumbers can have the advantage of artificial heat.

The management is of the simplest kind. About the middle of May the house is cleared out. A hillock is then formed under the centre of each light, by first making a foundation of inverted flower-pots or seed-pans, with a good body of broken bricks and tiles laid over, and then a heap of good soil. The house is shut up, and, if needful, the fire is lighted; generally speaking, however, the fire is not used at all, for when the chilly October days return the cucumbers have to be cleared out to make room for the geraniums. It may be observed, however, that to have means of supplying heat is a great advantage, for a shilling's worth of coke may save the whole affair from ruin when wintry weather breaks into the heart of the summer, and the columns of the daily papers are suddenly choked with reports of potato disease.

Strong plants are put out on the hillocks, and they are never stopped until they reach the roof. Then the points are pinched out. The side growths are carefully trained on temporary cords and wires, and as the growth thickens regular stopping and cutting out become necessary, but we stop little and cut less. Usually we begin to cut fruit in the first week of July, and go on to the end of September. The appearance of the house when the vines have got up is beautiful, and the amount of fruit produced is such, that to print the record of one good season would be to incur the suspicion of having searched for facts in the realms of fancy. One small point in the management we have found of great importance. It is to keep a clean stick inserted here and there in the hillocks. By drawing one out, we see in a moment what is the state of the soil as regards moisture. We call these "trial sticks," for the sake of a name, and have never done so well as since we made it a rule that they should be always in use. The hillocks are of course always growing. We put on crumbs of clay with a little rotten dung at first, but as the plants come into full bearing, we put on fat half-rotten dung, and the hillocks disappear, and the body of soil becomes a continuous bed. Into this bed we dibble cuttings of all kinds, double walls, shrubby veronicas, named sweet williams, anything and everything; and thus the cucumber-house pays its rent again and again, the shade of the vines and the frequent sprinkling being favourable to the rapid rooting of cuttings of almost any kind.

A HOUSE FOR WINTER CUCUMBERS should be narrow with a steep roof, ample heating apparatus, and a brick pit in place of a stage for plants. In a spacious house, and especially in a house with roof of low pitch, it is much more difficult to keep cucumbers in health during winter, than in such houses as are here figured. In a mild winter any house made comfortable in respect of warmth will answer, but when the keen east wind blows icy daggers against the glass, and discovers every crevice in the woodwork, the arrangements must be thoroughly good, or there will be an end of the cucumbers. One of the most serviceable cucumber houses we have had for winter work is represented in the subjoined figure.

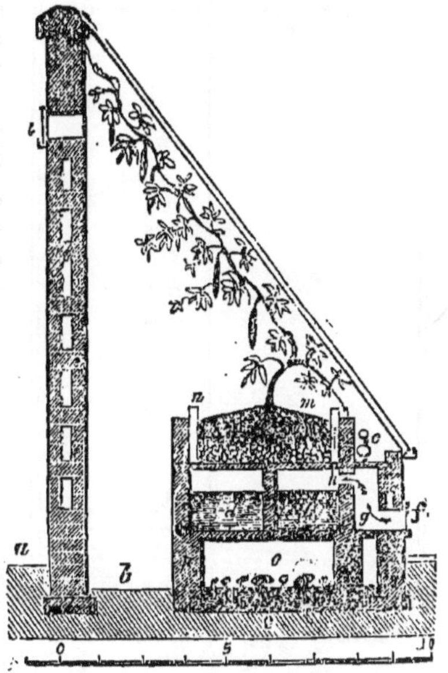

This useful house is built against the end of a shed, and is twelve feet wide and twenty-three feet long. At *a* is the ground level, below which the pathway, *b*, is excavated a foot and a half, and at *c* the excavation is a half-foot deeper, to form a bed under the tank. The tank, *d d*, is fifteen feet long, and is supplied by flow and return pipes, *e*, by a branch from the flow, to supply atmospheric heat. To keep up a circulation of air, as well as of heat, there is an aperture in the front wall, *f*, which can be opened, or closed, at pleasure. When opened, air is admitted under the pipes, *e*, into a chamber, *g*, from whence it passes through an opening, *h*, into the tank, and thus gets moistened, as well as warmed, before it enters the house, through the tubes, *n*, which are placed at intervals along the casing of the tank, and all of which can be closed, when necessary. After circulating round the house, the air escapes through the back wall, at *i*, and at this opening, as well as at *f*, the ventilation is regulated by a sliding shutter outside, the one in the back wall being also worked from within, by means of a cord over a pulley.

The tank is of slate, encased in brickwork, with a partition down the middle, to regulate the circulation of the water. When used for cucumbers and melons, a bed is made, *m*, a good depth of loose rubble being first laid down, for drainage, and the soil is added as required by the plants. Under the tank is an open space for a bed, *o*, and the heat, communicated to this, from the bottom of the tank, and the brick piers, *p*, suffices admirably for forcing mushrooms, rhubarb, asparagus, etc., but as the latter does best in light, sufficiently to colour the shoots, we have not often grown it there—for mushrooms it is admirable. From the front of the tank to the back wall, about a foot from the glass, is a wire trellis, to which the plants are trained. When the trellises are not all in use, we turn to use the back wall for greenhouse plants, on moveable shelves, and the return pipe, shown

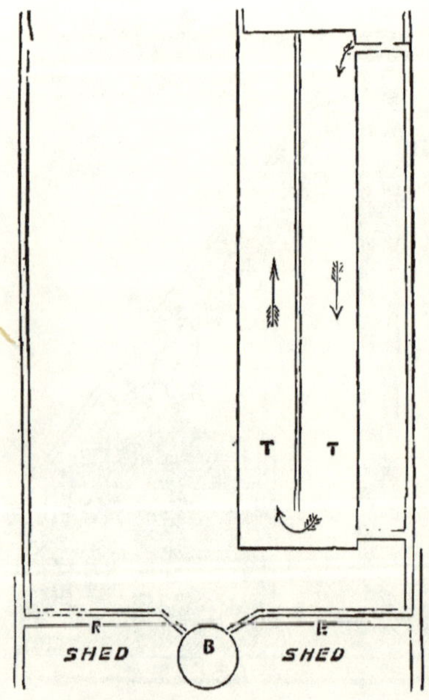

in the section, runs along the lower part of the wall, and gives sufficient heat to force geraniums, camellias, rhododendrons, cytisuses, etc., and beyond the tank we have eight feet of space, which we call the "cool end," and which is heated only by the return pipe, which leaves the tank and passes round a stage, before it takes a direct return along the back wall, to the boiler. This cool end is also used for greenhouse plants.

Referring to the outline sketches, it will be seen that the heating apparatus is in the shed where the furnace was originally placed for the flue. The conical boiler, *b*, is in the centre, the flow pipe leaves it near the top, and the return pipe enters near the bottom. The flow has two connections with the tank, one at the end nearest the boiler, and one at the end most remote; ether of these can be closed, by means of a stop-cock, and ii the fire has been allowed to get low, or if severe weather fenders it necessary to obtain a little extra heat quickly, we generally close one of the taps for a short time, until a brisk circulation is established. There is an extra length of pipe attached to the flow side, to carry heat beyond the tank into the cool end; but this we seldom use, the return pipe being almost always sufficient. The movement of the water from the pipe into the tank, T, is indicated by arrows, and the pipes are distinguished by the letters —F the flow, and R the return. By a little variation of these particulars, such a house as this might be used as an early vinery and peach house; the back wall and the trellis would afford good spaces for training, and instead of planting in the bed over the tank, it would be necessary to make a border at the back, and use the tank-bed either for plunging stove plants in pots, or planting them out in it. But as one particular form of house will not suit all tastes and circumstances, we present sections of four different but nearly related structures, well adapted for cucumbers, as also for forcing strawberries and kidney beans.

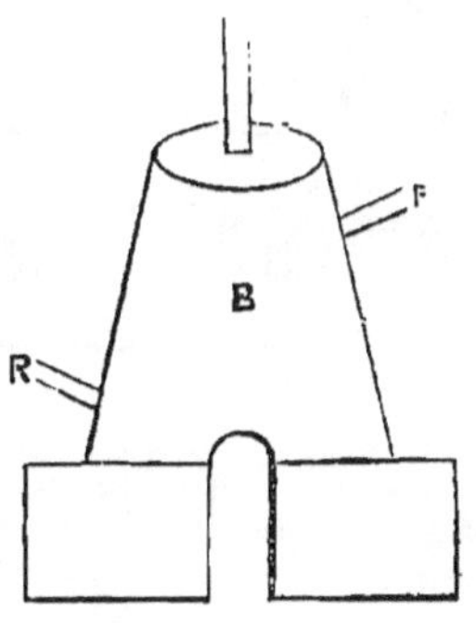

The lean-to houses are not the most desirable form for late autumn and mid-winter work, as they scarcely give sufficient light at that season, unless a portion of the back wall below the ventilators is of glass—say a 4 feet depth of glass running the whole length. Span-roofed houses are the most desirable on account of the greater body of light, and they are preferred by most practical men, because light exercises a great influence upon the flavour of the produce. When grown without the required degree of light, the fruit is bitter—so much so sometimes, in flat-roofed houses during dull weather, as to be positively uneatable.

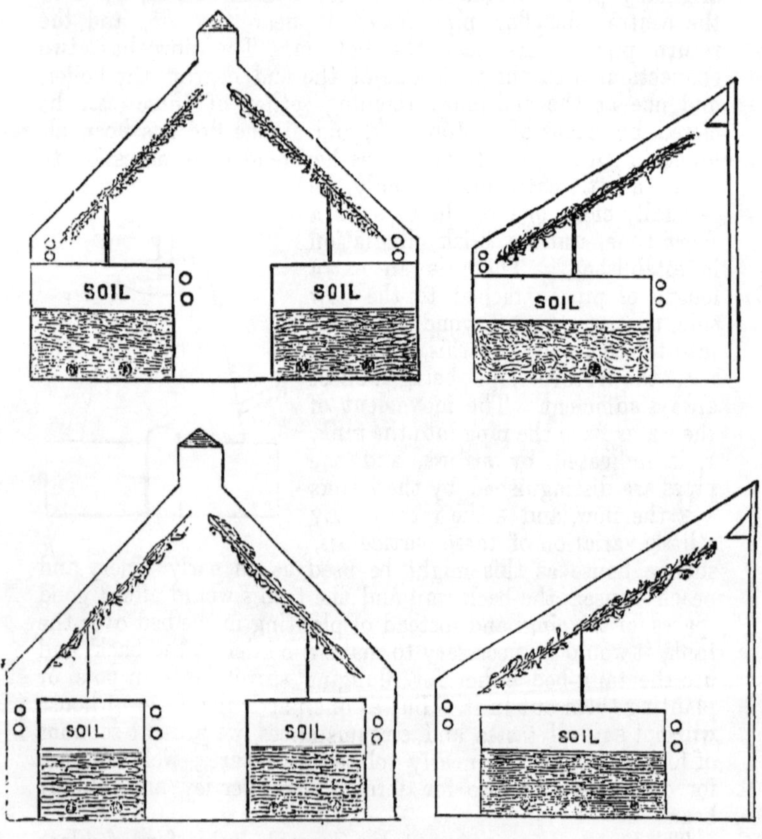

As will be seen in the sections here given, rubble is represented to be the means of conducting the heat from the hot-water pipes below to the soil above in which the plants are to be placed ; but we do not recommend rubble in perference to a hot-water tank. Although both cucumbers and melons may be grown to a high state of perfection upon rubble, it is not equal to a tank, the heat from which causes a moist atmosphere. The heat from a tank is also more sure and lasting. In any case where it is desirable to have a tank, it can be substituted in either of these sections in the place of rubble. The best form of tank for the purpose is constructed of slate, and partially filled with water, through which passes a flow and return hot-water pipe as explained above. In every case as much as 18 inches of soil must be provided; two feet is not too much as spring advances. The best materials for rubble are flints or brick-bats, two feet in depth, with a covering of coarse washed gravel, or some newly cut turves laid grass downwards. After the rubble is in its place, and as the soil is added to it, place some drain pipes three feet apart along the middle of the bed; let one end of them go down to the rubble, and the other end just above the surface of the soil. These are to be the conductors of water into the rubble below when a strong heat is necessary. To every twelve feet length of bed about four gallons of water must be used every other day; this must be poured down the drain tiles, to moisten the rubble, etc., below.

As regards the amount of piping, the small circles show no more than is actually necessary. If, in fact, no more is added than in the positions shown, there will be no extra amount of heating surface to fall back upon in case of severe weather in mid-winter. It would be well therefore to add, besides those shown, two more pipes in each case for top heat, to be used when wanted, and full control should be secured over the whole of them by valves to shut off and turn on at pleasure. This is assuming that 4-inch pipes will be used. If a size less is used—say 3-inch, then there ought to be more of them, that the heat may be mild and continuous. If only the same quantity of 3-inch pipes are used as shown in the diagrams, then it would be necessary in severe weather to make them so hot, to keep up the required degree of temperature, that the heat given off would be positively injurious even with the precaution of using evaporating pans upon the pipes.

A Pit for Winter Cucumbers will serve as well as a house where only a small supply of fruit is required. It should if possible be sunk below the level to economise heat, and a tank is very much to be desired; but a good make-shift structure may be adopted for the use of fermenting material, and where stable manure is always at hand, will be found economical as well as effective. The subjoined figure represents a serviceable pit for forcing cucumbers and kidney beans. The aspect is due south; the walls are 4-inch brickwork without pigeon holes; the width is five feet, and a length of twelve feet may be considered sufficient to begin with. It is surrounded with a trench two feet wide, enclosed by a 9-inch wall. The interior must have a deep bed of rubble, and on that a bed of two feet depth of soil, the surface of the soil being two-and-a-half feet from the glass. The heat is obtained by filling the trench with manure fresh from the stable, and occasionally turning it to renew the fermentation, and of course removing and replacing with fresh as it rots down and loses power. Very much will depend on management, but if the start be right a little pit of this kind will produce an immense quantity of fruit, and will be especially valuable in the early months of the year.

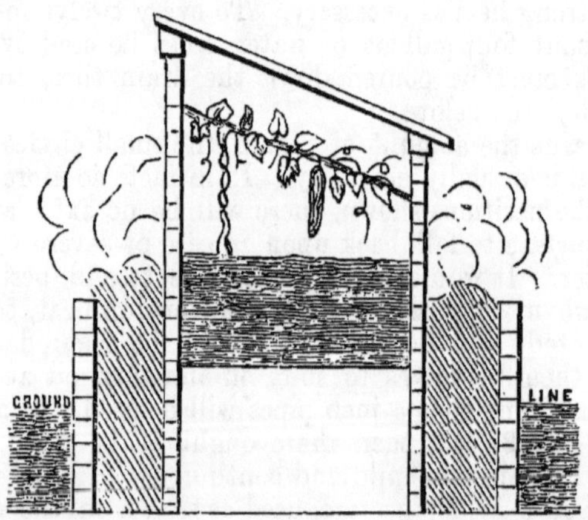

Winter Culture of the Cucumber. The secrets of producing cucumbers during the dull months of winter, in a condition fit for use, are few in number, and by no means difficult to understand. In the first place, it is no use to attempt to grow them, excepting in a properly constructed and sufficiently heated house. Hipped or span-roofed houses are the best, for cucumbers grown in winter in small lean-to houses are often bitter through an insufficiency of light. Secondly, sufficient heating power must be at command, to prevent the plants suffering from a low temperature in severe weather. Whether grown upon a hot-water tank or upon rubble, the heating medium must be sufficient to maintain a bottom-heat of 80°, for plants in a fruiting state will not continue so long with a less warmth at their roots. Thirdly, to have them through November, December, and the first two months of the new year, the plants ought to be raised either from seed or cuttings in the month of August previous, and planted out in the beds not later than the first week in September. Fourthly, the main object should be to encourage a vigorous growth during the earlier stages, and in doing this give plenty of air both night and day, to enable the new growth to be both stout and firm. Towards the end of September air must be admitted more cautiously, as the nights are sometimes cold and damp, and the fires must be started about the same time, to keep the temperature to its proper height, and also to expel any excess of moisture. Also bear in mind that a close stagnant atmosphere at this season of the year is a frequent cause of mildew, which must be warded off by timely attention, or the plants will soon be destroyed. Fifthly, you must not stop the young growth severely after it has reached the trellis. One or two pinchings of the strongest leaders, about the middle of October will suffice. After that time they will not make more growth than is needful for the production of fresh fruit.

As regards the temperature of the house up to that time, much will depend upon the state of the weather. If a nice growing temperature of 70° can be obtained during the day, and by early closing 60° during the night, the plants will be better without the aid of fire-heat. A high temperature in the house up to this time only creates a weak spindly growth, which, when winter comes with its long nights and dull days, is next to useless for the production of fruit. Care, too, must be taken not to over-crop through the first part of the season, if a continuous supply of fruit is required. The cultivator must aim at securing vigorous plants by the end of November without the use of artificial heat, and then they will be in good condition to go through the winter satisfactorily. Every leaf made after the middle of November must be preserved with the greatest care, for after that time no more are produced than are really required. The leaves must be kept clean and healthy by gentle syringings on the mornings of mild days, when air can be admitted to dry up the superfluous moisture quickly. A gentle fumigation of tobacco must be given directly there is the least trace of green-fly or thrips.

A temperature of 70° to 75° by day, and 60° by night, is a safe temperature for so dull a season of the year. In the spring, plants that have been in bearing for two or three months very often show signs of weakness; therefore, they must not be excited too soon. The middle or end of February will be plenty early enough, and then, as the days lengthen, a day temperature of 80° by fire-heat may be maintained. Previous to increasing the day temperature, give the surface of the bed a top-dressing three inches in thickness of very short rotten dung, the fattest that can be obtained, or, what is better still, equal parts dung and good lumpy fibrous loam: this should be warmed before being put on the bed. The surface roots will soon find their way into this, and in a short time throw new life and vigour into the plants. In March, syringing, both night and early morning, may be practised with benefit, and a humid atmosphere must also be maintained by the use of evaporating troughs, and by frequently damping the paths of the house. Cucumber plants absorb an immense quantity of moisture by their leaves. In a few weeks from this they will bear vigorously, and to keep them going, the roots must receive constant assistance by a good soaking with clear weak manure water once a week.

Open-Air Culture. The cultivation of cucumbers on ridges out of doors is a very simple matter, and if a warm sheltered situation is selected, the crops will in favourable seasons be most excellent. The beds may be from two to four feet wide, and in their formation, first mark the space they are to occupy and then take out the soil to a depth of twelve or fifteen inches, and lay the soil on each side neatly. The trench is then filled to one foot above the level of the sides with stable manure, in a condition somewhat subdued as to heat; litter, leaves, grass mowings, or other fibrous refuse may be added to the manure to increase the mass and assist in prolonging the bottom heat. The manure should be covered with about twelve inches of light and moderately rich loam, and the time for the application of the covering must be determined by the condition of the fermenting materials. If rank and hot, a few days must be allowed to elapse; but if the heat is mild, the soil may be put on at once, and in a few days afterwards the plants may be bedded out, and be protected with hand-lights, so long as protection is considered necessary. Glass may be dispensed with altogether in the production of cucumbers on ridges, but hand-lights afford such valuable assistance that they should be invariably brought into requisition if available.

By affording protection during the first two or three weeks, the cucumber plants can be put out early in May, instead of at the end of that month; and a gain of two or three weeks is effected. They should be strong and well established when bedded out, and be put in a line down the centre of the ridge at a distance of about thirty inches apart. The points will require nipping out as soon as the plants begin to grow freely, to encourage the production of side shoots, but no further stopping will be necessary. During periods of dry weather, maintain a sufficient degree of moisture in the soil, by regularly watering them over head through a coarse rose, and in the evening.

The Enemies of the Cucumber are many and various, but there is one way to keep them all at bay, and that is to keep the plants always growing freely without being subjected to any extreme whatever. Too much or too little of heat, air, or moisture will bring about a bad state of things in some way or other. The plant is often injured by excess of heat, and if this happens to be accompanied with deficiency of moisture, the entire substance of leaf and stem seems to be instantly transformed into green fly; the beginning of which at the back of the leaf is usually denoted by a change from a healthy green to a suspicious yellow. For all the insect plagues, fumigation with tobacco is the safest and surest remedy; for mildew, dustings of dry sulphur, and for any condition to which the term "disease" may be applied, the remedy must be found in restoring the vigour of the plants. To anyone in trouble about unhealthy cucumbers, we may recommend a careful perusal of the whole of this chapter; some points of which will probably suggest in what the disease originated, and how it may be cured. All the plagues known to the plant are, with few and rare exceptions, completely at the command of the cultivator to prevent them, but as to effecting a cure, that is sometimes impossible, and it is sometimes the cheaper process to destroy the plants than attempt to restore them to health.

It resembles many other plants in this respect, that it grows "like a weed" when all the circumstances that govern it are favourable. But it differs from many useful things that thrive under any circumstances, that it really is particular as to what it shall eat, drink, and avoid. The plant is extremely sensitive to extremes of any kind, and that is the main reason of the frequency of failures in its cultivation. Those happy cultivators who profess to know nothing of failure, and can always show us houses or pits, or both, gaily garlanded with cucumbers, have had their share of failures, and have become wise through the teaching of adversity. Observe, if you have the opportunity, how particular they are in ensuring perfect drainage; a rich and very mellow soil; a sufficient and constant h at, both of soil below and air above, and, not the least important of all, a proper degree of humidity. The cucumber loves heat, but may quickly become roasted or frozen out of existence; it loves a substantial soil, but sheer clay will kill it; for moisture it has a continual hankering, but is easily washed out of existence when supplied with more water than it can appropriate. Generally speaking, failures are the result of some extreme condition—too much or too little moisture; a temperature too high or too low; or, what is perhaps more often the case, a succession of extremes of the most opposite character, as for example, being suddenly deluged with water after having been allowed to become dry, or being subjected to a great heat after having for some time been too cold for existence.

One of the very first requisites to success is to make up the bed on a sufficient body of drainage materials. If the bed becomes sour and pasty through any excess of moisture, the plants will collapse and present all the appearance of having been killed by drought. Another requisite is to secure a suitable compost containing a large proportion of well-rotted turf from a loamy pasture, with thoroughly-rotted stable dung and leaf-mould quite free from mildew. To keep the heat at 70° to 85° is easy enough in the books, but much less easy in practice; so that probably nine-tenths of the failures arise from unfavourable temperatures. As regards humidity, cucumbers are as a rule fairly treated; they rarely suffer through insufficiency either overhead or under foot; but of course they occasionally get too much, and it often happens that the cultivator fails to perceive the relation of heat and humidity in plant-culture: the golden rule, that degrees of heat and humidity should correspond nearly, being sometimes ignored in the daily practice.

Two cases of failure have been lately brought under our notice, and both tell the same tale. An amateur who had acquired considerable experience in cucumber-growing, so that it became the custom for his friends and neighbours to visit his cucumber house as an entertainment, on one occasion got up such a scene as drove the parish crazy with delight. A pretty span-roof house was seen clothed from the ground to the ridge-line on both sides of the roof with gigantic-leaved vines, from which were suspended hundreds of cucumbers, the straightness and freshness of which were simply marvellous. This happy amateur invited a vast concourse of people to visit him on the day of the local show, and it was rumoured abroad that those who went would see some cucumbers. For a few days previous to the looked-for event the house was kept rather close because the weather was dull; but there were some bursts of sunshine which sent the thermometer up to 150 deg., and although master and man both knew how the temperature went, they agreed that as regards the cucumbers "they could stand it." The day of jubilation came, and the gardener sent for his employer very early in the morning, "just to look at the cucumbers." The great leaves hung like rags, the plants appeared as if cut through over the roots, and hurrying to that bourne from whence no cucumber returns. The master divined the meaning of the wreck, and simply said, "Thermometer 150 yesterday. Ah, we've overdone it." But he was equal to the occasion. He put mats on the outside to subdue the light, and smeared the roof inside with green colour to still further darken the interior, and also to create an optical confusion. They then plied the syringe until the leaves were drenched, and the very house was like a dripping well. The last trick was to lock the door, put the key into the gardener's pocket, and start him off to London, with instructions to keep away for twenty-four hours at least. In due time the guests arrived, and it was most unfortunate that the gardener had gone to town and taken the key with him. But they could see through the glass, and, as they were quite full of fun and half-full of champagne, they were soon satisfied, and carried our friend's fame with great noise round the world. The next day the house was cleared and the parish was pelted with cucumbers, and there the story ends. The other case is like it, but a gardener, having all his own way, was the acting hero. During the cold rainy days of June he kept his cucumber house quite close, being afraid of a chill. Very soon his grand vines that had been bearing abundantly, and were still young enough to continue fruitful, began to droop. We have just returned from an inspection; we found the plant all through the house loaded with all the vermin the cucumber is heir to. Having, by means of elaborate cross-questioning and putting down verbal traps in several places, elicited the confession that now and then—but, oh dear, not often—the glass had gone up to a hundred or so, and it might be a little beyond, and perhaps once or twice to 150°, and—there the confusion becomes too hazy, and we conjecture on our own account that the figure might have reached 200°; the end of it being that the plants were consigned to the rubbish heap.

Selection of Varieties.—New varieties of cucumbers appear periodically like meteors in the heavens, and a large proportion pass away almost as quickly and are not remembered. But occasionally a distinct and meritorious novelty appears, takes a permanent place in the lists, and acquires historical importance. The most useful are those of the *Sion House* type; the fruits of which are of smallish growth, a fine dark green colour, very slightly ribbed, glossy, and without spines. For winter work these are the best of all, and for a paying crop in summer, it is no easy matter to supersede them. The one known as *Rollison's Telegraph* represents this race admirably, and is universally esteemed. But the Sion House type have no special beauty, and when large handsome fruits are required, *Blue Gown* and *Daniel's Duke of Edinburgh*, may with great advantage be selected. Generally speaking, the black spined are the handsomest, being of a rich deep green colour, with a delicious bloom; but white-spined cucumbers have their merits, and one of the finest of this section is *Kirklees Hall Defiance.* It is of importance to avoid all those varieties that tend to coarseness, they are altogether undesirable for the supply of the table; they are not less disappointing when sent to an exhibition, for competent judges pay little heed to mere size in cucumbers, and will pass over many braces of monsters to favour smallish fruit well matched and finely finished. The larger the better within certain limits, but refinement of character is of the highest importance, and it is sheer folly to allow large fruits to hang so long that they become tough and uneatable, and tend to discredit the cultivator who ventures to present them in a competition. The following, in addition to the three varieties named, are suitable for exhibition :—*Henderson's Perfection, Champion of the World, Hamilton's Invincible, Lindlegana, Horticultural Prize*, and *Luton Hoo.* For general purposes, and more especially for family and market supply the following will be found useful :—*Berkshire Champion, Cuthill's Black Spine, Exeter Market, Carter's Model*, and *Tender and True.* The beginner in cucumber culture is advised to begin with Telegraph and Blue Gown, and when accustomed to the business, it may be found an agreeable pastime to grow a dozen to a score of sorts in large boxes in a roomy house for comparison of their merits, and for advance in practice.

CHAPTER XIX.

THE MELON.

"Ye gods that made me man, and sway in love,
That have inflam'd desire in my breast
To taste the fruit of yon celestial tree,
Or die in the adventure, be my helps,
As I am son and servant to your will,
To compass such a boundless appetite."

Pericles, I., 1.

THE MELON *(Cucumis melo)* is as closely related to the cucumber in its horticultural requirements as in its morphological characteristics. The cultivation of the cucumber, therefore, is a good preparative to the cultivation of the melon, which requires more heat, more light, and less moisture to bring it to perfection.

The melon is the noblest production of the kitchen garden, and well worthy of the high fame it has always enjoyed. The position it holds at exhibitions and in seedsmen's catalogues indicates its importance and value, for it rarely happens that there is a tame competition in the classes for melons, while the annual supply of new varieties to supersede all the old ones is great enough to show that honour and profit are regarded as the sure rewards of those who may succeed in effecting and establishing improvements. The melon agrees with most other garden plants in this, that its real improvement is a slow process, quite misrepresented by the so-called new varieties that are always current, and that appear to exist only to prove that between names and things there is often a great gulf fixed. Amongst these, however, occur from time to time distinct and useful kinds that mark a real advance in quality; and one of the most satisfactory improvements effected of late years is seen in the scarlet-fleshed class, the best of which are scarcely inferior in flavour to the best of the green-fleshed, which, until recently, enjoyed pre-eminence.

MELONS.—LITTLE HEATH AND QUEEN ANNE'S POCKET.

FRAME CULTURE.—The best melons are produced by rough and ready methods, and yet the fruit is not in any way adapted for the poor man's garden, for there must be a plentiful and constant supply of fresh manure to carry on the cultivation, and the produce is an article of luxury adapted only to the tables of the affluent. In great gardens melons are grown in houses heated with hot-water pipes, but they may be grown quite as well in frames, and in truth there is no system that suits the plant so well as the old-fashioned hot-bed, for its vapours and gases are more promotive of its health than the purer air of the nicely built melon-house, heated with hot water, and kept as dry and as clean as a drawing-room.

THE FIRST STAGE in the cultivation comprises the sowing of the seed and the nurture of the plants until they are strong enough to be planted out. The first requisite is a good hot-bed, and it need not be a large one, as another will be required for fruiting the plants. We raise a lot of melon plants with cucumbers, tomatoes, capsicums, globe amaranths, and celosias, in a frame only three feet in length by two and a-half wide, and find one good horse load of stable-manure twice turned suffice for the purpose.

A thin surfacing of rich mellow soil is spread over the manure to form the seed-bed, and the seeds are sown in rows across the bed when the heat is steady at 75° to 85°. In great gardens this sort of work is begun in January, and is carried on in substantial brick pits with the aid of an abundant supply of fermenting material. But in a small garden, where the appliances are of a less costly nature, the first week in March is early enough, for the bed is then considerably aided by sun-heat, and very much trouble is saved in the nursing of the young plants. The seed may be sown in pots and pans, but the bed is far preferable as producing stronger plants and occasioning far less trouble. Sow the melon seeds in rows six inches asunder, and the seeds three inches apart in the rows. When they are fairly up, and show the leader fairly rising, pinch out the points to compel the formation of two or three side-shoots in place of one leader. With careful watering and ventilating, if the heat continues steady, they will advance nicely, and soon become thrifty plants, ready for transference to the bed in which they are to fruit. The plants should be in the fruiting-bed within four weeks at least from the date of the sowing of the seed. We have in favourable seasons planted out within three weeks, but it is not well to move them until they are somewhat stocky.

It must here be observed that melons are usually grown in pots until ready for the fruiting-bed, and there can be no objection to the practice where there are skilful hands to carry it out. But the risks are many in pot-culture, as compared with the plan we recommend, and the bed system occasions less trouble. It is not at all uncommon to find young melon-plants in pots quite beset with red spider, owing to a little irregularity or neglect in air-giving and watering, whereas, when grown in a bed from the first, it is altogether unusual for fly or spider to touch them, for they are robust in growth, rooting freely, and if the bed should get a little dry, they do not soon feel it. Another remark must be made as to pinching out the point of the leader. When raised in pots, it is well not to stop them at all until they have been planted out at least a week, and then if they are stopped they make a nice growth from the lower eyes, and soon spread over the hillocks. But when raised in a bed they are so strong from the first that the stopping may be done earlier, and the result will be a gain of time in the formation of fruiting wood.

THE FRUITING-BED should be got ready in time, and should be formed with a good body of manure, that has been two or three times turned, with good capacious frames to cover it. When melon growing begins in January, the fruiting-bed will require to be lined as the heat declines, to maintain a proper temperature; but if we begin in March, sun-heat will finish the crop, if it is well started with a big sound bed of stable manure, that has been in some degree fermented, so as to produce a sweet and steady heat. In a sunless season, however, the heat must be kept up by linings, for the melon requires a bottom heat ranging from 70° to 90°, and an atmospheric temperature of 65° to 80°, with a rise of 10° during sunshine.

The usual way of ridging-out is to form a hollow in the bed in the centre of each light, and fill these to the surface with brickbats, or hollow tiles; then cover with a turf, grass sides downwards, and make a smallish hill of soil for the plants. The next thing is to put out two plants to every light, give a little water, and keep rather close and shaded until the plants make a start, and show by their free growth that they are well established. They are earthed-up as they advance, and thus the hills advance with the plants. It is no wonder that when the plants are raised in pots and treated subsequently as now described, they are frequently assailed with fly and spider, and give the cultivator incessant trouble to keep them clean and healthy. Our method is to make up good-sized hills in the first instance, using two barrows of soil, at least, to each, and shut up the frames for a few days; by this time the hills will be nicely warmed. Then we consider if the heat is too strong, and if it is we subdue it by ventilating, and very soon the bed is ready for the plants. We now lift them carefully with a trowel, and plant only one to each light, in the centre of the hillock, which is raised so as to bring the plant very close to the glass. If carefully handled, and aided with the syringe, and kept as close as possible, without allowing the heat to rise above 90°, they take hold of their new position at once, and make a splendid start, and thereafter give very little trouble; for fly and spider have no relish for plants so treated.

THE PROPER SOIL is a matter of some importance. The melon will not thrive in a light soil, and it is not well to incorporate with the compost any considerable proportion of manure; the top spit of a pasture, where the staple is a stiff brown loam, will answer admirably; but it should be laid up some time previously, to get rid of tipula grubs and wireworms, and to rot the fibre in some degree. Three parts of such soil, well chopped up with one part of well-rotted hotbed manure, will form a good compost, and in planting it will be well to fill in round the root with a mixture of fine soil—say equal parts of turfy loam, leaf-mould, and rotten manure, to coax the roots into immediate action.

THE SUMMER CULTURE is simple enough, but the attentions requisite must be regularly given, or disappointment of some sort will be sure to occur. In the first place there should be no shading from first to last, except when the plants are first put out, and even then it will only be necessary if the weather happens to be very bright, in which case two or three rhubarb leaves may be laid on the glass, for a few hours every day, to mitigate the fervour of the sun's rays. As to watering, we must differ from the books again, in recommending a more generous treatment than is usually prescribed, for melons are thirsty, and will be cleaner and more robust if regularly syringed overhead, and kept nicely moist at the root by regular watering of the hillocks. They will not endure the degree of humidity that cucumbers enjoy; but they are often kept too dry, and become the prey of various insect plagues in consequence. As to ventilating, that must be to some extent regulated by the heat of the bed and the state of the weather; but as the plants cannot be kept in health without plenty of air, it is desirable to ventilate as freely as possible—consistent with maintaining a proper temperature. With this in view, the cultivator will take care to have heat enough to render air-giving both safe and desirable. In many cases the dry system is adopted because free watering has been found to promote canker and damping at the collar. But if the drainage of the hills is secured in the first instance, by a foundation of rubble, and *soft tepid water* is always employed, and the bottom-heat is right, melons will enjoy more moisture than they usually obtain, and in return for it will give heavier crops and finer fruit.

The plants must be allowed to spread until they reach within six inches of the side of the frame, and then the point of every shoot must be pinched out. It may be remembered, however, that if they are never stopped at all, they will just as surely fruit, but judicious stopping causes a more plentiful production and more equal distribution of those secondary shoots on which the fruit is produced. It is customary to "set" the female flowers with farina from the males, but we have always found the crop to be as good in a bed where we never "set" a single flower, as in one that was most punctually and carefully attended to. We give the bees the credit of taking this task off our hands, for they are assiduous workers amongst melons and cucumbers.

In due time the fruit will appear, and the cultivator must have the courage to refuse nature's generous offer of many more fruits than the plant can ripen properly. As soon as a fair crop is set, persist in suppressing the flowers as they appear, and stop every fruit-bearing shoot at about four eyes beyond the fruit. And what is a fair crop? it may be asked. A large sort, such as Beechwood, may be allowed to carry half-a-dozen fruit, and a smaller sort, such as Scarlet Gem, may carry nine.

As the fruits swell, keep the plants going with a good heat and liberal watering, and if the leaves appear yellowish through having exhausted the hillock, water twice a week with guano water, made by adding half an ounce of guano to every gallon of soft water. If the roots run upon the surface much, cover them with a dressing of fresh soil at the rate of about a barrow-full to every hillock, taking great care not to bruise the stems or the leaves in the operation. As the fruits acquire their full size, discontinue syringing, and lesson the supply of water at the roots, and give air freely, but be careful the heat does not go down, for melons must be ripened in a good heat to have proper tenderness and flavour. Every fruit should from the first rest on a tile or slate, unless the plants are trained to a trellis, in which case it must have the support of a few strips of bass suspended from the trellis. Whenever an inverted flower-pot can be conveniently used for support it should be preferred to any other method. They must not be cut the instant they have acquired their proper colour, or they will be comparatively worthless; the signal for removing them is when they emit a powerful odour, and separate from the stalk at the slightest touch. After being removed they should be kept a few days before they are cut for eating.

IN SELECTING SORTS it is necessary to bear in mind that, as a rule, green-fleshed melons are the best. The *Beechwood*, *Small Egyptian*, and *Bromham Hall* are fine old sorts, that will render good service if the seed be true. *Bellamore Hybrid*, *Prince of Wales*, and *Victory of Bath* are newish varieties of the green flesh section, that may be trusted for beautiful fruit of the finest flavour. The best scarlet fleshed variety is *Scarlet Gem*, which requires more heat than *Little Heath*, which is in every way good, besides being hardier and more prolific. An extremely nice melon, with rich pink flesh, is *Princess Alice*, a handsome netted fruit of a buff-yellow colour. *Queen Anne's Pocket* is valued for decorative purposes, but for eating is comparatively worthless, or at the best only fit to amuse children.

HOUSE CULTURE.—If the amateur proposes to launch out in melon culture, a suitable house heated with hot-water pipes will be required. The practice will be precisely the same as in frame culture, except as regards the source of heat, which will be more certain, more cleanly, and more completely under control; but to counterbalance these advantages, it will be found that melons in houses are apt to be sooner and more severely beset with red spider than when grown with fermenting materials. The red spider *(Acarus tellarius)* is the only enemy to be feared, but unfortunately an enemy sure of conquest unless met with prompt and energetic action.

The one great necessity in the cultivation of the melon is *sunshine;* hence, although we may produce early melons and late melons, they are always, properly speaking, productions of the summer, and that is one great reason why they can be well done in frames, and there is no special advantage in growing them in houses. It must be understood, however, that sun heat, as a rule, is not enough for melons; to produce first-class samples, heat must be obtained from fermenting materials, or flues, or hot water, or some other method. Nevertheless, as sailing near the wind has a chance of its own for the adventurous, the production of melons may be attempted by those who cannot command the means to do the thing well, and they may come out of the conflict conquerors. Given strong plants to begin with, and an early, hot, and long-continued summer, a fine crop of melons may be secured by the cultivator who can combine skill with watchfulness and perseverance. We have grown as fine melons as were ever seen or tasted, with the aid of grass mowings only; and also without any heat at all in a house with summer cucumbers.

Melons in the Open Ground are likely to prove more plague than profit, but with good management, in a favourable season, a few fine fruits may be secured. Those who simply plant out melons and hope for the best, are very likely indeed to go unrewarded, for a systematic cultivation is required; and the principal object of all the arrangements must be, to make the best of the climate, to carry the plants safely through a period of trial, or enable them to derive the fullest possible advantage from a long spell of bright warm weather.

We are to suppose that the warmth of May has arrived, and that you have a sufficient number of melon plants in pots in a frame or warm greenhouse. Those who raise their own plants will of course sow seeds on a good hotbed some time in March, and keep their plants close to the glass and as freely ventilated as they will bear, so as to have them strong for planting out in May. A large body of stable manure about half rotted, will be required for forming hillocks. The manure when heaped up must be slightly moist, but by no means wet, for we want it to ferment and produce a gentle heat for a considerable time. The material may perhaps be obtained by pulling to pieces hotbeds that have done their work and got cold, or it may be necessary to purchase. In any case it must be borne in mind that the fierce heat produced by heaping up a body of rank stable dung is not required, but if it has been already fermented two or three times, and is getting short and solid, it is in just the condition required, for a good body of it will produce a mild lasting heat that will ensure a steady growth of melon plants, and enable them to become well established by the time the summer has advanced sufficiently for their fruiting. For

every hillock dig a circular hole two feet deep and a yard and a half across. Into this hole throw the manure, and pile it up in a conical form until it is about three feet high, taking care to beat it somewhat solid with the fork as the work proceeds. The top must be flat or slightly convex, and covered with nine inches depth of compost consisting of about one half stiff loam, and the other half bits of turf, leaf mould, and very rotten manure. A little clay may be added if the mixture is rather light, for melons require a substantial soil. About the middle of May, when the weather is favourable, put a strong plant in the centre of the hillock, and cover with a common h nd-light or bell-glass. If the sun shines fiercely, lay a rhubarb leaf over the glass, and tilt it slightly to give a little air. In this way you must nurse and coax the plant into free and healthy growth, and although it may appear not to grow at all for three weeks or so, if it only continues to look well you must be satisfied, for its roots will be running freely and getting firm hold of the station, preparatory to the work required of them.

It will be necessary now to provide for every plant a fifteen or twenty-inch cloche or bell-glass, and three stout pegs made of half-inch deal, two inches wide, regularly notched as shown in the figure, the lower part being shaved off for more convenient insertion in the ground. Drive in the stakes so that the bell-glass can be lodged upon the notches exactly over the centre of the plant, and can be raised or lowered upon the notches as change of weather may render necessary.

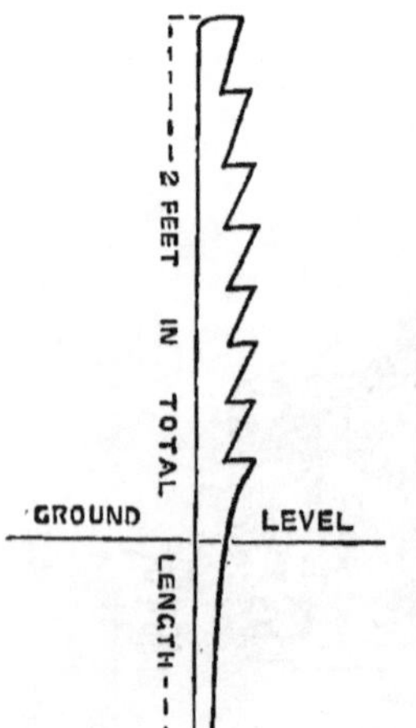

In regard to pinching and pruning there is very little to be done. As soon as the plant has made five leaves pinch out the centre, leaving four leaves. These will give rise to four leading shoots, which are not to be pinched or pruned at all, but must be trained out regularly with the aid of pegs or bent willow twigs, and be allowed to branch and subdivide in their own way. For the removal of the original bell-glass, the advancing size of the plant will be the signal. Take it away and put on the large cloche, resting it on the lowest pegs so as to afford the plant a very little air. As the season advances the cloche must be raised higher, but it must never be removed. It is intended to protect the centre of the plant to prevent canker at the collar, and save it from injury when heavy rains occur. Regular supplies of water must be given, of course, and the plants must be kept in the best health possible. When they come into flower, it will be advisable to "set" the fruiting flowers, but so many flies visit out-door melons that you will probably obtain as good a crop if you neglect this task; though when melons are grown in frames and houses, it is sometimes necessary to set the fruiting flowers.

If the weather is kind you will have melons, certainly not otherwise. A period of cold may be tided over by letting the cloches down within an inch or so of the ground, and putting old lights aslope to screen the shoots that show the forwardest fruits, but for the most part the elements have you at their mercy, and if you do not cut ripe fruit before September is out you will not cut any at all. As the season may smash up when a good crop is in want of only a little more time to finish it, you may cut the nearly ripe fruit with some length of stem attached, and ripen it in a warm greenhouse. The instant that the stalk of a melon begins to crack away from the fruit the ripening process is completed, and the melon should be eaten.

The *hillock system* may succeed so well that, having gained experience thereby, you may desire to extend the practice. The next step therefore will be to develop the *ridge system*. In place of hillocks make ridges, running north and south, put the plants four feet apart on the ridge, and the ridges far enough apart to allow plenty of room for traffic between. It will be well to protect with cloches, as advised for hillock culture; but miniature span-roof frames or A pieces, fitted with glass with a span of twenty inches, would be preferable, as protecting the whole line of the ridge, and they could be set on bricks, to raise them to the height required.

As a matter of course, the hardier kinds of melons are to be preferred for this culture, such as *Sutton's Tom Thumb*, *Monro's Little Heath*, *Gilbert's Ostrich Egg*, *Golden Gem*, and *Achapesnorrischer*.

CHAPTER XX.

SQUASHES, GOURDS, AND MARROWS.

"Go to, then; we'll use this wholesome humidity,
This gross watery pompion; we'll teach
Him to know turtles from jays."

Merry Wives, III., 3.

THE appearance of pumpkins and gourds on every cottager's fence proves that they are in universal request, and so easily grown that they might almost be classed with the weeds of the kitchen garden. To make a lengthy chapter on the cultivation of these useful fruits would be to tax the reader's time unfairly, for, given a certain few very simple conditions, and there is nothing more simple in all the horticultural practices.

The SQUASH, *Cucurbita melo-pepo;* the PUMPKIN, *C. pepo;* the POTIRON, *C. patira;* the VEGETABLE MARROW, *C. ovipera,* and the rest of this useful and variable family may be grown to the greatest perfection by very rough means, provided they have the advantage of a long hot summer. In a cold wet season they are scarcely profitable; but fair average conditions satisfy them, provided only they begin life well.

We will suppose that in a sunny sheltered nook in the garden, there is a great heap of earth derived from an excavation on the premises, or carted in for some special purpose, as for example, that the turf in it may be rotted down for the potting shed. On this mound a lot of gourds or pumpkins may be grown without the least injury to the bulk of stuff, and it scarcely matters what the stuff is, whether top spit of pasture laid up at some cost, or clay from a foundation, or mere rubbish, that no one knows what to do with. Let us make a profitable garden of this miniature mountain. In the first week of April we sow in pots seeds of the gourds intended to be grown, and put the pots on a sunny shelf in a greenhouse or on a mild hot-bed. As soon as the plants have about three rough leaves each, we knock them out and pot them separately in five-inch pots, and keep them in a frame or greenhouse. At the end of May we knock the mountain about to smooth its surface, and open holes in it about five feet apart every way, the stuff from which we spread about. The holes should be large enough to hold about a bushel of fresh stuff, which should consist of about equal parts of rotten dung and mellow loam. If the mountain happens to be made of good stuff already, a quart of fine stuff will be enough, but we suppose it to be rubbish, and so demand for each plant a bushel. When the holes have been filled, to provide a bed for every plant, we wait until they have been well warmed by the sun, and when the weather is calm we carefully turn out every plant into its prepared bed, press it in neatly, give it a little water, sprinkle a little soot round it to flit the slugs, and bestow a little nursing on them for a fortnight or so. The nursing consists of putting hand glasses over them if we have them, and these should be regularly tilted or removed entirely when the weather is genial. If there are no hand glasses, large flower pots must be at hand to put over the plants at sunset, and if the weather is bleak, they may remain on all day, for a little darkness will do them less harm than the frosty east wind, which will sometimes visit us even as late as the middle of June. Watering, in common with sheltering, must be regulated by the weather, but care must be taken not to overdo it. After standing stock-still for about a fortnight, the plants will begin to grow. When the weather becomes more settled, and you have accustomed them to light and air by sheltering less and less, you may cease your attentions and wait for your reward. It may be that they will occasionally want water, and that is about all they will want for the remainder of the season; you need not stop the growth, you need not fertilize the female flowers, you need not thin the fruit unless you want very large samples, in which case you must allow one or two fruits only to swell on a plant. A further aid in the production of extra large fruit is to give weak manure water in considerable quantity twice or thrice a week. By some such simple course of procedure, you may have gourds, pumpkins, and marrows, to any extent you may or can lay yourself out for.

An Early Crop of Vegetable Marrows may be very easily obtained by making up a very large hot-bed surfaced with one foot depth of turfy light loam, early in the month of

March, and sowing on it two or three seeds under the centre of each light. When well up remove the weakest and leave one, or at least two plants to each light. Give air cautiously, keep the heat down to 70° as the maximum, 60° being sufficient. The plants will grow rapidly and must have more and more air, the lights being drawn off for an hour or two on sunny days; frames and lights remove altogether when the season is sufficiently advanced. Caution must be experienced in respect of exposing the plants fully, because they will be less hardy than those planted out on hillocks. They will supply nice fruits at the end of May, and continue bearing abundantly to the close of the season. The smaller and more delicate varieties should be selected for this culture, the best for the purpose being *Hibberd's Prolific*.

The Culture in Beds is as simple as any other way and much to be recommended as a mode of preparing a piece of ground for cauliflowers or celery the next season, or to plant winter broccolis on before the marrows are cleared off. Mark out the beds five feet wide with two feet alleys between. Take out the earth one foot deep and lay it up in a ridge in the alleys; now fill in with half-rotten dung, fat and firm, to a depth of one foot, and then chop over a good body of the same stuff from the manure heap with the earth laid up in the alleys, and as the mixing proceeds spread it over the beds for a surfacing. If this is done in the last week of May or the first week in June, as the weather may suggest, the plants may be put out at suitable distances along the centre of each bed, and the protection of empty flower pots at night will suffice, unless the weather should become unfavourable. This system ensures for the plants a nice bottom heat, that lasts long enough to give them a good start, and the piece of ground so prepared will be in fine condition for the next crop. The smaller kinds of marrows, such as *Hibberd's*, the *Custard*, and *Moore's Vegetable Cream* may be put at four feet apart, but the common large sorts will require five or six feet, and even at that, will be much crowded before the season is over.

The Easiest Way to raise a crop of gourds or marrows may be described in very few words. It will be observed that in many gardens there is a glut of spinach, peas, beans, cauliflowers, and other summer vegetables for about three months in the summer, and then comes a lull, and vegetable marrows are in request. It not seldom happens that scarlet runners and vegetable marrows are somewhat in the way when produced extra early, because of the crowd of good things that are at hand to compete with them. But as the summer declines, the case is altered, and the things that were little valued in the time of great plenty, rise in value as the range of selection is contracted. To secure a supply of marrows in August and September is a matter of the utmost simplicity. You may go to a piece of rough ground that has been fairly dug over: if it is a mellow well manured loam, you may in the last week of May or the first week of June, insert seeds of gourds or marrows at proper distances, without making hills or taking any special pains. You will soon have a plantation, and the fruits will appear in plenty in somewhat less than two months from the time of sowing. If slugs abound, they will destroy the young plants, and that danger must be thought of in time; if drought occurs, the plants must have water. As for all the rest, leave it to nature, and take care always to cut the fruit while they are young, if they are required for cooking as summer vegetables.

During the past fifteen years we have every year grown seed of *Hibberd's Prolific Marrow* in order to supply the trade with a true sample; this variety being particularly liable to injurious crossing, if grown for seed in the vicinity of other kinds of marrows and gourds. We have in this business followed the practice above recommended. A piece of our rough clay land is dug over, and the line put down. A man takes a barrowfull of rotten manure from an old hot-bed, and with a spade takes out a spadefull of the clay and throws it aside, and fills the hole from the barrow; into this half-peck bed we insert a couple of seeds, and the work is done. We do not thin out the plants, but let them all fight for themselves, the holes being four feet apart each way. In the month of August the ground is literally covered with fruits, the size and shape of ostrich eggs, the greater part of which are left to ripen for seed. It is, therefore, evident that a short chapter should suffice for this subject, which is of none the less importance because there is not much to be said about it.

Uses of Gourds, Etc.—While many that are highly coloured make suitable drapery for fences, trellises, and screens, the large edible kinds are admirably adapted for clothing rough banks and half-waste places, a well selected group presenting in the latter days of summer a remarkable appearance. And here it may be proper to remark that the sorts usually grown for ornament are not edible, although a certain number of those that are most useful in the kitchen are magnificent things, considered from an artistic point of view. This is particularly the case with the squashes, of which there is a great variety of attractive forms. The mixing of edible and inedible, or as they usually called "poisonous" sorts together in a plantation is not advised, but it can scarcely be said to be fraught with danger, because the nauseous bitter flavour of the objectionable kinds will effectually prevent any one eating them, and as a matter of fact, we cannot find a record of a single case of poisoning through the eating of unwholesome gourds. As summer vegetables the marrows are invaluable. All the kinds may be used when ripe in the place of carrots and turnips, in soups and stews, and those with deep yellow high flavoured flesh, make excellent custards, being first slightly cooked, and then laid in slices with whipped eggs, milk, and the flavourings proper to custards. Not the least important of their uses is in the preparation of preserves and marmalade, the ripe flesh forming the basis of the conserve. The fame of pumpkin pie needs only to be mentioned to suggest a purpose to which the larger kinds are very commonly devoted in the country. Finally, where there happens to be a glut of fruit—as may happen when a collection has been grown for some special purpose—pigs and poultry will eat the flesh with eagerness, and thus the pumpkins for which there is no direct use will in time come to the kitchen in the shape of pork, chicken, eggs, and so forth.

SELECTION OF GOURDS.—The best for marmalade is the *Sicilian* or *Citron Gourd;* the best, perhaps, for custards, are the *Bordeaux Melon* and *The Turban;* the best for use as a winter vegetable is the *Round Warted Squash*, but all the squashes are available for the same purpose ; and the best for summer use, are *Moore's Vegetable Cream*, and *Hibberd's Prolific Marrow.*

CHAPTER XXI.

THE MUSHROOM.

"Ye elves of hills, brooks, standing lakes, and groves;
And ye that on the sands with printless feet
Do chase the ebbing Neptune, and do fly him
When he comes back; you demi-puppets that
By moonshine do the green sour ringlets make,
Whereof the ewe not bites, and you whose pastime
Is to make midnight mushrooms."

Tempest, V., 1.

THIS delicious fungus will often come without being asked, as on old rubbish heaps, and amongst cucumbers and melons; but when formally invited, it is capricious, and, at times, somewhat unpolite. Mushrooms are very easily cultivated *on paper*, and when you purchase spawn of a dealer you will probably be favoured with printed instructions for growing them on window sills, in chimney corners, and perhaps on the top of the eight-day clock that makes a husky throbbing in the entrance-hall. These toy systems will not obtain much attention here, for the simple reason that this book is intended to promote work rather than play, and a miniature mushroom bed is more delusive than the moonshine that promotes the growth of fairy-rings in the poetical world.

THE MUSHROOM, *Agaricus campestris*, may be studied to advantage as it appears from time to time in the fields. For several years in succession we may search for them in vain, but at last there comes a hot, dry summer, and instantly, on the occurrence of showers, the pastures will be covered with mushrooms. Heat promotes the "running," that is, the diffusion of the spawn, and a very moderate amount of moisture suffices to bring up the plant. The cultivation consists in imitating as nearly as possible the conditions that promote the growth of mushrooms in the meadow and by the roadside. The soil must contain a sufficiency of nitrates and phosphates, hence fresh short stable dung and good turfy loam are important aids. Darkness is regarded as essential, but the outdoor mushrooms proclaim that it is not. However, darkness promotes the kind of atmosphere that suits mushrooms, and hence the abundance and fine quality usually of mushrooms grown in dark houses. We shall commence the practical part of this chapter by describing the

MUSHROOM HOUSE.—If the cultivation of mushrooms is considered of sufficient importance to necessitate the erection of a house expressly for that purpose, the question of a few pounds should not prevent the erection of one large enough to afford an abundant and continuous supply. The site is of little consequence, provided it is placed contiguous to the frame ground or stable yard. The length of the house should be not less than twenty feet; the width should be twelve feet, neither more nor less. There should be two tiers of shelves on each side; these, to be large enough to hold a good body of materials, should be not less than four feet in width, and, for convenience of making up the beds and gathering the produce, this width must not be exceeded. These will occupy eight feet, and a space of four feet in width will be left down the centre for a pathway. In very many instances the pathway is much too narrow, often less than three feet, and as the materials have to be carried in and out with baskets, it requires two men to do the work of one, and the two together will not be able to move a certain bulk of stuff so quickly as one man with a barrow. The height must be sufficient for the bottom of the top bed to be thirty inches from the surface of the lower one, and to have a clear space of three feet above its surface. When the upper bed is only eighteen inches or two feet above the one on the floor, and the roof is close down upon it, it is back-breaking work to do anything to them, and their removal takes up much more time than is the case when the men can move about freely. Bricks set on edge make the best floor, and upon this the lower series of beds are formed, with a stout plank fifteen inches in width along the front to keep the materials up. The upper tier of beds may be supported by stout uprights of wood or four-inch cross walls, and the platforms may be formed with either wood or slate. A brick platform resting on arches is undoubtedly the best of all; but it is too costly to be recommended. The planks referred to for supporting the front of the bed should be held in their places by grooves formed to receive them, so that they can at any time be readily removed. Neither light nor ventilation is required for the crop, but it is desirable to have a window with a close-fitting shutter in a convenient position, to afford light whenever required. A very high temperature is not at any time desirable, and during the greater part of the year no artificial heat will be necessary, but in the winter season some assistance of this kind will be required, and therefore means of heating must be provided. To state the case briefly, a four-inch pipe should run round the wall, and be fixed intermediate between the surface of the lower and the bottom of the top bed. The pipe should be connected with a boiler heating one of the plant or fruit houses, for the purpose of avoiding the expense and labour incidental to an additional fire.

FORMATION OF BEDS.—To prevent any misunderstanding, it may be well to intimate that all indoor beds, whether in an old outhouse or in a first-class mushroom house, are made in precisely the same manner. Usually the beds are made exclusively with horse-droppings; but, apart from economical considerations, a mixture consisting of horse-droppings, short litter, and dry friable loam can be strongly recommended. By adding loam less manure is of necessity required, and the beds continue in bearing longer; and if there is any difference the mushrooms are of finer quality. Maiden loam rather rich in decayed fibrous matter is alone suitable for this purpose, and it should be employed in the proportion of about one-fourth of the entire bulk. The same proportion of short litter is the most suitable, and if there is any difficulty in obtaining a sufficiency take the requisite quantity of the long stuff, selecting that which has been well saturated with urine whilst in the stable, and chop it up into lengths of about two inches. When shaken out straight a man will, with a sharp bill-hook, and by taking a good handful at a time, be able to chop up the requisite quantity in a very short time.

When the droppings are procured from a stable on the place, they should be collected from the manure-heap about twice a week and spread out under cover, to keep them rather dry and prevent their exhaustion by fermentation, In purchasing manure it will be necessary to stipulate that it shall be new and contain a goodly proportion of droppings and short litter. When it comes to hand shake out all the short stuff and spread it out to dry; for when thrown into a heap in a moist state the fermentation quickly becomes so violent as to rapidly exhaust the manure. It must not, of course, be dust-dry, or it will not ferment at all; but in practice it is found that a very small amount of moisture is sufficient to ensure a mild and steady fermentation. A week or so before it is intended to make up the bed throw the manure into a heap to set it fermenting, and by the end of the week it will be quite warm enough for use. Frequent turnings at this stage are quite unnecessary, but it is well to turn it over once, and as far as possible to place the outside portion in the middle of the heap.

In the formation of the beds place an inch layer of loam over the bottom, and then proceed to fill in with the manure and loam; the latter must be perfectly dry and a little spread over each layer of manure as the work of filling proceeds, to ensure its being equally distributed throughout the entire depth. As each layer of three or four inches is placed on the bed let it be beaten thoroughly firm, for the spawn then runs more freely and excessive fermentation is prevented. Twelve inches is a good thickness for the bed, independent of a two-inch layer of loam, which should be applied after it has been spawned. The heat will, in all probability, increase rapidly during the first few days, and if it becomes excessively hot a few holes may be bored to allow the heat to escape; but it is much better to have the materials in proper condition, so that there may be no overheat, for with the escape of heat by means of holes referred to much of the ammonia, so essential in the production of mushrooms, will be lost. A careful watch must be kept upon the temperature, which ought not to exceed 80°. Immediately the heat commences to decline, and is about 75°, spawn the bed. Break the "bricks" up into pieces of about the size of a small hen's egg, and by means of a dibber insert them about twelve inches apart and regularly over the bed to a depth of three inches or so. Immediately after a bed has been spawned apply a half-inch covering of loam, or of perfectly dry cow-manure broken up to a powder and loam in equal proportions. In eight or ten days afterwards the spawn will commence to run, and an inch and a-half of either loam or a mixture as above advised should be spread over the surface. This should be rather dry and of the same temperature as the bed, if not a little warmer, as anything like a chill must be carefully guarded against.

MANAGEMENT OF BEDS.—In the after management of the beds the main points are to maintain them just moist enough for the development of the spawn and no more, and the house at a suitable temperature. Before a bed comes into bearing the temperature may range from 60° to 65°, but afterwards the mean should be 60°, as that temperature is the most conducive to the production of mushrooms of first-class quality; moreover, the beds remain in bearing much longer. As the house will contain beds in different stages—one only newly made up, a second just coming, a third in full bearing, and a fourth in all probability on the point of exhaustion—the temperature last mentioned will be found generally the most suitable. The beds will come into bearing in about five or six weeks from the time of spawning, and if made up as advised they will continue in bearing about three months. Beds in unheated structures may be made up from the early part of April until the middle of September; but after the last-mentioned month there will not be sufficient warmth to maintain them in a productive state. If the shed or outhouse is at all draughty, a good covering of dry hay or some similar material should be applied; and in all cases beds made in the month last mentioned should be covered after they have been spawned. Very little water is required, and, should the material become too dry, it must be applied in moderation, and of a temperature of about 75°. Very many failures occur through the beds being kept in too wet a state. Dryness merely checks production; for if the bed becomes too dry the spawn simply remains dormant, and directly the bed is again made moist it will begin to run again; but where the bed is too wet it perishes altogether. So long as the mushrooms are produced freely it may be safely assumed that no additional moisture is required.

OUTDOOR BEDS.—For these a sheltered and out-of-the-way place should be selected. They are formed with the manure in a fresher state than has been recommended for the indoor beds, and precisely the same as it comes from the stable. The sweetening so necessary when intended for hotbeds is not required; but to well mix it together and ensure its fermenting steadily, throw it into a heap and turn it over twice. The outdoor beds should be made in the form of ridges, three feet in width across the base and brought to a point at the top, with sides as sharp as they can be conveniently formed. The manure must be beaten firm, and when the heat begins to decline and the temperature of the mass is about 80°, spawn the ridges by inserting lumps of spawn in the manure in a similar manner and at the same distance apart as advised for the indoor beds. Then cover with two inches of nice loamy soil, and beat it well, and to make it thoroughly firm sprinkle it with water and then smooth it with the back of the spade. A covering of straw or long stable manure, about nine inches in thickness, must be applied; and to keep this dry lay mats or thatched hurdles over it. Outdoor beds require more attention and labour than those under cover, but the produce obtainable from them will afford adequate remuneration for all the labour that may be expended upon them. The manure will at the end of the season be available for dressing the kitchen garden, but it will not be so rich in nitrogen as manure which has simply been brought from the stable and thrown into a heap, and its value as a fertilizer will consequently be less. The outdoor beds may be made up during the same period as mentioned when speaking of the beds in sheds; and the last one may be assisted as the cold weather comes on by a good covering of warm fermenting materials.

Frame Culture.—It is not generally known that excellent mushrooms may be produced in pits and frames in which cucumbers and melons have been grown. There is nothing new about this plan of growing mushrooms, for it is well described by the late Rev. W. Williamson, in *Hort. Trans.*, vol. iii. The frame in which the main crop of melons is grown is prepared for the melons in the usual way, but at the last earthing up, which is deferred rather later than usual, the spawn is inserted about six inches apart in the fermenting materials then remaining uncovered, and care is taken to insert it rather thickly along the margin of the mound. The soil is then put in the frame and in due course the spawn finds its way over the bed. The dryness necessary during the ripening of the crop of melons prevents the appearance of many mushrooms before the melons are carried off, but as soon as the vines are removed, the beds moistened, and the frame closed, they will spring up in all directions, and continue to make their appearance for a considerable period; sometimes through the winter. The proper temperature must, of course, be maintained, and this will be a very easy matter in the case of beds heated with hot water. The temperature of frames on beds of fermenting materials can be maintained by means of linings, applied in the same manner as during the early part of the season. The Rev. W. Williamson states that he has gathered as many as two bushels of mushrooms at one time from a frame ten feet by six.

Cultivation in Boxes.—The long egg boxes, which are about six feet in length, two feet in width, and twelve inches in depth, are the most suitable, as they are capable of holding a good body of manure, and at the same time are not so big that they cannot be moved about if required. These should be filled with three parts horse-droppings and one part loam, in precisely the same condition as advised for the beds. It must also be beaten quite hard and spawned, and covered with soil in the same way. A box of this size will continue to produce nice dishes of mushrooms for a period of six or eight weeks. Large pots, pans, shallows baskets, or boxes of a smaller size than those mentioned may be turned to account in the same way. When filled they can be placed in a cellar, greenhouse, or similar place. About forty years ago Baron Joseph d'Hoogvorst, of Limmel, near Brussels, published a treatise on his system of growing mushrooms on shelves. These resemble troughs about a foot wide and twelve inches deep, and are fixed against the walls of stables and cellars, in tiers extending from the floor to the ceiling, with a curtain suspended in front to shut out light and air. According to the treatise, he gathered abundant supplies from the shelves, but they do not appear to possess any decided advantage excepting where the space is very limited. They are certainly awkward to fill, and owing to the small body of materials the beds made in them do not continue in bearing long. As remarked above, we do not believe in toy systems, and therefore, shall say no more on this part of the subject.

In Gathering the Crop it is important to cut them as low down as possible, for when a considerable portion of the stem is left it affords a harbour for maggots. At the same time care must be taken to avoid disturbing the small mushrooms with which those ready for the table are frequently surrounded. If not gathered in the form of buttons, they should be gathered immediately they have attained a fair size and before the gills assume a dark colour.

CHAPTER XXII.

THE HERB GARDEN.

"Medea gather'd the enchanted herbs
That did renew old Æson."
Merchant of Venice, V., 1.

THE HERB GARDEN, as an institution, has ceased to be, and, although it "lives in history," its claims on our attention as a matter of business, are few and small, as compared with what would have been the case had such a work as this been in hand three hundred, or even two hundred years ago. Nay, if we go back only a century we shall find the herb garden and the still-room, and the still-room maid in happy association, but they have all become memories embalmed for us in a peculiar odour of sanctity. The Herb Garden, therefore, in the historic sense, we are bound to ignore; but it remains for us to say something useful on the herbs that are commonly in request in private households, and as space is very precious, we shall begin by suggesting a method of forming a garden of herbs that will probably suit the requirements of the class in whose interests, more especially, this work is written.

FORMATION OF A HERB GARDEN.—The month of September is the best time in all the year for the formation of a herb-garden. For all the woody aromatic plants required for flavouring soups and meats, such as thyme, sage, etc., a dry, sunny, sandy bank is the best situation possible. The fragrance and flavour of these plants are much enhanced by a dry, rather poor calcareous soil, and full exposure to air and sunshine. A bank appropriated to such things might be made very pretty, for all these plants are at least sightly; some few of them are beautiful. It is quite proper for the gardener to have a plantation of these useful subjects, in order to supply quantities when required for drying, or for the preparation of any cosmetics, or other purposes; but it is desirable there should be a small, and we may call it a private, plantation, so situated that the ladies of the household may be able at any time, without difficulty, to obtain small quantities of such herbs as they require. Therefore it is we recommend the formation of a bank, in a sunny spot, to be planted with all such herbs as will thrive on it, and to be made as ornamental as possible; to which end may be added a few Provence Roses for the scent-jar, a few common Major Tropæolum (*vulgo* Nasturtium) for pickling, a Sweet Bay for flavouring custards, one or two trees of Variegated Rue, which is just as good as green rue for medicinal purposes, and *Calycanthus floridus*, for its spicy flavour; with whatever else may be deemed suitable for the situation. It must be remembered, however, that all aromatic herbs in common use will not thrive alike on a dry, sunny, sandy bank. Some require a deep, moist, rich soil, and of this class parsley and mint are notable examples. Places for such as these should be found independent of the supplies the gardener may be able to furnish, for they may be wanted when there is no one at hand to obtain them, and the kitchen garden may be too far away for a journey in wet weather. It is impossible to predicate the wants of every household; but, having found it greatly to conduce to domestic comfort to have herbs of all kinds scattered about the pleasure garden, though we have a complete and rather large collection of them all in their proper place, we propose these plans for the good of others, and have only to beg of each reader to accept, modify, or reject, as a consideration of individual circumstances may render advisable.

ANGELICA, *Archangelica officinalis.*—A coarse-looking plant of the Umbelliferous order. It grows five or six feet high, and requires a deep loamy soil and a damp situation. It is suitable, in fact, to plant out beside a lake or river. The stalks have a warm aromatic flavour; when candied with sugar, it is considered scarcely inferior to ginger as a carminative and stomachic stimulant. The root may be prepared in imitation of preserved or pickled ginger. In the north of Europe it is much used, and is believed to have the property of prolonging life. Angelica may be raised from seed, but it should be sown as soon as ripe. If seed is not obtainable, secure a plant, suffer it to seed, and sow the seeds as soon as they begin to fall, and a fine stock of plants will be the result. The plants usually die after their seeds are ripe; but if it is desired to keep them for several years, the flower-stems must be pinched out as soon as they are visible in spring.

Anise, *Traqium anisum.*—A half-hardy annual, used for garnishing or seasoning. Sow on the sunniest part of the border, in the first week of May, where it is to remain. The plants should be thinned, when up, to six inches apart. If seeds are wanted, it is best to purchase them, as they seldom ripen properly in this country.

Balm, *Melissa officinalis.*—This is a general favourite in the country, for its grateful lemon-like odour, and the refreshing drink which is prepared from it for the sick. It is a coarse-looking plant, growing two or three feet high. It will grow in any soil, but best in poor clayey stuff. Seed may be sown in April or May, but a quicker method is to obtain plants and part them. If required in any quantity the plants should be divided in September, and the pieces planted two feet apart.

Sweet Basil, *Ocymum basilicum.*—Bush Basil is *O. minimum.* Both are tender plants requiring to be raised annually from seeds. To secure early supplies, the seeds should be sown on a hot-bed in March, and the plants should have the care usually bestowed on tender annuals, and be planted out at the end of May, on light rich soil. If there are no conveniences for raising plants under glass, sow the first week in May on a sunny bank, and the plants will appear in the early part of June. Basil is used in soups and salads, and some prefer it to flavour peas instead of mint. If strong plants are put out at the end of May, seed may be obtained in September, but seed imported from Italy is far better than can be ripened in England.

Borage, *Borago officinalis.*—A rough-leaved rustic annual, producing the most lovely blue flowers. Sow in March, April, May, June, and September, to have a succession. The young tops have the flavour of cucumber, and are used in the preparation of a "cool tankard." In case of a scarcity of summer vegetables, the young leaves may be cooked as spinach. Bees are very fond of the flowers, and a rough piece of ground, not wanted for any particular purpose, might be sown all over with borage, both for the bees, and to give a cheerful air to what might otherwise be quite a waste.

Bugloss, *Anchusa officinalis.*—This is a rather coarse plant, with blue flowers in a cluster at the summit. The poorer the soil, the neater the growth and the longer it lasts. If sown in spring, on a sunny bank, it may be reckoned to last two years, and then will probably die, and leave behind it a great progeny of plants from seeds self sown. When it grows in sheer rubbish or between the bricks of an old wall it lasts many years, but in rich soil it becomes an annual. It has much the same properties as borage, and was anciently esteemed as a cordial.

BURNET, *Poterium sanguisorba.*—A pretty plant, requiring a very sunny, poor dry soil, doing well on sand, chalk, or bricklayers' rubbish. Sow the seed in March, April, and May, or multiply by division of roots, or by slips. Sometimes the seed will remain in the ground a year before germinating. It is used in cool tankards, soups, and salads.

CHERVIL, *Chærophyllum sativum.*—Also known as SWEET CICELY. A hardy annual, requiring a dry, sandy, or chalky soil fully exposed to the sun. Sow in March, April, May, and August, the last sowing being left to stand the winter. It is used for soups, salads, and for garnishing.

CHIVES, *Allium schœnoprasum.*—This is a valuable salad herb, as it gives to a salad the piquancy and pungency of the onion, in a subdued form, and is unaccompanied by those properties which render onions so objectionable; wherever salads are in request chives should be handy. Plant a few small tufts and leave them alone one whole season, after which cut the tops as required, but do not injure the roots. Any soil will suit them, but a sunny position is essential. If used for soups, divide the patches in March, and plant them a foot apart every way, in good soil. Take up the roots in November, dry them in a shed or kitchen, and store away for use. As a rule onions are to be preferred for winter soups, but for almost any summer dish requiring an onion flavour, chives are invaluable.

CLARY, *Salvia sclarea.*—An annual plant, the seed of which may be sown in April and May, on a dry sunny, sandy bank. Half a dozen plants will suffice for any family. It is used in soups, sauces, and in flavouring wines for the sick.

DILL, *Anethum graveolens.*—This is grown in quantities in some gardens, for the preparation of "dill water;" in others it is kept merely for flavouring soups and sauces, and for pickling. A dry, poor sand suits it, but it will grow in any rather light soil. The seed must be sown where the plants are to remain, and it is best sown as soon as ripe, for, if left till spring, it may fail to germinate. When grown in quantity, the seed should be sown in rows, a foot apart, and as they advance they must be thinned with the hoe to nine inches apart in the rows. As the umbels are valued as much as the leaves, the plant must be encouraged to flower. If the seeds are allowed to scatter themselves, a quantity of self-sown plants will appear the next spring, and these are sure to thrive, and furnish umbels in July and August.

FENNEL, *Anethum fœniculum.*—Sow in April and May; better still, as soon as the seed is ripe in the autumn. The early spring or late autumn are the best times to plant. If a quantity are required, sow on a bed of light soil in autumn, in drills six inches apart. The next spring, as soon as they begin to grow, transplant them a foot apart. It may be propagated by pieces of the root. If allowed to ripen seed, it does not last more than three or four years; therefore, where only a few plants are grown for occasional use, it is advisable to cut out the flower-stalks as soon as they begin to rise in spring. As in some families this is much used to flavour sauces for fish, it is worth making a bed expressly for it. This should consist of two or three loads of bricklayers' rubbish, in the form of a low mound, with a thin skin of any kind of loam on the top. It will, however, grow in any soil or situation, and is especially fond of chalk.

HOREHOUND, *Marrubium vulgare.*—It is best to obtain a root and propagate by slips, in a shady place; but seeds may be sown at any time. The best place for it is a dry sandy bank. It is a hardy herbaceous plant, much valued, when candied, for coughs and colds.

HYSSOP, *Hyssopus officinalis.*—A very beautiful plant, admirably adapted to adorn the dry, sunny, sandy bank. The *ezob* of the Hebrew writers has been the subject of almost endless controversy; in some of the texts it is probable that marjoram is intended. In Smith's "Dictionary of the Bible," Dr. Royle says that certainly the caper plant is sometimes meant. Our hyssop of the herb garden is a member of the Lipwort family, which is rich in aromatic plants, and is common in the southern parts of Europe. Sow in March, April, and May; or, better still, divide the plants any time in spring or September. They may be propagated by cuttings put under hand-lights all the summer.

LAVENDER, *Lavendula spica.*—This well-known garden favourite thrives best in a sunny, open spot, on a sandy soil, but will live almost anywhere, even in a sooty garden in the midst of houses. Cuttings of ripe wood planted firm in October will grow freely the next spring. Cuttings of young shoots soon form roots under hand-lights in spring and summer. When grown in quantity, the best way to propagate lavender is to cut a lot of ripe shoots their full length late in autumn, and leave them laying in heaps on the ground, exposed to all weathers till February, and then to insert them three or four inches deep in sandy loam, in rows a foot apart, and four inches asunder in the rows. At the end of the season, transplant them all, or thin them, leaving part to remain. Gather lavender when the flowers are beginning to expand; it is then most rich in its aromatic fragrance.

MARJORAM.—The summer marjoram, *Origanum majorana*, is an annual; the winter majoram, *O. heracleoticum*, and the common, or pot marjoram, *O. onites*, are perennials. All the sorts may be grown from seeds sown from February to June; the winter and common marjorams may be raised from slips or divisions of the roots in spring and autumn. The soil should be light and dry, but good, such as would grow a cabbage or a lettuce. When grown in quantity, the seeds should be sown in drills six inches apart, and the plants be thinned to six inches apart, when large enough for the hoe. The perennial sorts should be planted out in autumn, a foot apart every way. A plantation lasts several years, if every autumn the dead shoots are cut away, the soil between them carefully pricked over with a small fork, and a little fine earth is scattered amongst them. Gather, for drying, when the flowers are just beginning to open.

SPEAR MINT, *Mentha viridis.*—This invaluable herb loves a damp, rich soil, and should always be propagated by dividing the old plants, or by pieces of the roots. In every garden a plantation, however small, should be made every year, either in spring or autumn, and should be allowed to become strong before being gathered from. It is a good rule to grow a row on the same ground with the peas, to be handy to put into the basket with them; and to secure early supplies in spring, have a few roots on a warm sloping border, raised above the general level. For winter use it can be forced without any trouble, and the simplest way is to take up some strong roots that have not been gathered from all the summer, and pot them or put them in shallow pans, or boxes, in rich soil. This should be done at the end of August, and the pots or boxes should be left out of doors fully exposed to the weather. Do not cut down the green shoots; leave them for the frost to destroy. When the frost has cleared away the tops, put the pans or pots in a frame, and after a week or two transfer one of them to a warm greenhouse or forcing pit, and in three or four weeks the new growth will appear. Continue to introduce other batches as required, preferring always to force slowly than rapidly. If six weeks can be allowed, the shoots will be fatter, and the flavour richer than if forced in less time. If possible, leave a few pots full of roots in the pit or frame, as these will give shoots a full fortnight or three weeks earlier than mint can be gathered from the open ground. Water may be given freely to mint when forced, and it should be as near the glass as possible.

WOOLLY MINT, *Mentha rotundifolia*, is one of the most useful herbs of its class, and the very best kind of mint for the making of sauce to eat with lamb. The plant is coarse in growth, the leaves large, roundish, of a soft woolly texture, and very bright and grateful in flavour. The young tops should be pinched out and used quite fresh, and without washing. Mint sauce made quite thick with this mint will make even house-lamb at Christmas eatable, and such tame meats need some flavouring to justify the absurdity of eating them.

MARIGOLD, *Calendula officinalis.*—A showy annual, which should be grown on a dry, sunny bank, as although it will grow anywhere, it is never well flavoured when grown in rich, damp soil. Sow the seed where the plants are to remain; if in a piece, thin them to a foot apart. The thinnings may be transplanted if the seed-bed is not large enough for the supply of flowers required; the single dark-coloured flowers are the best for flavour. Gather the flowers when fully expanded, and dry quickly, and store away in paper-bags in a dry place.

PURSLANE.—*Portulacca oleracea* is the green purslane; *P. sativa* is the golden purslane. Sow in pans filled with sandy soil, in a warm greenhouse, or on a hot-bed in March, and plant out from those pans in May. Give scarcely any water at any time. Sow in the open ground during April, May, and June; if in quantity, the drills should be six inches apart, and the plants to be thinned to six inches. A dry, sandy bank is the proper place for them, and the hotter the better.

ROSEMARY, *Rosmarinus officinalis.*—There are varieties with golden-striped and silver-striped leaves. The soil cannot be too poor and dry for this useful shrub, which, when growing on a wall from self-sown seeds, is longer lived than when growing in a garden border. The hot sandy bank will, at all events, be a good place for it. It may be propagated from seed sown in March, April, and May, or from cuttings in spring; or, better still, by taking off rooted pieces, and planting them and covering them with hand-lights for a week or two, to assist their establishment. The plant may also be layered in summer—a process which consists in bending down a branch to the earth, and fixing it with a peg or stone, and covering the part which touches the earth with a little fine soil. If the branch is slightly cut or snapped without breaking it through at the part where it is required to root, the process is hastened, but roots are sure to be formed if this preliminary is neglected. When planted in quantity, a distance of ten inches apart every way must be allowed. Most of the preparations for promoting the growth of the hair consist chiefly of infusions of rosemary.

RUE, *Ruta graveolens.*—The "Herb of Grace" thrives well on the top of a wall, or on a heap of brick rubbish, or on a bank of chalky or sandy soil. The best way to propagate it is by cuttings of young shoots in May or June, put under hand-lights, but firm hard shoots may be planted in October, and they will make good plants the next season. Seed is a tedious method, but it may be adopted, and the best time to sow it is April or May. When grown in quantity, plant a foot apart. The variegated-leaved rue is a beautiful shrub for a rockery or wall. The only uses for rue are as a stomachic and to provoke appetite, and also to destroy worms in the intestines. For both of these purposes it is steeped in gin, and the gin is taken as a medicine. It is certainly effectual.

SAGE, *Salvia officinalis.*—The roast goose of Old England is scarcely less important than the roast beef; and so sage is scarcely less to be desired than horseradish. This plant requires a good soil, and an open, sunny position; shelter is desirable, for in hard winters sage is, in exposed situations, very much cut up. Cuttings may be made, in the month of April, of hard wood of last year's growth, and these should be planted in a shady place, and have water when the weather is dry. It is better, however, to wait till the early part of June, and then take cuttings of the new wood, selecting the strongest shoots on the outsides of the old plants. Remove the leaves from the shoots, except the last half dozen at the top, and insert the cuttings deep in newly-dug ground, in a shady place, six inches apart each way. Give them a sprinkle of water every morning, to keep the tops fresh and make the soil moderately moist. Of course, this need not be done during wet weather. Let them remain till the March following, and then transplant them to an open, sunny spot, one foot apart. Seeds may be sown in April or May, in a bed of light soil, in drills six inches apart. As soon as large enough to draw, the rows may be continually thinned, and the thinnings may be planted out, in showery weather, six inches apart, to gain strength for planting out for use. It is a good plan to destroy plantations of sage after four or five years' use, and begin again with young plants, as they are apt to become stumpy, and many of them die in the centre. The flavour of sage is so agreeable to some persons, that they put a leaf in the tea-pot to flavour the tea, and "they say" that tea so flavoured is a fine refresher for a weak stomach.

THYME, *Thymus vulgaris*, is the common pot-herb thyme. It grows best in a sunny situation, on stony or sandy soil, but it may be grown in rich garden soil; in which case it is rather tender in winter. When growing amongst stones, or on walls, the severest frost does not harm it. Thyme may be raised from seeds sown in fine earth in April or May, and will require to be thinned as the plants spread. It is far better, however, to divide the plants into little pieces, each with a few roots, in March or April, or, indeed, any time through the summer, if shading and watering are resorted to, that the heat of the sun may not destroy them. It is an exhaustive plant; therefore, after having stood some years in one spot, a fresh plantation should be made, and the old one should be destroyed, and the ground deeply dug and manured. Cut the tops for drying when the flowers begin to expand.

LEMON THYME is a lemon-scented variety of wild thyme, *Thymus serpyllum.* It does not come true from seeds, therefore, must be increased by parting the roots or by slips. A sandy soil is required for this; it thrives well in peat, but not in chalk, and in ordinary garden soils grows luxuriantly, and is sometimes used in place of box for edgings, and is better than box for green embroidery. The common wild thyme, *T. serpyllum,* of the heaths is as good as any garden thyme for flavouring soups, forcemeat, etc., therefore those who live in places where it grows in plenty may replenish their kitchen stores from nature's great herb-garden. The following are worth a place on the bank or rockery amongst Alpine plants :—*T. corsicus,* a little green-leaved annual, which comes up every year from self-sown seeds ; deliciously fragrant when in flower. *T. serpyllum lanuginosum,* a woolly-leaved variety of wild thyme, which makes a pretty patch on a ledge of rock, requiring scarcely any soil. *T. vulgaris variegatus,* with variegated leaves, makes a pretty tuft on a bank, and is almost good enough for an edging in the flower-garden. *T. azureus,* a delicate little rock plant, with minute purplish-blue flowers. Every known species and variety of Thymus is worth growing, and all are pleasantly fragrant except T. azoricus, which might be called a stinking thyme.

WORMWOOD, *Artemisia vulgaris.*—The common wormwood will grow anywhere, even in a shady border, where few other things will live, but, when required for a medicinal purpose, should be grown in the full sun. It is a hardy herbaceous perennial, of coarse, but not repulsive appearance. As it spreads fast, it is apt to become a troublesome weed, and it is therefore not advisable to plant it in any place where a neat appearance is a matter of importance. For medicinal purposes, it should be gathered in June, when in flower. It is a fine tonic bitter. Several very beautiful species of Artemisia are in cultivation in gardens. The variegated variety of A. vulgaris is a charming plant in spring, but becomes coarse in summer. *A. argentea* forms an elegant silvery bush ; it is not quite hardy. The southernwood is *A. abrotanum,* a plant which will grow almost anywhere, but is at home on a raised bank.

TARRAGON, *A. dracunculus.*—A favourite plant of the country garden, in some households prized for the preparation of tarragon vinegar, and it is much used, also, to flavour sauces. It gives an aromatic warmth to a salad. The soil for this plant should be poor and the position sunny. It is a hardy herbaceous plant, easily propagated by parting the roots. The tarragon plantation must be planted in the spring, the roots one foot apart; but where fresh leaves are required in winter and spring, plants that have not been cut from should be taken up in October and November, and be divided and planted in frames. In warm, sheltered gardens, a few plants on a dry border, facing south, may be pretty well depended on to supply fresh leaves all the winter. The flower-stems should be cut close over as they rise, unless seed be wanted. Those who like the flavour of tarragon should dry a little in summer for winter use, as the dried leaves have nearly as good a flavour as those freshly gathered.

CHAPTER XXIII.

THE STORAGE OF ROOTS.

"Hide those roots
That shall first spring, and be most delicate."
Henry V., II., 4.

THE proper storing of roots is a matter of great importance, and one that obtains much less than its due share of attention in gardens generally. Rough and ready methods answer very well when the store is small; but when a large family has to be provided for, suitable arrangements of a more systematic, and, we may even say, scientific kind should be made. The preservation of the stock in the best condition possible not only aids the table while it lasts, but prevents a common contingency of careless storing, the purchase of roots in spring to make good the waste resulting from unthrift. If roots become shrivelled through exposure to the air, or make much growth of white shoots or green leaves through being too warm, the quality is seriously deteriorated, and the money value in proportion lowered. It is something to have nice samples of old potatoes, turnips, carrots, parsnips, and beets in the months of May and June, for they may all be wanted, but it can only be done by good storing, the cost of which is as nothing compared with the result when there is any quantity of produce to be dealt with.

A few rough diagrams of storehouses for roots will perhaps convey more information than we could hope to afford by an elaborate essay. The requisites of a store are coolness, darkness, safety against the frost, means of ventilation, and convenience of access. As a matter of course, it is often possible to convert a common shed or stable, or toolhouse into a store for roots, but the primary conditions of success should be borne in mind, in order that the best may be made of materials ready at hand. Now for the diagrams.

The first represents a section of a lean-to store-room designed specially for small gardens, or for those places where it cannot be sunk below the level. It is represented as being hidden by shrubs and trees on both sides; indeed, this would be necessary to exclude frost unless the walls were of unusual thickness. If thickly belted on both sides by evergreen shrubs, and the roots covered over during very severe weather with straw or fern, very little harm will come to them, even if only a fourteen-inch wall at back and nine in front are used; and as a northern aspect may be adopted for such a building, there are but a very few places but can furnish a back wall ready for such a purpose. In general construction these buildings are pretty much alike, that is to say, brick or stone walls and tiled roofs are essential, and as the different kinds of roots should be kept separate, they should be placed on shelves, which should be of oak; the shelves are shown upon the sections in each case where they are in use. The bottom shelf should be kept about three inches above the floor, otherwise it will soon rot; potatoes may go

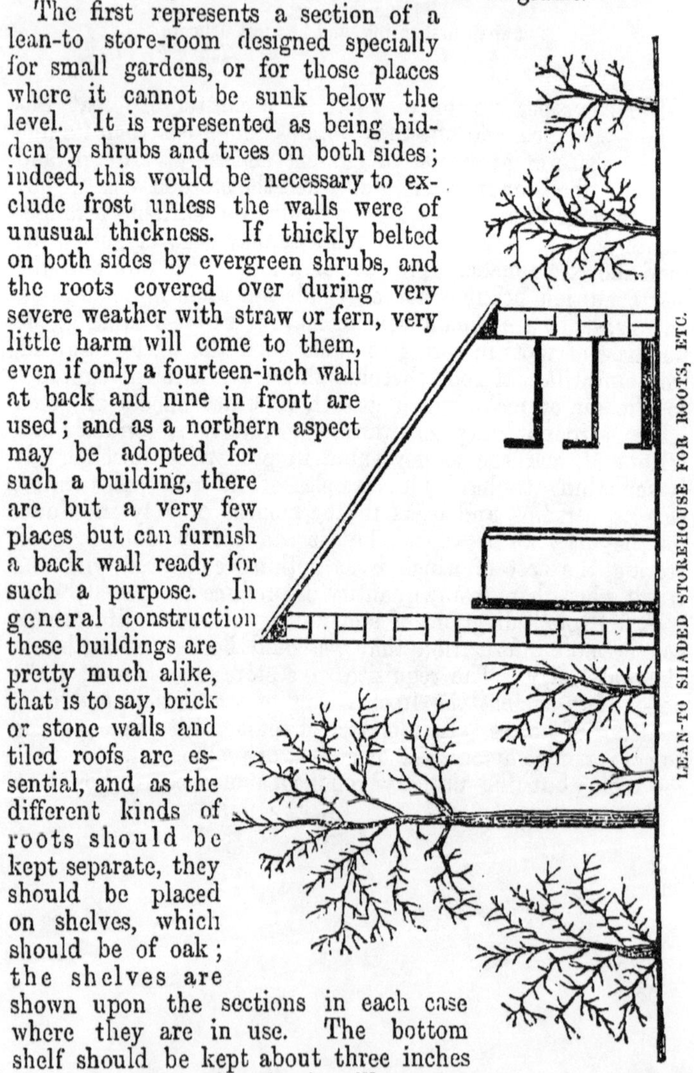

LEAN-TO SHADED STOREHOUSE FOR ROOTS, ETC.

on the bottom shelf, carrots, beetroot, etc., on the next, and the onions on the top. In every case means should be secured of admitting a current of air through the building. This may be done either with a small ventilator in the front wall or in the door, but taking care that it can be closed at pleasure. With a similar opening at the apex, a continual current of air may be kept up, which will render the atmosphere of the place as sweet and pure as the nature of the subjects which it contains will admit.

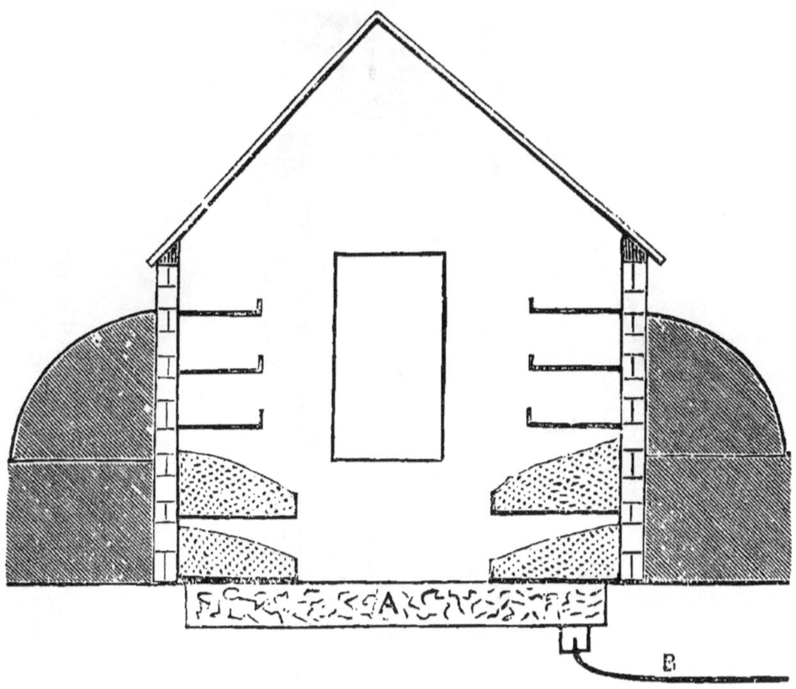

SUNK SPAN-ROOF STOREHOUSE FOR ROOTS, ETC.

A, rubble ; B, drain.

The second figure, if worked out, would make an admirable structure for such a purpose, and may be made capable of holding any quantity of produce. It should be sunk three feet below the level of the surrounding ground, and if in an

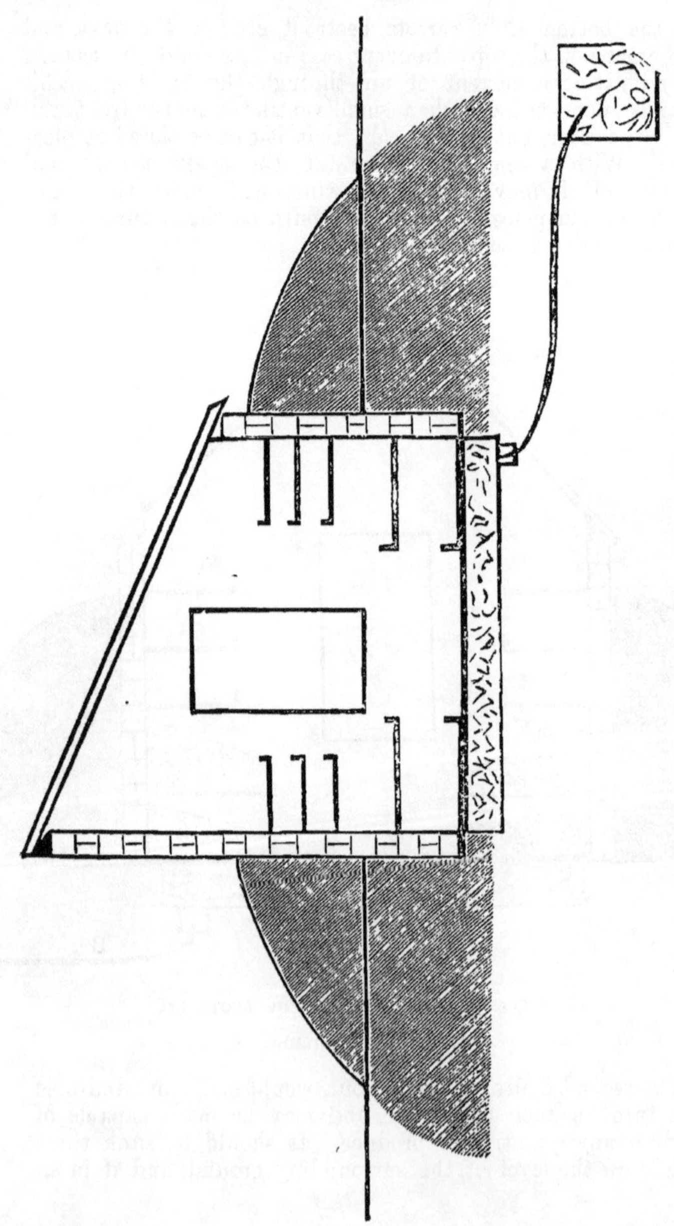

SUNK LEAN-TO STOREHOUSE FOR ROOTS, ETC.

exposed situation, a bank of earth should be thrown up on each side. When this is done the internal air cannot be affected by any amount of frost. When such structures are built for this purpose, it is important to remember that drainage is necessary, as any accumulation of damp either in the house or under the floor will to a great degree render the air of the place unsuitable for the purposes for which it was intended. To guard against this, the floor is laid on rubble A, which communicates by the drain B with a catch-water or cesspool, from which it soaks away, or is carried on to another drain. Generally speaking, if the catchwater is half filled with lumps of chalk it will absorb all the moisture brought by the drain B. Two shelves are shown on each side of the door which reach up to the ground-level. These are supposed to be for potatoes, while those above are for beet-roots, carrots, etc. This, as well as the next figure, must be entered by steps inside the house. If the banks of earth are considered unsightly, they are easily hidden by means of small shrubs or ivy.

The third figure is a well-arranged and suitable structure, and such as would serve the purpose of many good gardens now wholly deficient of such a building.

The fourth figure is an improvement on the old-fashioned potato clamp. D is a small raised mound of earth, over

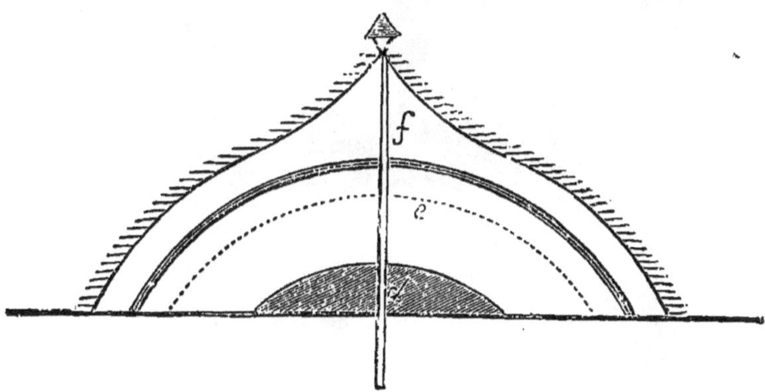

IMPROVED POTATO CLAMP.

which some straw is placed. This mound serves to drain the principal part of the clamp. The potatoes occupy the space

E, over which is a layer of straw; F is a vacant space beneath a rough-thatched roof carried to one centre pole, and above the potatoes. With an inlet of air in mild weather at about two places round the bottom, and with an outlet at the apex, a small current of air may be kept up to carry off the foul air which is always generated where there is collected a mass of vegetable matter, and this open space between admits of its being carried off most effectually, while the inner covering of straw and the thatched roof are a safeguard against frost. It may be proper to remark here that exposure to light very soon spoils the flavour of potatoes, and continued exposure renders them poisonous.

CHAPTER XXIV.

EXHIBITING.

"Perchance you wonder at this show;
But wonder on till truth makes all things plain."
Midsummer Night's Dream, V., 1.

THE healthy excitement of a horticultural exhibition tends in a most direct and powerful manner towards the improvement of the garden in all those departments which minister more especially to the spirit of emulation, and more or less on those that lie outside the field of competition. As a matter of course some gardeners who become fired with zeal in competing for prizes, are the worse for it in all their ways and their work; but the influence, on the whole, is beneficial and, generally speaking, it is to the employers' interest to encourage the contribution to the horticultural show of the products of the garden. In the every day life of the English gardener, there is much wearisome monotony, much dreary dullness, much unhealthy depression, and the horticultural exhibition affords a most agreeable and desirable change from the leaden routine; and the men who take an active part in the management, as well as in the competition, are usually found to be trustworthy and vigilant, and spirited in the discharge of their most ordinary duties. The bustle and consideration of detail, and the close association with men of experience and business tact, are of great service to a young man who associates himself with the working department of a flower show, and the hope of attaining a good position in the prize list, will quicken his activities to the great advantage of his garden work, if his mind is but fairly balanced, and bent on the attainment of respectability by the due discharge of every duty. The occasional mischief that results from the influence of the flower show, is seen in the neglect of certain departments in order that extra care may be bestowed on others, the garden as a whole being sacrificed that the subjects intended for exhibition may have attention disproportionate to the resources of the place. Of course the employer is to blame if this kind of mischief acquires any considerable proportions. It should be nipped in the bud, for a grand show of fuchsias or pelargoniums, or whatever else may be the gardener's *forte,* will not compensate for the chronic disorder of the entire establishment. It is not often this sort of thing happens. If we look round the garden of the man who takes the lead in the exhibition tent, we shall almost certainly find it well kept, productive, and in all important matters in advance of the average of establishments of similar extent and plan. As a matter of fact, the best gardeners are, nine times in ten, exhibitors by habit, and owe their advantage in gardening in great part to the information the exhibition affords and the spirit of emulation it excites in the minds of all who take an active interest in its promotion.

During the past ten years the exhibition of vegetables and roots has acquired immense importance, and a considerable benefit to the public at large is one of the results. From rough, unsightly groups of second-rate productions we have advanced by rapid stages to a high standard of taste and quality, so that now the displays of these things constitute a very attractive feature in the scheme of an exhibition. To secure a good place in a spirited competition in this department is well worthy the endeavour of a gardener who would obey the impulse of an honourable ambition.

The very first consideration of the intending exhibitor should be to ensure high quality. The young man will perhaps think more of size than beauty, and will be shocked, perhaps angered, when he finds that the judges have passed him by and bestowed rewards on collections that his would outweigh many times. The disappointment will teach him more than any book or even the counsels of his best friend. An interesting exemplification of the persistency of judges in looking for quality may be noticed in the customary judging of peas. Amongst the more important of the newer varieties is one named Superlative, which, to the learned in this business, appears by its immense size and peculiar distinctness of appearance, to be the perfection of a pea for exhibition, and yet it is usually passed over, and the day must be near at hand when none but the most ill-judging of exhibitors will be so unwise as to present it. The simple reason of its rejection is that it has no quality. Parallel instances might be cited to almost any extent, but we must economise space and be content to close this paragraph by saying that the search for quality in view of exhibition honours will benefit the employer's table and considerably augment the value of the aggregate products of the garden.

Success in great part depends on tasteful arrangement. All the subjects selected for exhibition should be neatly trimmed and sufficiently washed, so as to present a thoroughly nice appearance. The artistic element will be found to be of great importance, and given collections of equal value in respect of variety, growth, and quality, the one that is best put up will be entitled to the prize. As a matter of course, there are many ways of exhibiting vegetables, but the choice of receptacles will usually lie between baskets and trays, unless there is a specification on the subject in the schedule. The prettiest mode of exhibition we have seen for a long time is that adopted by Mr. G. T. Miles, of Wycombe Abbey Gardens, who uses a neat wooden tray of suitable size, and garnishes his vegetables with fresh green moss. The subjoined figure represents a collection of fifteen varieties put up in Mr. Miles's manner. The tray is four feet long, two feet wide, and two inches deep. It is fitted with a lid, which converts it into a box five and a-half inches in depth. It has a partition down the centre, and is used not only for the exhibition, but for the conveyance of the vegetables, with the exception of the cabbage and cauliflowers, which are carried in a basket and have a final trimming at the last moment when exhibitors have to quit the tent for the judges to make the awards. By packing in soft moss exactly as the samples are to stand, there is no further occasion to handle them, and they look as fresh when the judging is in progress as when they were first taken from the ground.

It would be well if those who prepare schedules would give special attention to this matter, with a view to ensure uniformity of plan in the presentation of collections, and the plan, of course, should be determined with a view to display the competitions fairly, and render them thoroughly attractive and useful. What is worth doing, is worth doing well; and it is no longer necessary to prove that vegetables and roots may be made pleasing to the eye as features of an exhibition.

FIRST-PRIZE COLLECTION OF FIFTEEN VARIETIES OF VEGETABLES.

CHAPTER XXV.

THE TOMATO, CAPSICUM, AND EGG PLANT.

"It is a most sharp sauce:
And is not well served in to a sweet goose."
Romeo and Juliet, II., 4.

THE plants to be treated of in this chapter are closely related botanically, and require nearly the same course of cultivation to ensure a profitable production of their beautiful and useful fruits. They rank in importance in the order of their names, the tomato being, in its way, a princely fruit; but the egg plant, which stands last in the trio, is of much greater value as an esculent than is known to the world at large, for the delicious aubergine is of this tribe, and not the only one of the number that deserves to be valued for delicious eating. These plants are all tender in constitution, though our summers are usually warm enough for their full development if planted out at a suitable time. But to do full justice to them, they should be made the best of as pot plants, for they are, without exception, ornamental and interesting, and a certain select few are highly attractive and valuable for decorative purposes, notably so the larger kinds of capsicums.

THE TOMATO, or LOVE APPLE, *Lycopersicon esculentum,* has of late years passed from the rich man's garden, in which it was exclusively located, and has become a citizen of the world, the welcome guest of every household, and the subject of the poor man's special care. And no wonder, for like its cousin, the potato, it is so thoroughly useful and so accommodating in respect of the cultivation it requires, that it suits every garden and every table, and, strange to say, gratifies every taste, for it was never heard that, when fairly presented, this noble fruit displeased anyone.

A SUMMER CROP OF TOMATOES may be secured by a very simple course of procedure. At the end of March or early in April sow a few pots of seeds of any of the large red kinds, the *Common Red* being as useful as any, though less handsome than the named kinds. Any light rich soil will serve for them, and the pots must have a warm place if possible; but if they stand on a sunny shelf in the greenhouse they will do very well. In due time the plants will appear, and when they have made two or three rough leaves they should be potted singly in small pots, in light soil, and made quite firm, and kept in a sunny place in a pit or greenhouse, where, however, they must have plenty of air. At the end of May these will be strong plants, and must be put out of doors to harden them for a week or so, and then a sufficient number should be planted out in the hottest place that can be found

TOMATO ON TRELLIS.

for them. Be not troubled about the sort of soil that is best, for, in truth, sunshine is their first and chief requirement. We have for many years grown the principal supply for the household by planting them next the walls of greenhouses, and instead of preparing borders for them, have simply planted them in the gravel walks, opening for each a hole with a trowel, and packing the roots in with a handful of leaf mould or nice compost to assist the plant at the first start, after which it had to find its food amongst the stones and brickbats. When so situated the plants need regular watering, and it will be good for them when the fruit is swelling, to give them a watering with liquid manure twice a week, though, if this be neglected, they will nevertheless produce an abundance of good fruit provided they have occasional showers and much hot sunshine. As they advance in growth they must be nailed in like wall trees, and have a little pruning to keep them in order. As soon as fruit appears nip out the point of the shoot bearing the fruit, and so continue, taking care not to check the growth too much or the vigour of the plants will be injuriously reduced. If it is inconvenient to nail in the growth, a trellis may be provided by attaching to the wall a sufficient breadth of cheap wire netting, to which the shoots may be loosely tied, for as the shoots swell rapidly, they will soon be cut if tied close, but the ties must have some strength, because of the weight of the fruit they will very soon have to bear.

If any plants are left over from the planting, it will be advisable to fruit a few in pots. Put them into ten-inch pots at once, using a strong soil, with a handful of smallish pieces of brick intermixed. Pot firm, keep in the house in the fullest light possible, and encourage growth, but take care to let them have plenty of air, or they will be injuriously drawn. As soon as requisite put a strong stake to each and tie in the leader, which stop at about eighteen inches. From the middle of June put them out of doors on a hot pavement or on a border, choosing for them, in any case, a position fully exposed to the sun, and where it will be convenient to water them regularly. In case of bad weather, as not unseldom occurs even in the very midst of the summer, take them into a house for a time and bring them out again when the weather has mended. These pot plants will not occasion much trouble, and a very moderate amount of attention will ensure a fine crop of fruit. The advantage of pot culture is the certainty of the result, for in a bad season, when tomatoes in borders are a failure, the pot plants will save the credit of the garden by providing the house with ripe tomatoes. If the season is unkind throughout, they should be grown under glass from first to last.

Towards the end of the season the plants will cease to bear, and the later fruits will not ripen out of doors. Those of them that are fully grown may be ripened by cutting them with a length of stem attached and hanging them up in a sunny greenhouse, and the smaller green fruits may be appropriated, while plump and good, for pickling.

THE WINTER SUPPLY can only be secured by skilful management and suitable conveniences. Tomatoes are supplied to Covent Garden Market all the winter through, but from the end of February to the middle of April they are decidedly scarce, and it is not unusual for the supply to cease utterly in the month of March. To obtain a winter crop it is advisable to sow the seed from the middle of June to the middle of July, and there should certainly be two sowings. They must be grown in pots out of doors from the first, and shifted on as they require more room, until they are in nine-inch or ten-inch pots, beyond which it will not be safe to go. A rich loamy soil must be employed, and the pots must be drained with extra care. The pots must not be plunged, but rather be exposed to the sun, as the plant can bear roasting with advantage if taken care of in respect of watering. Do not stop until fruit appears, and then nip out the points of the fruit-bearing branches. Keep them securely staked, and move them occasionally, to prevent the roots finding their way into the bed or border they stand on. House them in September in a structure that will afford them plenty of light and a

TOMATO TRAINED TO HOOPS.

temperature of 60° to 75°. Keep them cool at first by ventilating freely, but be careful not to carry the cool treatment too far, and indeed, they must have the help of fire heat from the time they are taken in, to render more safe the necessary ventilation. An occasional syringing on a fine morning will do them good, and when they are bearing freely they should be assisted with weak liquid manure.

THE SPRING CROP is best secured by striking cuttings in December and January. These should be shifted on until they fill eight-inch pots, which is the utmost space to be allowed them. There must be no stopping, they must have all the light possible, and as regards temperature, should have the same range as advised for the winter crop.

SELECTION OF VARIETIES.—As remarked above, the *Common Red* will answer every purpose if appearance is of quite secondary importance. It will be observed that the first flowers that appear on the tomato plant are usually, in the common red variety, fasciated, that is, two or three flowers are amalgamated, and the appearance is that of a "double" flower. These fasciated flowers produce fasciated fruits, which are characterised by deep furrows and dark broad rough seams, which mark them into distinct divisions, and produce a very ugly appearance at the crown. If the double flowers are pinched out, and the plant is allowed to swell off only a moderate crop of fruits from single flowers, the Common Red will produce fruit scarcely less handsome than the named varieties; but when left to itself, the earliest and largest fruits are generally ugly ones. The most distinct of the named sorts are *Hepper's Goliath*, and *Trophy*, which are especially valuable for exhibition; for general usefulness, combining beauty and productiveness, *Earley's Defiance* is first-rate. The *Orangefield* and *Powell's Early* are good. The *Upright* and the *Common Yellow* are scarcely worth growing. Amongst the fanciful varieties that may be safely commended, a first place must be given to *Carter's Green Gage*, a smallish spherical fruit of a greenish-yellow colour, remotely resembling a green gage plum. The *Pear-shaped*, *Cherry-shaped*, and *Red* and *Yellow Currant* are interesting as pot plants, or for adorning a rough trellis; but where a few useful tomatoes only are wanted, it is sheer waste of time to sow seed of any of these small-fruited varieties. On the other hand, the amateur who has any fancy for growing a collection of tomatoes may take this comfort for his encouragement, that every one of them, from the largest to the smallest, may be turned to account for the manufacture of tomato sauce, and heaven forefend that any of us worthy people should ever lack of that delectable compound.

A word on the cooking of tomatoes may not be out of place here. The simplest way is to put them into a hot oven for about ten minutes, and then serve them without any more preparation. They should swim in their own gravy, and have no flavouring or improving whatever. With a dish of chops or cutlets, or with any roast meat, but more especially with mutton, tomatoes hastily cooked, without any addition whatever, are invaluable, and the refined palate will declare the Love Apple to be a tremendous competitor of Homer's Lotus. To prepare tomato sauce is an easy matter. Boil the fruit with a very little water. Rub through a tammy cloth: to every quart of pulp add half-an-ounce of garlic and one ounce of shallots, and salt to taste. Boil again for half-an-hour, then strain, and add to every quart of clear sauce a quarter-of-a-pint of vinegar, and bottle and seal down. It may be useful to add that tomato sauce should be of good colour and thick, and savoury. It is best to put it into small bottles, because after a bottle is opened the sauce will not keep long.

THE CAPSICUM that produces the Guinea pepper of commerce is *Capsicum annuam*, a pretty plant, but much surpassed in beauty by the Cherry pepper, *Capsicum cerasiforme*, and the Bell pepper, *Capsicum grossum*. All the varieties are easily grown as pot plants, and in a good season ripen their fruits perfectly, if properly managed, in the open ground. The middle of March is early enough for sowing the seed, and a good return may be ensured by sowing as late as the end of April. Sow in shallow pans, in light soil, and place the pans in a stove or on a hotbed. Those to be grown in pots should be potted singly in thumbs as soon as they show their rough leaves, and kept in a warm place, such as the sunny end of the greenhouse, or the cool end of the stove, to promote free growth. They should be in the full light, and have air during genial weather, so as to be kept sturdy and strong from the first. Any light rich soil will serve for them; such as fuchsias require will answer perfectly. From thumbs they should be shifted to sixty size, thence to forty-eight size,

YELLOW CAPSICUM, PRINCE OF WALES.

and thence to eight-inch, in which they may remain for fruiting, for they do not usually require any larger size. They make fine conservatory plants, and in all their later stages may be grown in a sunny greenhouse or frame without the aid of artificial heat, and should have air night and day during hot summer weather.

Border Culture of small pepper is of a simple nature. Sow in pans in April if there is the convenience of a hotbed or stove, but if not sow in a frame the first week of May, and as soon as the plants begin to crowd one another, prick them out to four inches apart in the same or another frame, or if more convenient, thin them as they stand, and pot the thinnings. The border should be next a fence or wall facing south, and should be raised somewhat above the level of the adjoining walk. A rather poor sandy soil is to be preferred to one of great depth and richness. The plants may be put out at the end of May a foot to a foot and a-half apart, and if the weather is cold, they must be protected with hand glasses or frame lights, and have a little extra care until they begin to grow vigorously, after which they may be fully exposed, and all they will require will be regular watering.

Selection of Varieties.—For ornamental purposes, the following are the best: *Cherry Red*, *Long Red*, *Yellow*, *Green*, and *Carter's Prince of Wales*. For salads, the best is *Sweet Spanish*.

The Egg Plant, *Solanum ovigerum*, is an annual of somewhat coarse growth, producing flowers resembling those of the potato, which are followed by fruits of various shapes and colours, all of which are edible and wholesome. The variety which produces white fruit is the best known, and is the one generally cultivated for ornamental purposes, its fruits bearing a close resemblance to fowls' eggs. This, however, is the least valuable as an esculent, and therefore when egg plants are grown for the table, the common white variety is not worthy of attention. They are strictly greenhouse plants, requiring the same cultivation as balsams or capsicums. Ours are grown in a house devoted to summer cucumbers, which do not shade the egg plants over-much, and these last occupy vacant places on the beds in which the cucumbers are planted, saucers being placed bottom upwards for the egg plants to stand upon to prevent them rooting through into the borders that are occupied with the roots of the cucumbers. The seed is sown in pots or pans in March or April, and has the advantage of a mild hotbed to start it into growth. As soon as the plants are large enough, they are potted singly in thumb pots, the soil being light and rich, as for fuchsias or balsams. They are kept rather close and warm until they have made a fresh start, and thenceforward they require very little care indeed, for the same amount of warmth and air and atmospheric moisture that suit the cucumbers suit them also perfectly. They are shifted on as fast as they fill their pots with roots, until they occupy eight or ten-inch pots, after which they are allowed to become pot-bound, and they soon flower and fruit freely. The culture may begin in February for an early supply of fruit, but the young plants will require a good hotbed or a snug corner in the stove to keep them going until the season is sufficiently advanced to enable them to take their places without harm in the greenhouse. Regular supplies of water they must have, of course, and as they begin to show fruit, it will be necessary to increase the supplies, and to aid them further with weak manure water. Every plant must be tied to a neat stake in good time, but usually they will not want support until they are in their fruiting pots. Let them swell all the fruit they show, and if by this time the weather is unusually hot, they may be put out in the sun in a spot sheltered from the wind, and they will enjoy the change. We have, however, always obtained handsome plants and fine crops of fruit without removing them from the cucumber house. In a very hot season, egg plants fruit freely in an open border, but, as a rule, it is waste of time to plant them out.

SELECTION OF VARIETIES.—The *Common White*, as remarked above, is the handsomest, and therefore the best for ornamental purposes. It is too tough and fibrous to be of any use for the table, and therefore should not be grown as an esculent. The *Giant Purple* produces immense globular or elliptical fruits of a beautiful violet or blackish-purple colour. This is a good table fruit. The *Green Thibet* is the largest of all, the colour dull green with occasional patches and streaks of purple. It is a mass of delicate pulp, with very few seeds, and most delicious when nicely cooked. The *Black* is a large fruit of a very dull, deep purple colour. It is handsome and curious, but of less value for the table than the green. The *Scarlet* fruited is a very tall-growing plant, flowering and fruiting later than the rest, and requiring more heat than suffices to bring them to perfection. It is not worth growing unless it can have stove heat.

When egg plants are regarded as subjects for the art of the cook, they are called *Aubergines.* Under that head in all cookery books will be found directions for dressing them. We have had them served in all possible ways, and the one we prefer is our own—it is the simplest too, and that we think is a recommendation. Two or three large green or purple fruit are sliced up as thin as lemon peel, the seeds being carefully removed. They are fried of a fine brown in fresh butter, and served hot with a cut lemon and cayenne pepper. There is nothing finer to accompany a sweetbread or a cutlet.

CHAPTER XXVI.

HORSERADISH.

That same cowardly, giant-like ox-beef hath devoured many a gentleman of your house: I promise you your kindred hath made my eyes water ere now. I desire your more acquaintance."

Midsummer Night's Dream, III., 1.

BULLY BOTTOM does not so address the pungent root that forms the subject of this chapter, but a very near relation thereof. However, the phrases fit the case so well that there should be no apology needed for the present borrowing of honours intended for Master Mustard Seed. It does not appear that Shakspeare brought the real flavour of horseradish into any of his quips, or images, or allusions, although indeed, the ineffable Jack Falstaff likens Justice Shallow to "a forked radish, with a head fantastically carved upon it with a knife," and there could be no radish so suitable for a grim presentment of "a man made after supper of a cheese paring," "the very genius of famine," and known to the ungodly as a "mandrake." Let it pass, though like ginger, it be "hot i' the mouth."

THE HORSERADISH, *Cochlearia Armoracea*, is usually classed with the salads, and it may also be classed with the tap roots. But it is so distinct in habit and uses, that we prefer not to class it at all—it is sufficiently important to have a chapter to itself. It is a well-doing hardy plant that will pay its rent and something over on any good soil without any cultivation whatever. It loves a deep strong loam and to be near water, and when once it has got firm hold of a piece of ground, it is as difficult a task to get rid of it as to draw a young lion's teeth. Nevertheless this thrifty earth-biter answers promptly and generously to good cultivation, and wherever there is a convenient market it is one of the most profitable roots that can be grown.

As it requires two years to grow handsome roots of horseradish, and as when once planted it is likely to remain as a permanent occupant, an odd corner, remote from the rotation cropping, should be assigned it. For thirty years we have had a plantation—left as a legacy from a former holder—and from this we annually dig a sufficient supply, which is stored for use, and thus we obtain an abundance of stout straight roots, with the least trouble imaginable. The plump crowns tell where the good roots are, and the small crowns are never touched. Every autumn we spread over the piece a coat of half-rotten dung, or sprinkling of guano, and thus it is maintained in its power of production. Should we live to see the crop degenerate, we shall trench up the piece and pick out all the roots, and put it under rotation cropping, so as, by frequent use of spade and hoe, to kill out the horseradish entirely. The market culture varies with the nature of the ground and convenience of the cultivator; Knight's method will suit a deep sandy soil. In November trench the ground three feet deep, and leave it rough. In February mark out the ground in four-feet beds, and one-foot alleys; then take from the first bed nine inches of the top soil, and lay it upon the adjoining bed, after which take out an opening at one end of the bed, in the way of trenching, to a depth of fifteen inches. On the bottom of this trench put at nine inches apart the sets, which should consist of plump crowns cut two inches long. Set them with the crowns upright, and cover with earth taken to form the next trench, in which plant sets as in the first. Proceed in this way, making the trenches eighteen inches apart in ground of average strength, but in strong ground they should be two feet apart. The number of the beds and the length of the beds the cultivator must determine for himself, but before doing so, he must consider his requirements, and must not expect to dig until the roots have grown two seasons. There should, however, be twice as much land prepared in the first instance as will be required, and if more than one bed is planted, there should be left a blank bed between, which the first year can be covered with an annual crop, such as small seeds, salads, etc. In any case the bed planted must have nine inches of soil taken from it and laid on the adjoining bed that is to be sown with seeds. A series of beds managed in this way will be high and low alternately, the low beds filled with horseradish, the others with annual crops.

In the following February eighteen inches of the earth

from the unplanted bed or beds must be taken off and spread lightly over the horseradish plantation, and the lowered bed or beds must be treated as the others were in the first instance to form a plantation to succeed the first.

In the autumn following the first plantation will be in condition to be lifted. Trench out the roots with care, and you will have a grand crop, such as no haphazard routine will produce, either in respect of beauty, or quality, or bulk.

Poor land may be made productive of good horseradish by trenching two feet deep and putting a good body of fat stable manure at the bottom of the trench. To plant land so prepared make holes eighteen inches apart and fifteen inches deep. Into each of these drop a crown or small root cutting taken from close under the crown, and fill up the holes with sand or coal ashes.

Where the conveniences offer the temptation, very fine horseradish may be grown on raised beds, and the crop may be cleared away without leaving a particle of the roots on the spot as a plague for ever. When clearing out ditches and cutting down woodland walks, and in other ways making a lot of loamy stuff mixed with weeds and waifs that you know not what to do with, have it laid up as it comes to the rubbish yard, in banks four feet wide at the base, and three feet high, the top being nicely rounded. Into the sides and crown of this bed insert at eighteen inches apart each way—putting down the line lengthways of the bed for every row—sets formed of "thongs" or pieces of small side roots cut to lengths of six to nine inches. Let this ridge stand for three years and then clear it out. The crop will pay for the making, and something considerable to boot, if only prudently marketed. In places where alterations and improvements are in progress, this is a good way to economise heaps of rubbish.

The Uses of Horseradish are pretty well known, but probably to many readers of this book a few words on the subject may prove useful. It should first be remarked that the dug roots suffer by exposure to the air in some degree, and therefore they should never be left carelessly about for any length of time, but be buried in earth, from which they may be removed as required. The large imported horseradish is many degrees inferior to freshly-dug roots from the garden, but being large, they answer very well for hotels and restaurants, and wherever else large quantities are required and must be prepared in haste.

Few people know the proper flavour of horseradish, for the very important reason that it is the most evanescent thing of its kind we have to do with in the management of the table. Let any one taste a few shreds of the root as they are freshly scraped, and then, having put a few aside, taste them in the course of an hour or so. In the first instance the taste will be intensely pungent, harmonised by an agreeable sweetness. In the second instance you have a dry chip scarcely at all pungent, destitute of sweetness, and the properties that balanced it have gone away. To enjoy beef with horseradish, one condition requisite is that the vegetable should be fresh, and it is not at all unusual for the root to be scraped an hour or so before it is wanted, the consequence being that it is neither so white nor so fragrant, nor so brightly agreeable to the palate as it would be if served quite fresh. It must be admitted there is a little difficulty in putting horseradish on the table. It should look like foam, and emit a delicious fragrance. It is the case in many kitchens that various small jobs must be got rid of in good time, and so it happens that horseradish is scraped too soon and is put in some warm place to spoil as fast as it can. The way out of this difficulty is very simple. At a convenient time the horseradish may be made ready, and should be at once put into a small basin or tureen, or any other vessel in which it can be covered closely, and so be preserved from the action of the air. A basin with a saucer on it will generally answer the purpose. Put it in the coolest place you can find, and there leave it until the last moment. Then shake it up with a fork, and serve it as required, and you will find it scarcely less fragrant and full-flavoured then when first prepared, and the compromise between time and quality is effected.

Horseradish Sauce.—The best way to prepare this is to roughly cut up some fresh roots and put them into spirits of wine, and keep tightly corked. When the sauce is required, have ready some rich melted butter made with milk, or any of the approved forms of white sauce, and add a few drops of the tincture until the desired flavour is obtained. The bottle must always be kept closely corked, for both the spirit and the flavour are exceedingly volatile. This same tincture or essence may be mixed with fresh mustard and a little red pepper to produce a piquant sauce for a devilled chicken, or to accompany a broiled steak. If not mixed until wanted, it will be appreciated no less for its refreshing fragrance than its fiery flavour.

Another mode of preparing a sauce is as follows: Grate on a clean grater till you have sufficient, then put it in a sauce tureen with a little salt, mustard, vinegar, and a very little pounded loaf sugar (this last must be added very cautiously, or it will spoil all). Mix the ingredients well together, and add enough thick cream to make the mixture of the consistence of sauce, stir gently once or twice and your sauce is ready, and should be sent to the table as soon as possible.

HORSERADISH VINEGAR is often useful, and is easily prepared. Add to a quart of vinegar four ounces of freshly-scraped horseradish, an ounce of minced shallots, one clove of garlic, and as much red pepper as will impart a slight warmth, special care being taken not to use too much. Let it stand for a week closely corked down. Then strain it through a cloth and bottle it for use.

HORSERADISH SALAD is obtained from the crowns when grown in a warm place in the dark. It should be as white as snow, and quite tender, with a pleasant sweetish pungency. A little of it mixed with a salad improves it greatly for such as prefer warmth in a salad, and it is good enough to eat alone at times. But if it is at all green or tough it is not to be desired; hence the necessity of growing it quickly and in the dark.

SCURVY GRASS, *Cochlearia officinalis*, is a near relative of the horseradish, and like it, pungent and antiscorbutent. Though in old times of great renown as a stimulant to digestion, and a remedy for scurvy, it is now but little thought of, improved habits of living having rendered such correctives unnecessary. The natural habitat of this plant is the salt marsh and muddy estuary, and therefore, in cultivating it, a damp situation should be chosen. The plant produces root leaves which are large, heart shaped, and hollowed like a spoon; hence it was formerly known under the name *Spoonwort*. It is grown from seeds, which are sown as soon as ripe, in June or July, and are afterwards thinned to eight inches apart. In the following Spring the leaves may be gathered. A few plants should be left untouched every year to supply seed.

CHAPTER XXVII.

FORCING.

> "A cause on foot,
> Lives so in hope, as in an early spring
> We see the appearing buds; which to prove fruit,
> Hope gives not so much warrant, as despair,
> That frosts will bite them. When we mean to build,
> We first survey the plot, then draw the model;
> And when we see the figure of the house,
> Then must we rate the cost of the erection:
> Which if we find outweighs ability,
> What do we then, but draw anew the model
> In fewer offices; or, at least, desist."
>
> *2 Henry IV., I. 3.*

THE proper treatment of various vegetables for ensuring supplies in advance of the natural season has obtained attention incidentally as appeared necessary in the preparation of the foregoing chapters. It is necessary, however, that a brief chapter should be devoted to the subject of forcing in general, for the means at our command for expediting the growth of plants contribute in a very marked degree to the increase of our comfort and in not a few instances constitute the most important, because most profitable business of the garden.

Two considerations confront us at starting. Glass houses and fuel are costly, and all the preliminary arrangements should be ordered with a view to the accomplishment of a maximum of work with a minimum of expenditure. An amateur may easily err in the adoption of contrivances that are expensive in the first instance, and a perpetual burden of expense to keep them in repair and usefully occupied. The very first care should be to do the best with the roughest means, say a good brick pit, and a bed of leaves to produce a gentle heat costing nothing and resulting finally in production of clean leaf mould for the potting shed. The management of fermenting materials is a matter of the utmost importance, not only because, as a rule, they produce a certain degree of heat at little cost, but because generally speaking better work may be done with their aid than with hot-water pipes. The last-named are however the surest, cleanest, safest of heat diffusers, and so far economical that market growers, who must make things pay, trust much more to hot water than to fermentation in all their more important winter work in the production of vegetables and flowers. The reader interested in this subject may be advised to turn to the chapters on frames and hot-beds, for the proper use of these is the first thing to be learned in the practice of forcing. The next phase of the business is that of the forcing-house proper, on which it now becomes our duty to speak in detail.

A FORCING-HOUSE adapted for supplying early vegetables and flowers may with advantage be constructed in a span roofed form, and should be snug and compact, with no more headroom than is absolutely necessary for the work. The most useful and inexpensive structure for forcing small things, such as flowering plants, kidney beans, asparagus, and strawberries, is a span roof house seven feet high from the path to the apex, and from ten to twelve feet wide, inside measurement. The outer wall of a house of these dimensions, whether entirely above or partly below the surface, should be three feet high and support side lights eighteen inches high, upon which the lower ends of the rafters must rest. Side lights of a greater height are not desirable, because the difficulty of maintaining an equable temperature is increased in proportion to the increase in the surface of glass. To maintain a temperature moderately uniform is of so much importance that some cultivators prefer houses without side-lights, but the additional light which finds its way into the house is of so much importance to the occupants during the short days that they are decidedly advantageous. It is not needful that they should be moveable, but as the houses can be turned to account in the cultivation of many things during the summer season, which are all the better for a free circulation of air amongst them, the little additional cost in fixing the lights so that they can be opened and shut at pleasure is not worth considering. The roof can be fixed, or be formed with rafters and moveable sashes, but in either case the arrangements must be such as will allow of air being admitted, as required, near the apex. The walk must of necessity be down the centre of the house, and the width should be full three feet. On each side of the walk beds must be formed by the erection of walls three feet in height and four and a half inches in thickness.

In districts where a plentiful supply of leaves or other fermenting materials can be obtained, hot-water pipes underneath the beds may be dispensed with, but where there is a likelihood of any difficulty in obtaining the fermenting materials, the plunge beds should have the pipes fixed underneath to maintain a sufficiency of bottom heat. In the arrangement of the heating apparatus a flow and return pipe should be fixed on each side close to the outer walls, and just above the level of the bed if there are no side lights; and in houses provided with these the top pipe should be on a level with the wall plate. In addition to these a double row of piping on one side of the walk will be required. For houses not exceeding ten feet wide three-inch pipes will be large enough, but for those of greater width, say twelve feet, four-inch pipes would be preferable. For bottom heat two rows of three-inch pipes underneath each bed will be requisite,—the flow and return to be nearly level, the flow being rather the highest, and to be fixed nine inches to the right and left of an imaginary line down the middle of the bed, and about four or five inches above the bottom. A platform nine inches or so above the top of the pipes will be required for the support of the fermenting materials, and this may be formed with slabs of stone or slate, sheets of galvanized iron or boards. If boards are used they must be placed an inch or so apart, to allow the heat from the pipes to pass readily through to the bed.

The Plunge Bed.—Leaves gathered in a moderately dry condition form the most useful of all the fermenting materials for forcing; they give off a moderate degree of warmth, and retain their heat for a considerable length of time; consequently, there is no risk of the roots being burnt with an excess of heat, as is the case when stable manure is employed, neither does the necessity arise for frequently replenishing the beds for the maintenance of a proper degree of warmth. Tan is also suitable for the formation of plunge beds; it heats steadily and retains its warmth for a very considerable period. Indeed, a tan bed may be kept in working condition for an indefinite period without the necessity arising for its being entirely remade. When the heat has declined below a certain point, by removing the plants from the bed, turning them over, and adding a little fresh tan, the heat can soon be brought up to the proper pitch again. It will be needful to remove at intervals the decayed portion of the tan, because if allowed to remain it will prevent the bed heating satisfactorily, and afford accommodation for worms, which, as a matter of course, will soon find their way to the interior of the pots. To remove this powdery stuff, the result of decay, is the most simple matter possible, as you have only to sift the tan and to throw on one side that which will not pass through the sieve, and to remove the other entirely from the house. In remaking beds which have been sifted put in the bottom of the bed as much new tan as will, with the remaining portion of the old material, bring up the beds to the proper level again, and then spread the old tan over it. By this arrangement the heat will be sufficient for promoting a healthy root action.

With hot-water pipes underneath the bed, the material immediately over the platform will in a comparatively short time become as dry as dust, and when this occurs the bed must be turned over and the dry stuff intermixed with the bulk of material, or the heat will not pass through, and in consequence the pipes will become of but little service. This remark holds good with reference to all the fermenting materials, but it is especially applicable to tan.

In alluding to the beds, reference has hitherto been made to fermenting materials only, and before proceeding further, it is desirable to explain that when hot-water pipes are provided, fermenting materials may be dispensed with altogether. If they can be obtained without an extravagant outlay, they should be employed. But if the materials have to be purchased at a considerable outlay, the cultivator should rely entirely upon the heat from the pipes. Something must be provided in which to plunge the pots, and for this purpose either sand or cocoa-nut fibre refuse can be employed. As a great depth of either of these is not required, the platforms should not be placed so close to the pipes as advised above; a depth ranging from fifteen to eighteen inches will perhaps be the most suitable, and as the warmth will be derived entirely from the pipes, special care must be taken to prevent the bottom layer of the material remaining in a dry state for any length of time.

All the plants suitable for forcing will derive immense assistance from a genial bottom heat, and the pots should be partly or wholly plunged in the hot bed. Some amount of judgment must at all times be exercised in plunging the pots, because on the one hand there is a risk of the roots being injured by an excess of heat, and on the other of their not receiving the full benefit. If the temperature of the bed does not exceed 70 degs. and is not likely to go any higher when the plants are brought into the house, the pots can be at once plunged to within an inch or so of the rim without the least danger of the roots being injured. But should the temperature be in excess of 70 the pots must be partly plunged or be stood on the surface of the bed, according to the extent of the excess, and whether the heat is on the increase or decline.

TEMPERATURE AND HUMIDITY.—The temperature of the house, technically termed top-heat, must vary somewhat according to the state of the weather outside and the character of the principal portion of the plants with which the house is filled. Speaking in a general way, it should range between 60 degs. and 70 degs.; but if the weather happens to be very severe, it may fall to 55 degs. without injury to the plants. In many instances, especially when a considerable number of plants have just been brought into the house, it will be desirable to allow a little fall. This, however, is a matter which must to a certain extent be left to the discretion of the cultivator.

A moderate degree of humidity in the atmosphere is of no less importance than a genial temperature and a brisk bottom heat. This can be produced by occasionally pouring water upon the floor, sprinkling the walls, hot-water pipes, and surface of the bed, and by syringing the plants. The temperature of the water poured upon the floor or sprinkled on the walls on each side of the pathway is of no consequence whatever, but that with which the surface of the bed is sprinkled and the plants syringed must be of the same temperature as the house, or a few degrees higher. Tepid water must also be used for watering, as a chill to the roots, such as would be caused by the application of cold water, is injurious. The ventilation of the forcing house must receive careful attention, for although the plants will not require much air, the ventilators must be opened a little way, whenever the weather is favourable, to maintain the atmosphere in a thoroughly sweet condition.

A Forcing Pit adapted for a small garden may be constructed and kept at work with but little outlay considering the returns it should make, for in the summer and autumn a few nice pines might be grown in it, and by potting a few suckers from time to time, they would be kept for succession without in any way interrupting the winter work in forcing French beans, asparagus, potatoes, &c. The subjoined figures represent a pit that has for some years been usefully employed in this way :—

The wood plates that rest upon the walls, as also the rafters, are "red wood deal," three inches by four inches, with a spline upon them to separate the lights exactly as in ordinary pits and frames where the lights slide up and down. The lights used are also the ordinary kind, only having handles with which to slide them up and down with, fixed at the lower instead of the upper end. These lights are about seven feet long; the rest of the roof is covered with a fixed light, under which the moveable lights slide freely for the purpose of giving air, or of carrying on necessary operations in the front part of the pit. The pit is sunk below the ground line, the better to admit of its being covered up on cold nights—a matter of considerable importance, as by so doing, we not only save a considerable amount of fuel, but also, by arresting evaporation and radiation from the glass, preserve a suitable degree of moisture in the atmosphere.

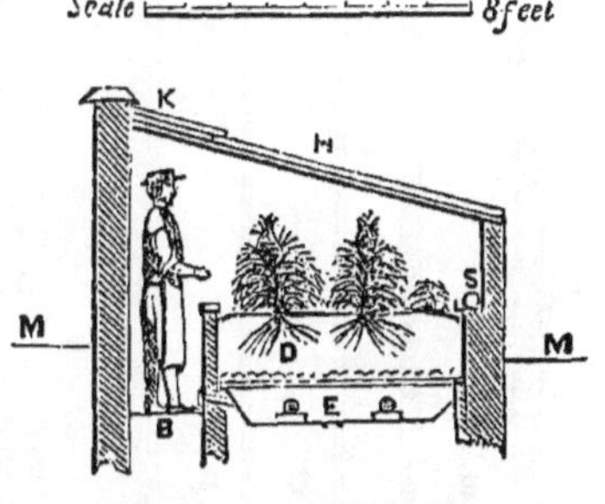

SECTION OF FORCING PIT.

For heating so small a house, a very small boiler would be sufficient, unless other pits or houses are attached to it, or

A, stokery, five feet deep ; B, back path, two feet wide ; C, chimney, but if the flue could be carried into some other it would be better ; D, bed of soil for plants to be planted in, six feet wide ; E, chamber in which two-inch flow and return pipes are fixed for bottom-heat ; F, flow, which is also two-inch pipe as far as S, where the stop valve is fixed ; G, this pit may be attached to any apparatus already at work, if it be sufficiently powerful. Generally speaking, one large apparatus is much easier managed and more economical than a number of small ones. If, however, a small one only is wanted, a comparatively large furnace should be made, and a furnace door large enough to admit a good sized shovel, for nothing can be more trying to the temper of a stoker than the baby furnaces fixed by some country tradesmen.

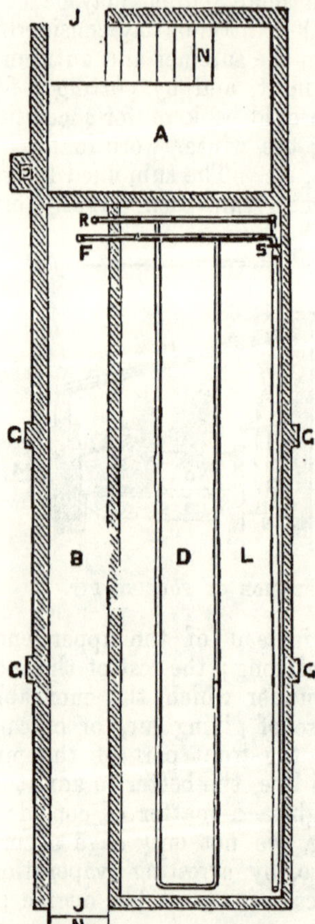

GROUND PLAN OF FORCING PIT.

On referring to the plan, it will be seen that a flow and return two-inch pipes are shown in a chamber under the bed in which the plants grow; this space being separated from the bed of soil above by a loose flooring of oak slabs or rough boards. These two small pipes for bottom heat, will be found to give sufficient warmth to the soil without excess, except it should be in very severe weather, when a good deal of fire heat is used in order to maintain the atmospheric heat; then, at such times, the excess can be let into the house by opening the drain-pipes, laid through the wall for that purpose, whilst in summer, when but little atmospheric heat is wanted from the pipes, bottom-heat may be given, independent of the large pipes, by turning a stop valve at S.

piers; H, sliding lights, seven feet long; these slide under the fixed lights, K, so as to admit of any necessary operations in front part of house being done from without, as well as for air. J, door; T, flow and return four-inch pipes, with vapour troughs; M, ground line; N, steps; R, return pipe.

The two four-inch pipes should have vapour troughs upon them; otherwise, it will be difficult to maintain sufficient moisture in the air for the well-being of the plants.

A Combined Vinery and Mushroom House is represented in the figures that follow, the former being specially adapted for the amateur who would enjoy an occasional hour's work in

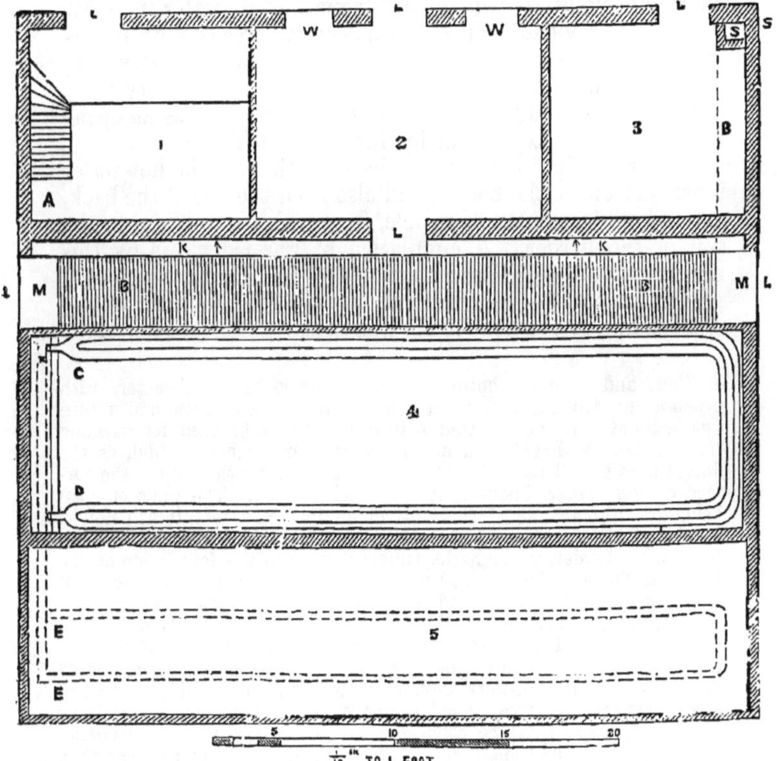

GROUND PLAN OF EARLY FORCING VINERY.

the forcing of grapes, mushrooms, asparagus, and sea-kale. It will be observed that in this scheme the vines are planted inside the house. The principal part of the border is also in

A. Hot-water boiler. B. The smoke-flue carried along under the floor, and covered over with three-feet-wide iron-grating to form the walk.

the house, and that which is not so, is covered by shutters, or lights; if the latter, all the better, as the gardener would find the space inclosed above the border useful for a hundred purposes, without interfering with the vine roots, such as wintering salads, hardening off plants, etc.

The border is placed upon a thick layer of open stones, burrs, or bricks, by which all stagnation of water is most effectively provided against; drain-pipes, three or four inches in diameter are also laid across the border under every arch formed in the front wall, and consequently under every vine, as these arches must be set out so that each vine has an opening for its roots to pass out by, into the outside border.

The drain-pipes will convey the warmth from the hot-water pipes laid under the border, and also from the flue at the back, throughout the mass of rubble, from which it will rise to the soil of the border. A circulation of warmed air is by this arrangement secured to the interior of the house, which will greatly benefit the inmates, and often in cold weather render the opening of the ventilators unnecessary. Should too much

C. Flow, and D return hot-water pipes, four inches in diameter, with evaporating troughs cast upon some of them. E E. Flow and return two-inch hot-water pipes, fitted with stop-valve, to be used for warming the border. F. Front wall of vinery built on arches as high as the dotted lines go. This wall must be fourteen inches thick up to the surface of the border, above that nine inches thick. The walls on plan being drawn to a scale of one-tenth of an inch to a foot, it will not be necessary further to specify them. G. Pipe drain which passes down the front of the border, through the rubble that forms the foundation of the border to flue B, to be open at both ends, which will cause a circulation of warm air under the border, and one of these drains should be laid under each arch. H. Shelf for strawberries, etc. I. Ventilators, twelve inches deep at front and eighteen inches deep at back of house; as many of these ventilators as can be got in should be used, indeed, there should only be sufficient brick-work between them, for them to slide over when open, thus opening exactly one-half of the length of the house, both back and front; they should be connected the whole length by means of an iron rod, and should slide in grooves upon metal bearings; they can then be opened or shut by a cord passing over a pulley, where they are *not within reach*, or by a simple handle or knob, *where they are so.* J. Roller, and blind of canvas; in early forcing this will be necessary, both for protection by night, and occasionally for shade by day, especially when the vines are resting in July and August. K. Border, eighteen inches wide, for fig-trees. L. Doors. M. Flag stones against doors. N. Shutters over outside border. P. Water drain laid along the front of border. S. Chimney. W. Windows. 1. Stokery. 2. Potting-shed. 3. Mushroom-house. 4. Inside border for vines. 5. Outside border.

air be admitted by this means, a plug could be made to drop into the end of some of them, at the end terminating in the outside border, marked A on the plan.

The borders being all covered, and the means of warming them provided, the roots of the vines could be got into a state of activity before the house is finally closed. As these borders would entirely depend upon the gardener for their supply of moisture, it must be given with no niggardly hand, as the vine, when in growth and carrying a crop of fruit, requires plenty, which should not be given quite cold ; it should also occasionally contain a good dash of the drainage from the stable or cow-house, to keep up the fertility of the soil.

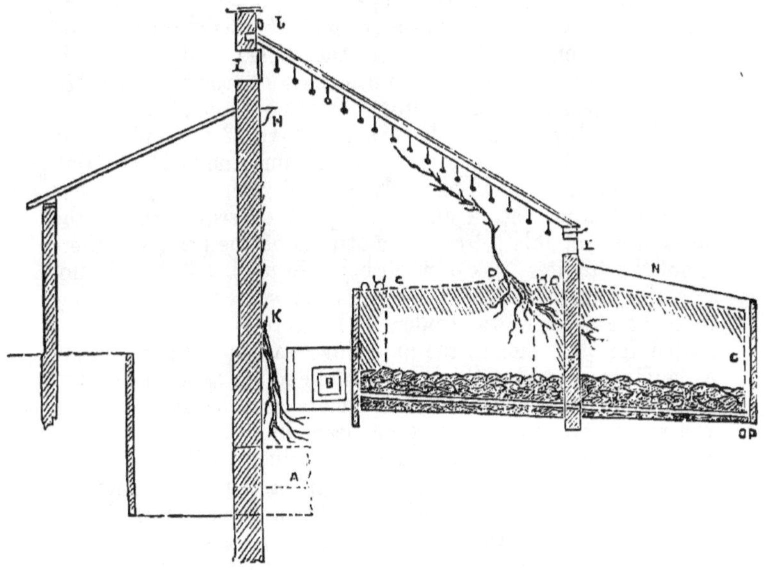

SECTION OF EARLY FORCING VINERY.

The subjects usually brought into the forcing-house are kidney-beans, potatoes, and strawberries. On each of these a few remarks will in this place be appropriate. In respect of sea-kale, asparagus, and other subjects that are forced in pits and frames or in the beds they permanently occupy, information will be found in the chapters which treat of their cultivation generally.

FORCING FRENCH BEANS.—In the production of a supply of French beans during the winter and spring months, a structure in which a temperature ranging from 65 deg. to 75 deg. can be maintained without difficulty is of primary importance, for they cannot be cultivated with any degree of success without a liberal degree of warmth. The form of structure in which they are grown is of no consequence whatever, provided the plants can enjoy a sufficiency of warmth and full exposure to the light. Heat and light they must have, and if they are well provided for in these respects, and the watering pot and the syringe are employed judiciously, and with rather a liberal hand, there will not be much difficulty in obtaining excellent crops.

A small lean-to or span-roof house which during the summer season is devoted to cucumbers and melons, is admirably adapted to the requirements of the winter crops of French beans, but good crops may be obtained from plants placed in the pinery. The atmosphere of the pine stove is rather too dry for them, and by the time the last gathering is made the foliage will be badly infested with red spider, but this is not a matter of any very great consequence, for the pines are well able to resist the attacks of the pest, and there is not the slightest risk of their being injured. But it is not so with grape-vines, for they are most susceptible to injury from the attacks of red spider. Therefore, if the space can be spared for the beans in the pine stove—as, for example, upon a shelf near the glass—take advantage of the spare room; but no matter how much space in a vinery may be at command, you must never attempt to grow beans in it, for when the red spider makes its appearance upon the foliage of the beans, it is practically impossible to prevent its spreading to the vines.

The selection of a suitable variety for forcing is a rather nice point, because the very finest of the sorts differ much in productiveness when grown under glass. The neat dwarf variety known as *Sir Joseph Paxton* is the very best for forcing. *Newington Wonder* is also good.

When a supply is required for as long a period as possible, make the first sowing about the middle of August, and the second about the middle of September. Sow in eight-inch pots seven beans in each, and stand the pots on a hard surface out of doors. It is a very good plan to stand them in a line by the side of a broad walk in the kitchen garden, for they can be watered and receive other needful attention without any difficulty, and they will, at the same time, enjoy full exposure to the light and air on all sides. The worms can be readily kept out of the pots by placing them upon a plank laid down, or upon bricks, or saucers turned bottom upwards. Some time towards the end of September both batches must be removed to the house or pit in which they are to be grown, and receive the assistance of a temperature of about 70 deg. by day and 65 deg. by night. If the weather sets in cold early in September, the first batch should be taken indoors and the second sowing be made in the house. The house must be ventilated freely at first, so that the change shall be felt as little as possible. But after they have been indoors for a fortnight, the admittance of air must be considerably lessened, and the ventilation, in a large measure, be regulated by the weather. The last week in December will, as a rule, be quite soon enough to make the third sowing to succeed the September batch. Beans sown in November or early in December are not, as a rule, of much value, for owing to the deficiency of light the growth is weak, and a very indifferent crop is the result. After the December sowing successive batches should be started every fortnight or three weeks, according to the space at disposal, and the requirements of the household. The number of pots forming each batch must also be regulated in a similar manner, but a batch consisting of less than thirty pots will not be of much service, because of the length of time that will necessarily elapse before it will be practicable to obtain a good dish. It is not, of course, suggested that the table should be supplied with beans every day, but there ought to be enough plants to afford a dish twice a week during the time each batch is in bearing.

The autumn sowings are recommended to be made in the pots in which the plants are to remain; and this may be done in the case of the batches started in the winter. But there are one or two reasons why the practice is not desirable, and chief among them is economy of space. It is preferable to sow in five-inch pots seven seeds in each, and as soon as the first rough leaves are developed, to shift into pots eight inches in diameter. Five plants only are to be allowed to remain in each pot, and two plants must consequently be removed if all the beans come up. This is best done immediately after it can be seen whether any of them have been injured in the repotting. In repotting put them rather low, so as to bury an inch or so of the stems. When sown in the large pots, the pots should be filled to within about two inches of the rim, and when the first rough leaves are developed add an inch and a half of soil, and in doing so exercise sufficient care to avoid bruising the stems, which at that stage are rather tender. A compost consisting of good loam four parts, and leaf-mould and well-decayed manure a part each, can be recommended as in every way suitable for beans.

From the time the pots are moderately well filled with roots until the last gathering, the supply of water to the roots must be liberal, and once a day at least the syringe must be plied vigorously. During periods of bright frosty weather, when it is imperative to keep the fire going briskly, a syringing twice a day, morning and evening, will be most beneficial. As soon as each batch comes into bearing, liquid manure of a moderate degree of strength should, if there is no great difficulty in obtaining a supply, be applied alternately with the clear water, or once or twice a week, as may be most convenient. The liquid manure must, of course, be of the same temperature as the house when used.

Forcing the Potato.—The only satisfactory way of obtaining very early potatoes is to grow them in pots, but successional supplies may very well be obtained by planting out on beds heated with pipes or by means of a fermenting material. In this case, however, it would be found best, in most cases, to start the sets in pots and plant them out when the pots are well filled with roots, because the preparation of the beds would be delayed, and whatever plan tends to the economy of space in the forcing pit, is worthy of special attention. In growing for market, the system of planting out in beds must be followed, but for producing small supplies for a household, the earliest may with advantage be grown in pots from first to last, and for the successional supplies the usual pits and frames will be available. It is not necessary to discourse at length on this subject, but we shall endeavour to be explicit in order that the beginner may enter on the business with the aid of our advice with a fair prospect of success. About the middle of December we shall look out a sufficient number of sets of the earliest sorts, such as *Alpha*, *Veitch's Ashleaf*, *Early Rose*, *Sandringham Kidney*, *Extra Early Vermont*, *King of the Earlies*, *and Early Coldstream*, which are all adapted for forcing. If restricted to two varieties, should prefer *Alpha* and *Veitch's Ashleaf*. The sets selected should be about the size of a bantam's egg, and not at all or very little sprouted. They should be placed in shallow boxes, be lightly sprinkled with water and put on a shelf in a warm house, full in the light, the temperature to be about 50 degs. In the course of a week they should be looked over and every sprout except the best at the nose-end to be rubbed off. They should be again packed in the shallow boxes only one layer deep and with all the nose-ends upwards to encourage the growth of one stout, short sprout to each. They must be regularly sprinkled with water, but only enough to keep them slightly damp to nourish the sprouts and prevent shrivelling.

At the turn of the year they should be potted in 48-size, in light, rich compost, each set to be covered with quite an inch of soil to encourage the roots that come out from the base of the sprout. They should now be put in a temperature of 60 degs. by day and 50 degs. by night. The watering is a delicate business, and you must take care they do not obtain too much, and, as a matter of course, the water should be of the same temperature as the house. If kept near the glass and judiciously ventilated so that they are never punished by cold currents of air passing over them, the haulm will be healthy and short-jointed. If it is not so you must not hope for a handsome dish of potatoes, for everything depends on ensuring a healthy leaf-growth from the very first.

In due time the pots will be full of roots and the plants will be handsome little bushes. They must now be carefully shifted into 8-inch or 10-inch pots, and be put low down in the pots because the tubers will be formed in a cluster above the set. A series of shifts from size to size will never do, as one alone is allowable, and this should be to pots sufficiently large for the crop to finish in, or to beds prepared for the purpose and likely to maintain a sufficient temperature for a sufficient length of time. This shift completed, the heat must be raised to 70 degs. by day and 60 degs. by night, the supply of water be increased and a constant change of air must be secured by very careful ventilation, the air being made to pass over a warm surface before reaching the potatoes. The watering is still a delicate business, and a drop too much will be as harmful as a similar excess in another way. They must stand very close to the glass and precautions must be taken to avert mischief on those occasions when sharp frosts are apt to touch the tops of plants in warm houses, for if you lose your leaf growth you also lose your potatoes. Mats or shutters must be in readiness for emergencies, for as the day lengthens the cold strengthens, and it is not unusual for potatoes in the forcing pit to be seriously damaged by the formation of a coat of ice close over their heads on the glass of their domicile. By uncovering a plant now and then the progress of the tubers can be seen. As they attain towards a proper size for the table reduce the supply of water and increase the heat to 80 degs. by day and 70 degs. by night, and be not afraid if on sunny days the thermometer goes up to 90 degs. or even higher. The fear of heat on the part of the cultivator is the cause of the watery softness that commonly characterises forced potatoes. To render them mealy and nice you must promote the absorption by them of solar light, for potatoes are made of sunshine.

As regards the compost, it may be said that it should contain a little of everything good. It should be light, gritty, moderately rich, and decidedly calcareous. If a prescription be required the following will answer,—three parts turfy loam to one part each of rotten hotbed manure, old mortar broken small, and the charcoal and burnt earth from a garden smother. If such a prescription cannot be followed make such a mixture as would grow fuschias nicely, and add to it a considerable proportion of pounded oyster shells. If you have at command a mellow sandy loam that suits potatoes, use three parts of that to one part of old manure and half a part of small plaster or pounded oyster shells.

In shifting to the fruiting pots special care must be taken to ensure perfect drainage, for any lodgment of water or pastiness of the soil will be fatal to success.

Potatoes potted in the first week of January should be quite ripe by the middle of April, and by carefully removing the largest without disturbing the stool you may begin to send them to table in the early days of March, or even at the end of February. On the 15th of March, 1876, Messrs. Hooper and Co., of Covent Garden, presented to the notice of the Fruit and Vegetable Committee of the Royal Horticultural Society a fine sample of the Alpha potato, the result of a very simple mode of forcing adopted by Mr. Barker, of Littlehampton. The sets were planted on the 13th of

January in large pots, which were placed in a greenhouse facing south, the only protection from frost being a single flow and return pipe. On the 7th of March the crop was lifted. The tubers were of good size, the colour delicate white like wax, with a faint tinge of rose about the eye. When growing in pots they had a very pleasing appearance, owing to the naturally compact growth and beautiful colour of the haulm of this variety.

A good bed of leaves is a great help in the production of early potatoes, because of the mild continuous heat and sweet atmosphere they generate. Put on it six inches of a suitable mixture and plant out from pots when the plants are strong and the days are rapidly lengthening, and thenceforward the most important point in the cultivation is to water them carefully, and always with water of the same temperature as the structure they are growing in.

THE STRAWBERRY is a difficult subject to force, and yet like everything else very easy when you are used to it. When "pushed" on in a high temperature the berries have but little flavour, but slow forcing with plenty of light and air produces a crop equally rich in colour and flavour, and wonders may be done by the aid of *shelter only*, as in a ground vinery, a very freely ventilated frame, or on shelves near the glass in a cool orchard house.

In any case, whether for early forcing or to be fruited late in a cool house, the business begins in the open ground in June. You must fill a lot of 60 sized pots with rich soil pressed in very firm, only one flat crock being put into each pot. Take these pots to your plantation with a lot of pegs cut from old birch brooms and fix in every pot a promising runner. This is a simple business, but it must be well done, for we want the earliest roots obtainable from the little crowns at the ends of the runners. They must be regularly watered and looked after, *constancy* being the quality most required in a forcer of strawberries. In from fourteen to twenty days after pegging down the runners they will be sufficiently rooted to be separated, but you must not separate them until they have made a good root hold, and in this business judgment is required. As soon as possible, however, cut them off and carry them away and pack them close together in a sunny corner and keep well watered for about a week. Then let them become a little dry, and shift into 32 size, without in the least breaking the ball. They should not suffer the least check in this operation, and the object of letting them get a little dry is to promote the turning out in complete balls without injury to the roots. In this potting a rich firm soil should be used, say turfy loam two parts, the top crumbs from a bank of clay one part, and fat hotbed manure one part, the pots to be carefully drained, but with a view nevertheless to cramming into them as much fat soil as possible, for the strawberry is like an alderman and must have good food and plenty; it cannot live on chips or potsherds. In the potting process the stuff should be hammered as if for the foundation of a house, and as there is (or was) a famous house known as "Strawberry Hill," you may when potting strawberries for forcing consider yourself a master builder in the employ of one Horace of the blue Delft and Chinese pagoda persuasion, and not without the ambition requisite to the production of a second Horatius Flaccus.

The stock should now be ranged on a bed of coal ashes in an open spot, and have the most regular attention,. with a view more especially to regular watering. Keep the plants growing, and as their roots reach the sides of the pots the crowns will swell and ripen perfectly. To winter the stock brick pits are to be preferred, and they should be put away about the middle of October. As a rule we get a touch of frost some time between the 5th and 15th of October, and this touch of frost they should have and no more, unless it happens that they must be stored in the open, in which case they must take whatever weather comes.

The way to store them out of doors is to put them up in stacks under a wall or fence facing north, for the coldest and dryest place is the best for them. Lay the pots in a double row, layer upon layer, and sprinkle between as the packing proceeds any dry stuff that is at hand, such as tan, coal ashes, or leaves, to prevent the razor-like rush of air through the pile that will surely take the life out of the roots. They must not have any water while laid up in dock in this way.

The result of successful forcing lies in the first instance on the gradual introduction of the plant to a growing temperature. If you make a rush at it you get nothing. You may rush but your plant will not; it has a way of its own. Remove from the stack to the frame, from the frame to the cool house, and so on, allowing a week at least between every remove. When taken into the house in which they are to fruit the pots should be stood on troughs or pans or beds of rich soil; indeed, fat fresh stuff from the cow byre or sheep-fold will suit them, and they will soon send out roots through the pots to enjoy the banquet. The secret at first is to secure early roots, the secret at last is to feed the roots liberally. If a batch of forced strawberries should be short of moisture for one day, the fruit would drop or prove of the poorest quality, and the same sad end would follow if they were put into a high temperature too suddenly, or if, in his anxiety for early fruit the cultivator should forget to give them a reasonable supply of air. The slower the forcing the better, and in a domestic garden, the middle of January is soon enough to begin. At all events a hundred plants started in the middle of January will, as a rule, give five times more fruit than the same number started in the middle of December, to say nothing of the superior colour and flavour of the later grown samples.

STRAWBERRIES AT CHRISTMAS are desired in some extravagant households. The best way to secure them is to follow the plan of the gardeners of Copenhagen, where it is the custom to present friends with ripe strawberries on Christmas Day. The system adopted is to sow the seed of the alpine strawberries in July and August, and by securing strong plants in pots in good time, to force them slowly in pits with low pitched roofs.

THE COOL CULTURE OF BRITISH QUEEN and other first-class sorts to ensure large handsome well flavoured berries about a month or six weeks in advance of the open ground crop should be carried on with the aid of troughs, which afford the plants more food than it is possible for them to obtain in pots by any method of watering or encouraging them to root through. The troughs should be eight inches deep, seven inches wide at top, and five inches wide at bottom, with holes at the bottom to let off surplus water. The plants should be grown in pots in the usual way, and in October should be well established in six-inch pots with plump well ripened crowns. Having had a rest in a cool pit, and allowed to go nearly dry, they should be taken into a house at a temperature of 50 degs. and allowed to slowly start into new growth. As soon as the buds are visible they are planted in the troughs, in a mixture of turfy loam, road sand, and fat manure, and then put upon a shelf in the vinery or strawberry house and kept moving slowly in a temperature of 60 degs. They must have plenty of air when in flower, and when a reasonable (and rather smallish) crop of fruit is set, the remainder of the flowers and young fruit should be picked out, for it is only by limiting the crop that you can ensure a fine sample. The more slowly they come along the better, provided they do not stand still through lack of attention. If kept near the glass and well ventilated the berries will be large, highly coloured, and in flavour perfect.

THE SELECTION OF SORTS for forcing is a matter of great importance. *Black Prince* and *Keen's Seedling* have had the lead for many years, and are not likely soon to be superseded. The following are suitable for forcing, and should have a trial in every garden where the earliest strawberries are required:—*Lucas*, *Leon de St. Laumier* (syn. *Vicomtesse Hericart de Thury*), *Eclipse*, *Marguerite*, *Prince Arthur*, *Sir Harry*, *Sir Joseph Paxton*.

CHAPTER XXVIII.

THE FRUIT GARDEN.

Gard. Go, bind thou up yon' dangling apricocks,
Which, like unruly children, make their sire
Stoop with oppression of their prodigal weight:
Give some supportance to the bending twigs.—
Go thou, and, like an executioner,
Cut off the heads of too-fast growing sprays,
That look too lofty in our commonwealth;
All must be even in our government.—
You thus employ'd, I will go root away
The noisome weeds, that without profit suck
The soil's fertility from wholesome flowers.

Richard III. 3.

A SMALL chapter on a large subject must omit many things that might, or should, be said. To draw a hard and fast line between the vegetable garden and the fruit garden is impossible, and fruit culture must have a little of our attention. To obtain under certain rather commonplace circumstances, a sufficient supply of useful fruits to meet the ordinary wants of an average household, is not a difficult matter where the conditions are fairly favourable. The demands of the kitchen are continuous, and the selection of fruits for a kitchen garden should be governed by the consideration that a moderate supply of useful fruits in all seasons is much more to be desired than a glut of a few kinds in the later days of summer, to be followed by a blank for the rest of the year. The prudent planter will be cautious therefore in respect of planting varieties of apples and pears that ripen early and soon pass away, because at the time when the Joanneting apple and the Doyenné d'été pear (to name these as examples merely) are in perfection we have also bush fruits and stone fruits in plenty. So again, a very large proportion of the most delicious dessert pears ripen in October, and unless special care be taken, the fruit garden is likely to be too largely occupied with this class, while the later ripening sorts, such as Easter Beurré and March Bergamot may be neglected. In the plan of a kitchen garden at page 15, provision is made for a considerable supply of fruit in con-

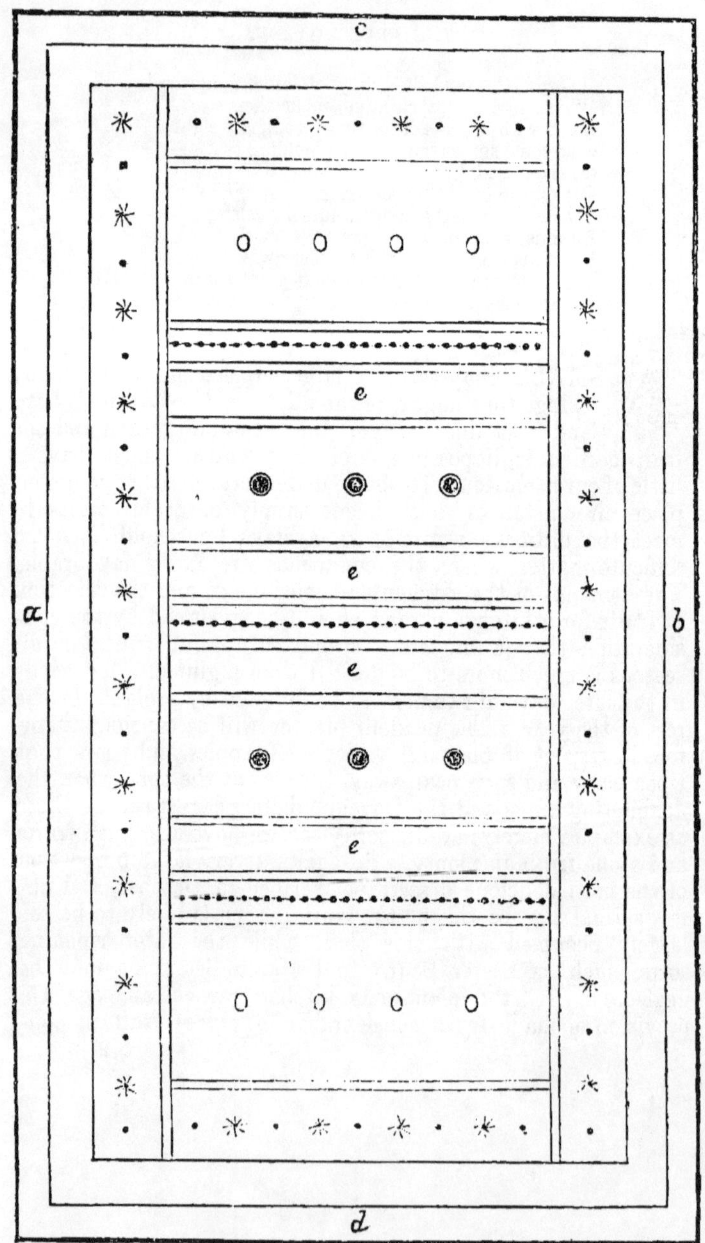

GROUND PLAN OF SMALL FRUIT GARDEN.

nection with a supply of vegetables. But this chapter would be incomplete if a plan for a fruit garden were omitted from it, and we are enabled to meet the requirement by presenting a plan for a small fruit garden designed by M. Burnevich, of Ghent, who has described this garden in his "Die Burgerlijk Fruitkweek." In adopting the plan we do not adopt the varieties of fruits he recommends, because they would not suit the English garden, and as will be seen presently, we have our own preferences in respect of varieties.

The ground plan shows the general arrangement of the garden, which is about 90 ft. in length by 50 ft. in breadth. Of course the dimensions may be enlarged if desired, but the above is useful as an example of what can be done in a very limited space. We will suppose that the ground has been carefully dug over and set out, and that it now awaits planting.

The wall *a*, facing the south-east should receive, reckoning from the corner N, twelve peaches trained in U-shape at 4 ft.

PEACH TREE TRAINED U-SHAPE.

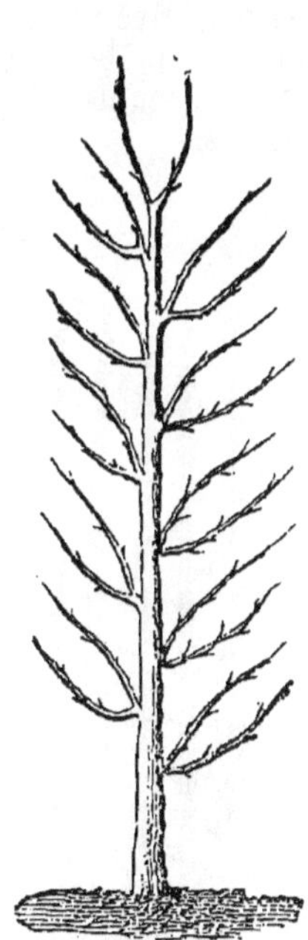

GRAPE-VINE TRAINED AS VERTICAL ROD.

apart. Next to these 10 grape-vines trained in vertical rods. The remainder of the wall may be allotted to 6 five-rod espalier pears.

The bed at the foot of the wall, which is only 2 ft. 4 in. wide, may be set with early strawberries, in tufts at distances of 15 inches apart.

The opposite wall, *b*, facing the north-west, has a less advantageous aspect, and should be reserved for early pears and a few cherries. In soils well suited to the apple we may try a few early sorts, such as *Devonshire Quarrenden*, *Gravenstein*, *Borovitski*, *Reinette de Hollande*, *Bedfordshire Foundling*, etc. The bed at the foot of this wall may also be set with strawberry plants, giving the preference to some late variety, which with this aspect will continue in bearing until the autumnal frosts set in.

The wall *c*, which has a south-west aspect, should be planted as follows:—Starting from the angle N, first, four apricots with five vertical rods each, fastened up so as to leave spaces of 15 in. between the rods. Six pears trained in like manner. A couple of plums may be substituted for two of the apricots.

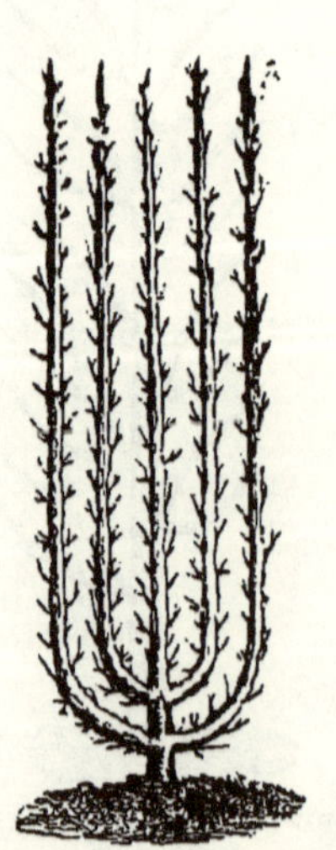

ESPALIER PEAR OF 5 RODS.

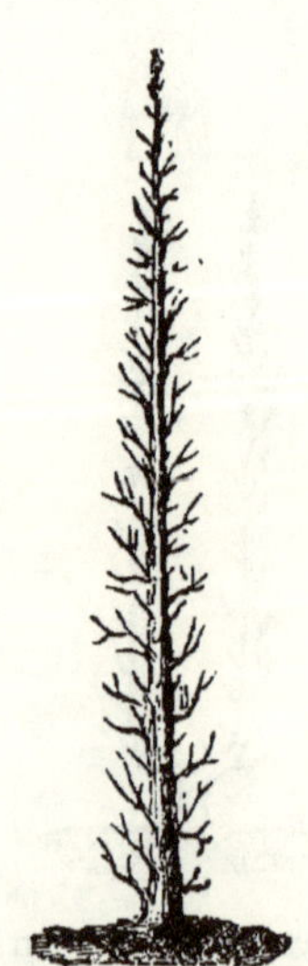

PEAR TREE, SINGLE VERTICAL ROD.

The wall *d*, with a north-east aspect, may be put to the same purposes, and planted like wall *b*. It should be reserved for autumnal pears.

In the beds, which are also 5 ft. in width, the asterisks (*) represent fusiform standard pears, alternating, in the beds facing walls *a* and *b*, with red, white, and black currant bushes; and on the smaller beds opposite the walls *c* and *d* with gooseberry bushes with bowl-shaped heads and short stems.

Around these beds on the sides next the paths are apples on

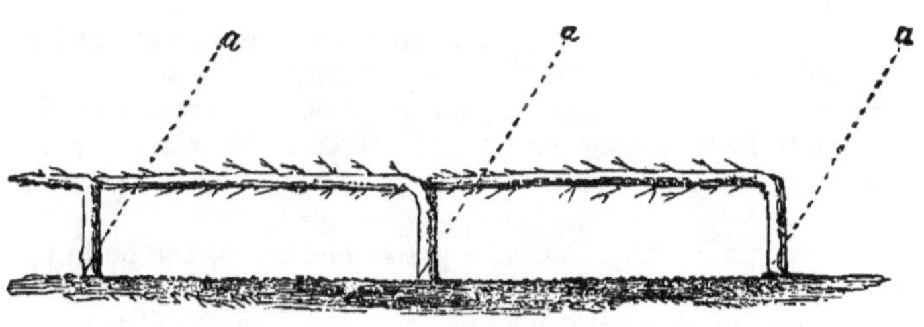

APPLES TRAINED IN HORIZONTAL RODS.

Paradise stocks, trained in single horizontal rods. The other portions of the beds are set with strawberry plants.

The three transverse trellises running across the interior of the garden, and which do not exceed 7 ft. in height, may be planted thus: The middle one with pears, trained as five-branched palmette candelabras; the other two with apples trained in fans, with six branches each in clayey soils, and four only in light ones. Lastly, by o are indicated apple trees, and by ●, six pyramidal pears.

In place of these pyramids we may put apples in half or full sized standards. The beds *e* should be left for minor purposes — such as growing pot-herbs, flower-seeds, setting cuttings, and the like.

The first business in planting a fruit garden is to consider the capabilities of the place. To produce good fruits requires a combination of favourable circumstances; a deep strong soil, a kind climate, and some amount of shelter. The manner in which particular places differ in their capabilities engages our attention, wherever we go in the exploration of gardens. Thus, the most productive English fruit garden known, that of Mr. Webb, at Calcot, near Reading, every kind of fruit, without a single exception, prospers and produces, and apples, pears, stone fruits, and nuts are particularly profitable. And yet, at the distance of only half a mile from that spot, a garden in which the soil appears to be of the same quality, and which enjoys almost similar advantages in respect of shelter and good management, all kinds of fruit trees succeed with the exception of pears, and these have baffled every attempt to establish them as profitable occupiers. To determine in advance what fruits may or may not be grown in a particular place is impossible, but generally speaking, the texture of the soil, and the known conditions of climate, and other governing circumstances, enable anyone possessed of experience in such matters to make a pretty safe forecast of what may be attempted in fruit culture with a reasonable prospect of success.

It very rarely happens that a place selected for the building of a residence and the formation of a garden, will not produce fruit of any kind at all. The walls of the house and the enclosing fences afford positions for fruit that the climate may be too unkind for if planted in open quarters, and as regards the soil, while it is impossible to alter the natural staple on a large scale, the preparation of borders for a few useful fruits next walls and fences is not a formidable task, for there are few places, however bleak and barren, that will not furnish a top crust of old turf and a heap of muck from a stable or a cow byre, by the aid of which a border may be formed for a few pears, or plums, or peaches, or even in an extreme case for the hardiest of apples, such as Hawthornden and Carlisle codlin.

The novice in fruit culture may be perplexed by the consideration that the planting and pruning and general management of fruit trees are matters of such difficulty that none but a ripe expert can reasonably expect to succeed. But the consideration is not worth considering. If the trees and the soil and the climate do not suit each other, the general management will not do much to reconcile them, although it must be admitted that the masters of fruit culture do overcome difficulties that less experienced persons would be defeated by. But given suitable conditions and suitable sorts, and the trees being of good make and shape and properly planted to begin with, and the novice may dismiss from his mind the subject of pruning and take a plain resolve never to prune at all. This declaration must be taken *cum grano*, because a cross branch may sometimes be cut away with advantage, and it may be desirable sometimes to remove dead wood and to shorten the shoots of young trees that are somewhat spare in their furniture. But it is a fact that it is not necessary to systematically prune any fruit tree or any fruit bush of any kind whatever. When the question is asked therefore, how shall I prune this or that? our reply is, you need not prune at all, neither an apple tree, nor a pear tree, nor a plum tree, nor a currant nor a gooseberry bush. You need not even prune or support the raspberry, for when left alone the stools throw up no more rods than are needed, and they are perfectly self-supporting, and they bear such prodigious quantities of fruit that a few years experience of the non-pruning system will convince any one that systematic pruning is systematic folly. These remarks do not of course apply to trees on walls or espaliers. They are in an artificial form, and must be kept to that form by judicious pruning. But even these are usually pruned too much, and their vigour is proportionately reduced, while as to the frequent cutting and pinching of pyramid and bush trees, that current works on fruit culture recommend, it is for the most part waste of time and injurious to the trees that are the subjects of it.

The reader will not need to be told that the question of pruning has two sides, and the practice has the sanction of ages in its favour. Having studied all the modes of pruning, and being familiar with many of the best fruit gardens in which pruning is practised with rare dexterity and praiseworthy perseverance, the writer of this little book does not hesitate to advise the man who desires to obtain ample supplies of useful fruits in the simplest and surest manner, to give up pruning altogether and let nature have her way. The fruit will come, and perhaps the crowding of the head of the tree which the books tell you to prevent by free use of the knife, may prove by the shelter the crowded growth affords, the very reason that your unpruned trees are fruitful, when others in the district that are "perfectly" pruned produce nothing at all. When you hear of an apple tree producing forty bushels of apples, you may be sure the owner has not devoted much time to the pruning of it. In one sense a tree left alone prunes itself. The long rods become clothed with fruit spurs, and in time these produce fruits. The weight of the crop brings the long rod down, and an arching pendant habit characterises, more or less, every fruitful tree. Now as the branch inclines to the horizontal its vigour is reduced, and thus fruit production checks growth, whereas pruning promotes growth, and by so doing postpones the production of fruit.

THE APPLE will thrive in places where no other large fruit will live, and as it flowers late, bad climates and bad seasons affect it less than most other fruits. For the orchard and to dot about the paddocks and home farm, apples on crab stocks are the most useful, but for a small garden bush pyramid trees on the true Paradise stock are the best. As there are many so-called "Paradise" stocks in the market, it is important to secure the best, which is known in the trade as the *English* as distinguished from the "French," the "Dutch" and others. But trade names are often deceptive, and the apple stock intended to be recommended now for the formation of dwarf trees is the *Pommier de Paradis*, that has been proved in the trial ground at Chiswick to supersede in compactness of growth and precocity of production the "English Paradise" and the "miniature Paradise" employed by Mr. Rivers, the "Dutch Paradise," and several others that do not favour either a compact growth or a healthy habit in the trees grafted on them. In addition to the true Paradise, the Doucin, and Scott's Paradise, which is employed by Mr. Scott, of Merriott Nurseries, Crewkerne, Somerset, may be recommended as favouring neat growth and early fruitfulness. The crab stock has been too much neglected of late years, owing to the eager pushing of trade interests in objectionable Paradise stocks, but we have nothing else on which to raise free growing, handsome, long lasting, and highly productive trees, and when an orchard, in the proper sense of the term, is in contemplation, we are compelled to look to this stock for the carrying of the more robust growing and profitable sorts of apples. Espalier apple trees are scarcely to be desired, as the close pruning they are necessarily subjected to induces canker by lowering the vigour of the trees; and where the roots are frequently punished by the spade, as must be the case with espaliers on the borders of the kitchen garden, decrepitude is soon manifested, and the

best aftercare will but rarely restore the trees to health. In the fruit garden proper the case is different, for espalier and cordon apple trees are necessary features there, and a bower walk formed by apple trees trained over forms a pleasing and useful form of approach.

The apple is the least particular in respect of soil of all our fruit trees, but a deep strong loam suits it best, and although drainage is not a matter of primary importance, a soil that holds much stagnant water in winter will not produce healthy trees.

A SELECTION OF APPLES must in any and every case have relation to the local circumstances. Thus the famous Ashmead's Kernel thrives nowhere so well as in the neighbourhood of Gloucester; the beautiful and useful Blenheim Orange produces many crops of the most beautiful fruits on light soil in the southern counties, but is comparatively useless on the heavy clay lands in the northern suburbs of the metropolis. The following are such as combine good qualities with adaptiveness of habit, and will suit for the northern and midland counties generally. Those marked with an asterisk are to be preferred in forming a small collection.

TWENTY-FIVE SORTS OF CULINARY APPLES.—*Alfriston**, *Aromatic Russet*, *Beauty of Kent**, *Bedfordshire Foundling*, *Blenheim Orange**, *Cox's Pomona*, *Costard*, *Echlinville*, *Gooseberry Pippin*, *Keswick Codlin**, *Mank's Codlin*, *Winter Codlin**, *French Crab*, *Dumelow's Seedling** or *Wellington*, *Flower of Kent*, *Gloria Mundi*, *Lady Henniker*, *New Hawthornden**, *Norfolk Beefing**, *Kentish Fillbasket**, *Lord Suffield**, *Northern Greening*, *London Pippin**, *Royal Russet**, *Yorkshire Greening*. These are all adapted for orchard and garden culture.

TWENTY-FIVE SORTS OF DESSERT APPLES. — *Ashmead's Kernel**, *Baddow Pippin**, *Braddick's Nonpareil*, *Cellini*, *Cornish Gilliflower*, *Cockle Pippin**, *Cox's Orange Pippin**, *Court Pendu Plat*, *Fearn's Pippin**, *Knight's Downton Pippin*, *Golden Harvey*, *Golden Pippin**, *Irish Peach**, *Juneating*, *Hubbard's Pearmain**, *King of the Pippins**, *Lord Burghley**, *Newtown Pippin*, *Nonsuch*, *Northern Spy*, *Reinette du Canada*, *Ribston Pippin**, *Scarlet Nonpareil*, *Worcester Pippin*, *Wyken Pippin**.

THE APRICOT is occasionally met with in the south of England as a standard tree, and in that form is rather to be regarded as a curiosity than a profitable tree, for it is only about once in seven years that these standards ripen a fair crop of fruit. As a rule this fruit requires the hottest wall that can be found for it, and it should also have a deep border, for if in a shallow border, a hot summer causes the death of large branches, the Moorpark variety being peculiarly liable to this mishap. During a term of very hot weather it is advisable to shade apricot and peach trees on south walls to moderate the heat to which at midday they are subjected. The employment of apricot stocks is much to be desired, for the plum stock commonly used certainly favours the sudden dying away of large branches which occurs from time to time in almost every garden. The best varieties for a small place are *Moorpark*, *Shipley's*, *Breda*, and *Turkey*.

THE CHERRY is a troublesome fruit where birds abound, but there is a way out of that difficulty. Cherries grafted on the Mahaleb stock form pretty dwarf trees, that are eminently fertile, and a plantation of such may be covered with old fishing nets while the fruit is ripening, and thus at a small cost the crop may be saved without any slaughter or noisy scaring of the birds. The subjoined figures represent two methods of protecting. If it is intended to protect the trees on

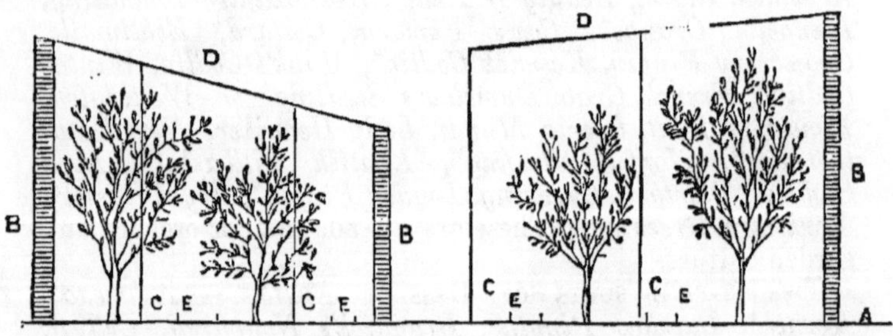

an outside border, or "slip," as it is usually called, it is simply necessary to have cross pieces, D, resting upon the garden wall and boundary wall or fence, B B, and supported by uprights, C C. In protecting the trees on an inside border, the cross-pieces, D, must be supported at one end by an upright, C, as here shown. E E E E in the two sketches represent rows of strawberry plants, which could be thus protected without additional cost. A is of course the ground-line. It would also be a capital plan to have cherry trees trained to the wall and gooseberry and currant bushes on the border, with strawberries between, so as to have the various fruits ripening about the same time altogether. The netting and supports can be readily removed from place to place, and any fruit it may be desirable to protect be covered without difficulty. It is not necessary to provide doors, as it is so very easy to arrange the netting so that the gardener can pass through close to the wall. Standard cherries are so handsome in flower that they are peculiarly suitable for planting in a paddock or playground, as well as in the shrubbery. A well drained sandy soil suits the cherry well, but any good soil as a rule will produce good cherries.

A SELECTION OF CHERRIES should comprise the *Morello*, as the most important, because in most places a north wall suits it perfectly; it is immensely productive of a most useful culinary fruit, and the birds do not like it. The following are the best of the several classes:—*Belle d'Orléans**, D; *Black Tartarian**, D; *May Duke**, D; *Black Eagle; Bigarreau Napoléon*, D; *Elton*, D; *Florence*, D; *Coe's Late Carnation*, D; *Kentish**, K; *Belle Magnifique*, K; *Morello**, K; *Frogmore Early Bigarreau**, D; *Royal Duke*, D; *Werder's Early Black*, D.

THE CURRANT is so accommodating that it is almost waste of words to speak of the soil it requires, but a very few words will suffice. A sandy or calcareous soil suits red and white currants better than peat or clay, and on the other hand the black currant prefers a damp loam or clay, and is rather poor on a calcareous or sandy soil. But we find them all thriving in the same gardens on all kinds of soils, and they usually bear well in seasons when all other kinds of fru ts are swept away by May frosts. The red and white are usually pruned back to within a couple of inches of the old wood, and when so treated they produce finer berries than when left unpruned. On the other hand, if left unpruned, they bear an enormous quantity of fruit, the rods being clothed with bunches to the very tip. As for the black currants, it is not customary to prune them at all, but if very large berries are wanted, a few strong bushes should be cut down to the ground and allowed to throw up only half-a-dozen stout rods the next season. This proceeding entails the loss of a season by the trees cut down, so there is no profit in pruning the black currant; the profitable way is to leave him alone. The best sorts are *White Dutch*, *Raby Red*, *Red Grape*, *Black Naples*, and *Lee's Prolific Black*.

THE GOOSEBERRY may be grown in a great variety of ways, and in places where, owing to adverse circumstances, the production of useful fruits is a matter of difficulty; this humble but useful berry should be largely cultivated. No one will touch a gooseberry while grapes or peaches are at hand, but when we are shut up to well-ripened samples of greengage gooseberry or the more famous Crown Bob, we feel that the world is still worth staying in, and shall easily find a lot of young people of precisely the same opinion. The gooseberry thrives on any good garden soil, and is the better usually for the protection of a wall or hedge. But to bring it to the highest perfection of which it is capable, a deep sandy, well drained and highly manured soil is requisite. The great berries that are weighed to the fraction of a grain by the serious censors at a gooseberry show are the result of very careful cultivation, the trees being systematically pruned so as to spread the growth equally to the air and light, and the crop being severely thinned and abundantly fed with liquid manure. But a row of useful sorts grown for the household use may be left alone as regards pruning, and the produce will surpass by ten times that of trees of the same size kept closely pruned in on the spurring system, for the more open and symmetrical and artistic the form of the tree the more surely will the east wind in the month of May secretly strip the fruit from it, while the unpruned tree will protect all its fruit with its own buxom leafy growth, and give you pecks to the other tree's pints. In places where first-class fruits cannot be grown, it is a good plan to plant gooseberries in all sorts of aspects and on walls and fences, for the uses of the fruit are innumerable, and a well-made gooseberry wine comes nearest to champagne of any of the many imitations of that delectable fluid.

A SELECTION OF GOOSEBERRIES should include the *Warrington* as the most useful of all for culinary purposes. Then we may add the following, the most desirable of which are marked with an asterisk:—Red—*Champagne**, *Crown Bob**, *Red Globe*, *Rough Red**, *Companion**. Yellow—*Glory of Oldport*, *Leader**, *Yellow Champagne**. Green—*British Queen**, *Green Gage**, *Greenwood*, *Turn-out*. White—*Queen of Trumps*, *Large Early White**, *Whitesmith**.

THE GRAPE VINE so rarely produces handsome and well flavoured fruit on the open wall in this country that we might be excused for omitting mention of it in this work. But good table grapes are grown on open walls in a few well managed gardens; and we have tasted many excellent samples of sparkling wines and clarets made from English vineyard grapes, and therefore the subject of grape culture must have some attention here. If we could put all our readers in the way of supplying their tables with such home-made wines as have been systematically produced by Mr. Roach Smith, the well-known antiquarian of Strood; and Mr. Fenn, the well-known pomologist of Woodstock,—to name but two amongst many friends who have acquired fame as amateur wine-growers—we should consider this book worth more than its weight in gold. But we can only say that wine making, in common with many other pastimes, cannot be very directly promoted by book teaching, and the novice must reach perfection by an apprenticeship, which will include a certain amount of blundering, against which no general directions will provide.

OUT-DOOR VINES.—To insure good grapes in the open air the vines must be cultivated—that is to say, they must be planted in suitable soils and situations, and must have careful management during the growing season. More frequently than otherwise the cultivator, rather than the climate, is at fault; the vines are planted without reference to the suitability of the situation, and left pretty much to themselves, and the climate is blamed for the inferiority of the crop.

A south aspect is best suited to outdoor vines, although with careful management they will do well trained to walls facing south-east or south-west, and that aspect should, if possible, be set apart for them. They also do better trained to high walls than they do to low ones; and walls not exceeding eight feet in height may be more profitably employed in the cultivation of the peach, pear, or cherry, than in the growth of the grape vine. Fences also are objectionable, because of the cold current of air which continually passes through the crevices that exist, even in the best constructed fences; and which materially reduces the temperature of the air in contact with the foliage and fruit. Dwelling-houses having suitable aspects present unusually favourable conditions for the production of outdoor grapes, because of the great height of the walls and the large surface they present for the development of the growth. They should therefore be turned to account for that purpose, especially as it can be done without any sacrifice of appearance, for the grape vine is beautiful in summer, and not unsightly in winter.

The construction of the border is second only in importance to the selection of the aspect. The border should be about eight feet wide, and three feet deep ; if the situation is cold and wet, it should be elevated above the surrounding level, and the soil kept in its place by a neat nine-inch wall. The soil should be excavated to a depth of four feet, if the border is to be entirely below the level, and a layer of rough stones or brickbats, twelve or fifteen inches in thickness put in the bottom. The space can then be filled with three parts turfy loam, one part horse droppings, and one part lime rubbish. There is, of course, no objection to the use of bones, but they are too expensive to be employed in borders for outdoor vines. It is not, of course, necessary to have the borders entirely below or above the surface, but they may be partly above and partly below, according to the exigencies of the case. Even in dry, warm situations no objection whatever exists to their being elevated entirely above the general level. The drain to the lowest part of the border should connect with the main drains, to carry off the water which collects in it. If the natural soil is a deep fertile sandy loam, decidedly dry and warm, there is no necessity for a prepared border for outdoor vines. Plant in the natural soil and be content.

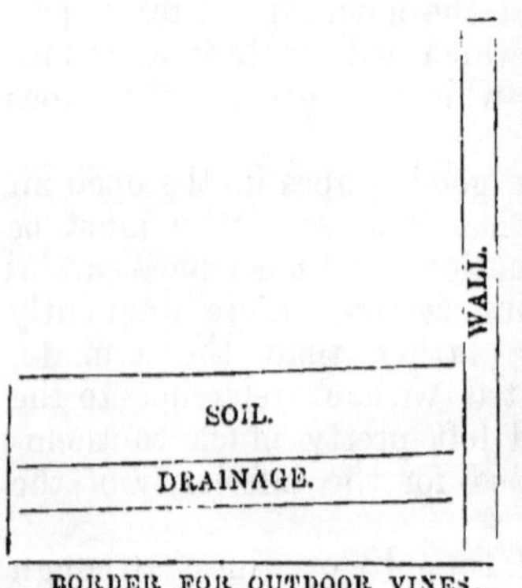

BORDER FOR OUTDOOR VINES.

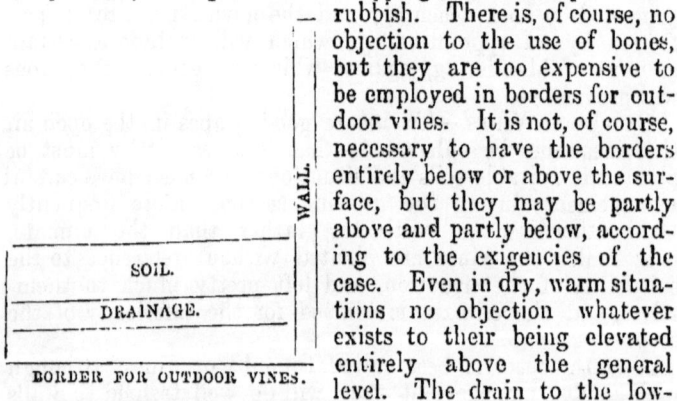

Grape vines in pots can be planted at almost any time, but October is the best month in which to plant vines taken up from the open border. The manner of planting when the vines are intended to cover the walls of a dwelling-house is clearly shown in the figure, and when they are planted in the manner indicated, the whole of the wall space can be covered without interfering with the windows or the light in the slightest degree. A slight alteration may be made in the planting if it is considered at all desirable, and four vines, two on each side of the door, may be planted instead of having two on one side, and one on the other, as in the present arrangement.

The advantage of having two sets of vines—one set for the top and the other set for the lower half of the wall—is very considerable, for outdoor vines bear better when trained on the long-rod system, and it is seldom that twenty feet of well-matured rod is produced in our short summers. When the walls do not exceed twelve feet in height, one set of vines will be quite sufficient, and for ordinary walls they should be planted at a distance of four feet apart, and each vine allowed to carry four rods, two fruit-bearing canes and two young ones for bearing the following season. In planting them out of pots, carefully loosen the roots round the outside, and plant them deep enough to cover a few inches of the stem, from which healthy roots will be emitted in a short time after planting.

The long-rod system of training, by which a constant succession of young wood is maintained, is the most desirable for vines in the open air. The first season after planting they should be cut back to within about fifteen inches of the base. In the spring the two top buds should be selected for training horizontally, one to the right and the other to the left; and when the one on the right has attained a length of eighteen inches, and the one on the left six inches, they should be trained perpendicularly up the walls. These, if strong and well matured, may be left their whole length at the winter pruning, and, the following spring, two young rods should be trained up, at a distance of twelve inches from the base of the others—that on the right of the main stem, on the inside, and that on the left, on the outside of the perpendicular rods. By this system the latter will always be kept at a regular distance apart, and the lateral growth will have ample space for development. For forming the second rod on the left, it will be necessary to select a strong shoot at the base of the first, and train it the proper distance horizontally, and then take it up in the manner mentioned above. If more than two bearing rods are required on each vine, a new cane, in the manner here mentioned, can be taken up each season, until the requisite number is obtained.

After the space is fully occupied, the canes which have borne fruit should, at the winter pruning, be pruned back to within a few inches of their base, and the young canes indicated by the dotted lines shortened back to their proper length, and allowed to bear a crop of fruit the following season. In the spring, a number of shoots will push from the base of the cane pruned back in the winter, and the strongest must be selected for training up to take the place of the one

LONG ROD TRAINING OF OUTDOOR VINES TO WALLS OF DWELLING HOUSES.

removed. This, in its turn, will have to take the place of the present fruit-bearing cane, and, again in its turn, have to make way for others; the young canes should be stopped once during the summer, when they have attained about half their length, to strengthen the lower buds, and they should also be stopped when they have attained their full length.

If the canes are short-jointed, it will be necessary to remove a portion of the lateral growth, when the vines start into growth in the spring. As a rule, the laterals should be about nine inches apart on each side of the rod, and a bunch of fruit left to every alternate lateral. After the bunches are formed, the laterals should be shortened back, and all sub-laterals removed as fast as they make their appearance, to afford the fruit the fullest exposure to the beneficial influence of the sun. The bunches will require thinning lightly when the berries are of the size of very small peas, to enable them to attain their full size, which it is impossible for them to do when they are left unthinned, as is usually done in the case of vines in the open. But when grapes are grown for wine making solely there is no occasion for thinning.

PROPAGATING VINES raised from eyes are the best for outdoor, as they are for indoor planting, but cuttings afford the readiest means of raising a stock, and, with ordinary care, strike very freely. Some time in November select moderately short-jointed and medium-sized shoots, that are well matured; fasten them together, in a bundle, and insert them temporarily in the border, and protect from severe frost. Early in March cut them into lengths of three or four joints each; remove the two lowest buds, and plant them firmly in well-prepared soil in the open border, deep enough for the bud nearest the top to be just above the surface. With a little attention in watering, and keeping clear of weeds, the larger portion will be nicely rooted by the autumn, and be in good condition for planting, or they may be transplanted and planted out in their permanent quarters the following autumn. In propagating vines by layers, it is simply necessary to select a well-ripened shoot, and after cutting it half way through, in a slanting direction, on the side that will be lowest when it is pegged down in the soil, and then fastening them just below the surface. This should be done some time during October or March, and a small piece of potsherd placed in the wound, to prevent its closing. One bud only should be allowed

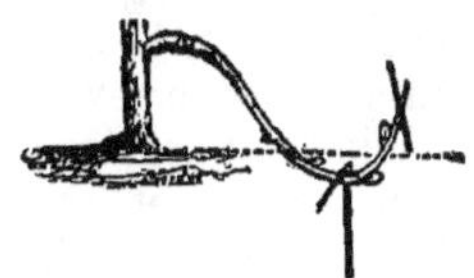

LAYERING THE GRAPE VINE.

above the surface, and the others rubbed off. The layers, under ordinary circumstances, will be well rooted by the end of the summer, but it is generally preferable to defer taking them off until early in the autumn.

GROUND VINERIES offer a fair compromise between the open wall with its uncertainties and the well-built glasshouse with its costliness. A ground vinery is a glasshouse in miniature, its form is that of a narrow frame, in the style of our A frame, described in pages 38 and 39. The smallness, and hence the cheapness of the ground vinery is not its only recommendation. One special virtue it has in economising the heat of the earth, which of course is but a reproduction of the heat of the sun, for the use of the grape vine, a heat-loving plant. In the most distinct manner possible, a ground vinery is a trap to catch a sunbeam. The village carpenter can make a ground vinery as well as anybody, but if the ready-made thing is required, it may be obtained from Messrs. Boulton and Paul, of Norwich, or any of the builders of greenhouses who do not disdain small work.

The management of a ground vinery is extremely simple, the one primary rule being that the vine is laid horizontally on a pavement of slates, or on cross bars over a trench, and is covered with a glass frame, which can be ventilated without difficulty. Usually the frame is placed on a foundation of bricks, from which a certain number of bricks are omitted to form pigeon-hole ventilators, which of course can be closed easily when very severe weather prevails, but which are usually left open to ensure a slow and soft, but constant movement of the air within the structure. The vines may be managed on the long rod or the spur pruning system. The last named has proved the best in our experience, and it consists in simply cutting back the side shoots every year and leaving the main rod intact. This is a very pretty mode of grape culture, costing but little for a first start, and affording a most delightful pastime, with the prospect always of a nice crop of really good table grapes. Given a healthy vine and a good season, the one important point in the management is to thin the crop severely. First, cut away all the small bunches while they are in flower, reserving about one bunch to every foot length of the main rod, and afterwards thin out the berries severely, the time for thinning being when they are scarcely so large as peas.

The common Sweet Water grape furnishes nice fruit for tarts, and a very fair preserve may be made of ripe grapes of any kind, but in the preparation of it the pulp must be pressed through a sieve of suitable size to remove the stones, and owing to the juiciness of the fruit, it requires plenty of cooking to reduce it. As for wine making, we cannot go into that subject here, but given plenty of grapes, it is neither a difficult nor a costly business to produce a wholesome and palatable wine suitable for daily use in the household.

THE BEST VARIETIES OF GRAPES for walls are *Esperione, Miller's Burgundy, Royal Muscadine.* For ground vineries *Black Hamburgh, Buckland Sweet Water, Foster's Seedling, Madresfield Court Muscat.*

GROUND VINERY AND PROTECTIVE BEDS.—The object of combining two systems of cultivation is to economise the glass and make it pay interest on its cost the whole year round. Mark out a piece of ground 66½ feet long and 36 feet broad. If the greatest length lies east and west it will be better than any other direction, but it does not much matter what is its direction provided it lies open to the sun, is well drained, and enjoying a little shelter from north-east winds. *It must not be overhung by trees.* Mark out all round a 4-feet walk; perhaps a narrower walk might do, but the walk has to serve also as a border for the roots of the vines, and there must be a certain amount of wheeling all the year round, for manuring the beds, etc. Next mark out divisions across the piece 3½ feet wide and 1½ feet wide alternately. At the end of every alternate bed plant two vines; the other beds are to be reserved for cauliflowers, saladings, and other subjects that require protection.

The next business is to provide the glass frames or "Vineries." Seven-feet lengths will do to begin with, but the arrangement is for every vine to have 14 feet of glass ultimately, which makes each separate length 28 feet. The frames are to be 42 inches wide, to accommodate two vines each, and the beds will be the same width throughout, with alleys of 18 inches width between. Let us suppose, then, that the whole affair is finished. We have in the six compartments marked A, 24 vineries, making a total run of 168 feet of glass, and as there are two vines in each, the total length of bearing rods is 336 feet. Let us suppose the vines to produce one bunch to every foot run, and if the bunches

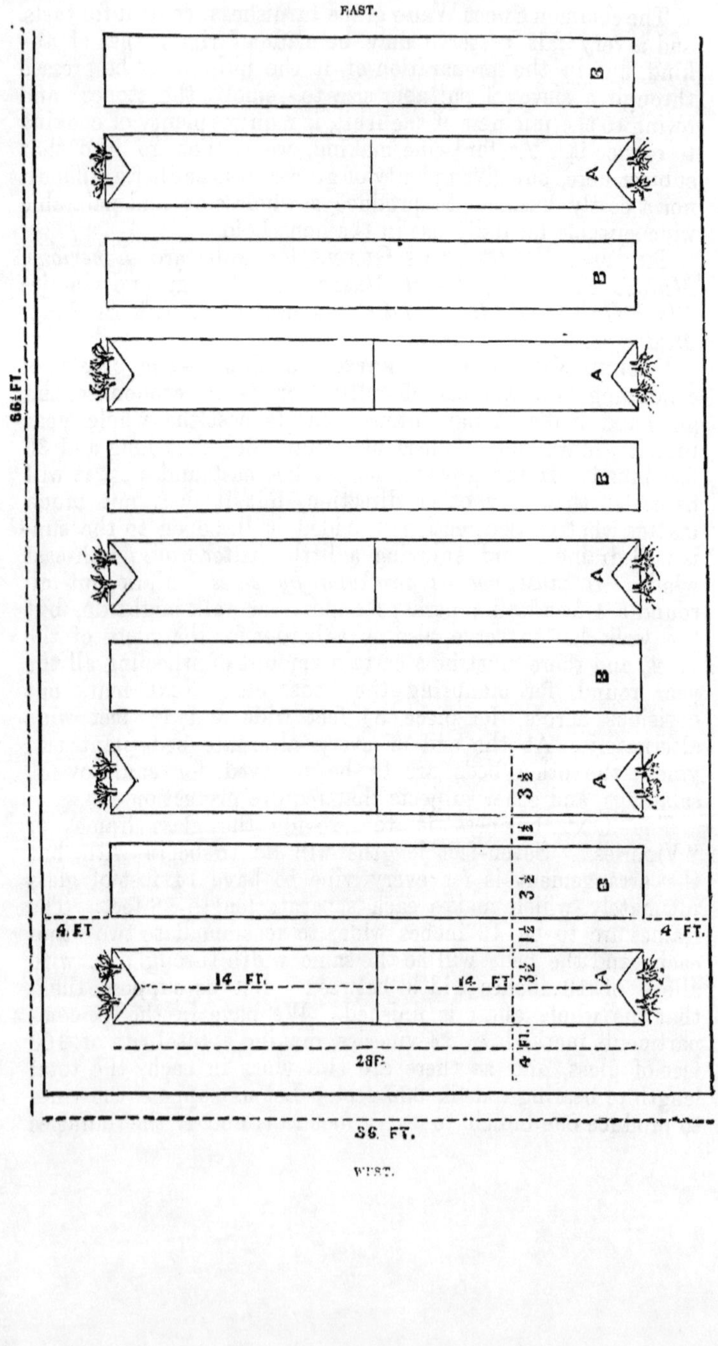

EAST.

B

A

B

A

B

A

B

A

B

A

66½ FT.

4 FT. 4 FT.

14 FT. 14 FT.

3½ 1½ 3½ 1½ 3½

4 FT.

28 FT.

36 FT.

WEST.

only average one pound each, we may expect an annual supply of 336 lbs. of grapes, so we may set down our ultimate expectations at from 300 to 400 lbs.

The beds marked B are to be cultivated the whole year round with useful vegetables, one important part of the routine being to plant them all in autumn with cauliflowers, lettuce, endive, sweet herbs, or the hardier kinds of bedding plants. As soon as the weather becomes wintry, the glass frames are to be removed from the vines and placed over these beds; they are to be placed on bricks, of course, to allow of ventilation, and during very severe weather mats must be put over, and the ventilating holes must be stopped with moss or straw, or half bricks inserted. A total length of 168 feet of protected beds would be of immense value to those who prize early cauliflowers, lettuces, and such other subjects as would be kept through the winter in them. Instead of having to lift and replant them, as is the case when we winter them in frames, they would simply remain where planted in autumn, the lights being removed from about the end of April or later, according to the state of the weather. This would expedite the maturation of the crop considerably, as there would be no check from lifting or sudden exposure of protected plants to cold winds, which is the common case in kitchen garden routine, for the frames would be put on the cauliflowers at night and on the vines all day, at that critical season when winter and spring are contending for the mastery. The only effect of such treatment would be to retard, not injure the vines; and as such things as hardy lettuces and sweet herbs of most kinds do not need protecting so late in the season as cauliflowers, vines desired to be started early might have their glasses put on about the first week in April.

The diagram contains only ten instead of twelve compartments, the space at command for it, necessitating the removal of two.

NECTARINES AND PEACHES require substantial borders and brick walls; to grow them as standards or free bushes is not advisable, for it is only about once in seven years on an average that they ripen their fruit fairly well in any position unless aided by a wall. We have for many years past grown such fine *Royal George Peaches* and *Elruge Nectarines* on east walls exposed to open meadows in the cold valley of the Lea, that we cannot consistently object to east walls in any district south of the line of the Trent. But south and west walls are preferable, and in very sunny seasons it may be advisable to give the trees a little shade at midday to moderate the excessive heat to which they are subjected when grown on south walls. When in any degree exposed, they should not only have protection, but be roughly pruned so as to leave a protective bristling of breastwood, which can be removed when the fruit begins to swell. A short wiry growth of projecting shoots is a very effective protection, costing nothing and really contributing to maintain the health of the trees.

THE BEST NECTARINES for walls are *Balgowan, Early Newington, Elruge, Hardwicke Seedling, Lord Napier, Pineapple, Violette Hâtive, Pitmaston Orange.*

THE BEST PEACHES for walls are *Bellegarde, Early Beatrice, Early Rivers, Early York, Grosse Mignonne, Prince of Wales, Royal Charlotte, Royal George, Noblesse, Barrington, Walburton Admirable.*

THE PEAR is exacting but accommodating. In many gardens that have a good soil and are well managed, it is a difficult matter to grow pears, whereas in others that appear to be no better off in respect of conditions, pear trees grow vigorously and produce fruit abundantly. As in the case of the apple we have free stocks for large trees, and dwarfing stocks for small ones, so in the cultivation of the pear, the pear stock grafted with a vigorous variety produces a tree of great stature and fine proportions, especially if never touched with the pruning knife, but the quince stock produces small trees, which may be trained as pyramids, cordons, and in other forms at the convenience or caprice of the cultivator. It is in respect of its compliance with the requirements of the pruner's art that the pear is especially accommodating. In cases where systematic pruning cannot be practised, bush and pyramid pears on the quince may be allowed to grow naturally, and they soon become handsome and fruitful, and as regards mere usefulness, are to be preferred to the most carefully trained trees. On the other hand the pear is best of all trees adapted for fancy training, and when skilfully managed makes a good return.

A SELECTION OF THE BEST PEARS.—Those marked with an asterisk are the best for a small collection for STANDARDS :— *Aston Town, Beurré de l'Assomption**, *Citron des Carmes, Jargonelle**, *Brockworth Park, Williams's Bon Chrétien,*

Dunmore, Ne Plus Meuris, Forelle, Winter Nelis, Seckle, Swan's Egg, Beurré de Capiaumont*, Autumn Bergamot*, Napoleon, Beurré d'Aremberg, Beurré d'Amanlis*, Louise Bonne of Jersey*, Fondante d'Automne, Easter Beurré*, Catillac*, Belissime d'Hiver, Souvenir du Congrès*, Windsor.*

FOR BUSHES AND PYRAMIDS.—*Alex. Lambre*, Bergamotte d'Esperen*, Beurré de l'Assomption*, Beurré Clairgeau, Beurré d'Aremberg*, Beurré d'Amanlis, Beurré Diel*, Brown Beurré*, Beurré de Rance*, Beurré Easter*, Beurré Goubault, Bon Chretien*, Broom Park, British Queen, Brockworth Park*, Conseiller de la Cour, Délices de Jodoigne, Doyenné du Comice*, Doyenné Defais, Doyenné d'Eté*, Duchesse d'Angoulême*, Eyewood, Fondante d'Automne, Forelle, Glou Morceau, Hacon's Incomparable*, Huyshe's Victoria, Louise Bonne of Jersey*, Monarch, Prince Albert, Souvenir du Congrès*, Suffolk Thorn, Winter Nelis*, Yat, Zéphirin Grégoire.*

FOR WALLS.—*Bezi Mai, Beurré de l'Assomption*, Beurré Diel*, Beurré Bosc, Brown Beurré, Goubalt, Brockworth Park, Chaumontel*, Marie Louise*, Knight's Monarch, Ne Plus Meuris*, Hacon's Incomparable, Thompson's, Graham's Autumn Nelis, Glou Morceau, Jargonelle*, Winter Nelis*, Josephine de Malines*, Easter Beurré*, Louise Bonne of Jersey, Beurré Rance*, Alexandre Bivort, Pitmaston Duchesse d'Angoulême, Souvenir du Congrès.*

THE PLUM resembles the pear in many respects, requiring a similar strong soil, and being amenable to similar management when required in any particular form on a trellis or wall. As a rule, however, the plum answers best in the form of an unpruned bush, grafted low and planted in a sheltered situation. The strong growing kinds make noble standard trees, and when well made in the nursery should never afterwards be pruned at all. The more delicate kinds of dessert plums require the help of a wall in most cases, but whenever fruit can be obtained of any given variety from trees in the open border, it will be found superior in beauty and flavour to the produce of the wall. The same is the case with pears.

A SELECTION OF PLUMS.—The best for STANDARDS are *Victoria*, Pond's Seedling, Belle de Septembre, Denniston's Superb, Diamond*, Gisborne's, Prince Englebert*, Kirke's, Early Orleans*, American Damson.*

FOR PYRAMIDS AND BUSHES, OR TO TRAIN ON WALLS.—*Early Favourite**, *Green Gage**, *Jefferson*, *Mirabelle*, *Golden Gage*, *Reine Claude de Bavay**, *Guthrie's Late Green.*

THE RASPBERRY is less accommodating than the black currant, but will endure partial shade very well. Its most important requirement is a deep, moist, rich soil. As for many years past we have given up pruning and training raspberries, we are bound to say that we shall never return to the practice unless it be to prove the folly of the procedure. Plant the canes four feet apart, in one long row, or if in many rows let the rows be five feet asunder. If the land is suitable for them, they will in the next season throw up a few strong stout canes, and every year afterwards just as many canes will appear as are wanted, and these will arch out slightly to enjoy light and air, and will not need any support whatever. On the other hand, if the soil is poor and thin, and the canes are planted thickly, pruning and training will be needful, and the worst of all ways to treat them is to tie them in bundles to upright stakes. When we say that in a strong soil with plenty of room between, they do not need pruning, it is not to be understood that the dead canes that have borne fruit are to be left. They must be removed for the sake of tidiness. But there is one golden rule that must be followed. The ground must never be dug between or near raspberries, but a thick coat of fat manure should be spread amongst them some time in the autumn or early in the spring. It is advisable to make a new plantation from single canes fairly rooted about every seven years to allow of the destruction of old plantations that are wearing out.

THE BEST VARIETIES are *Red Antwerp**, *White Antwerp*, *Fastolf,** *Prince of Wales Double Bearing.* Of these the two specially marked are sufficient for almost any garden.

THE BLACKBERRY may be treated in the same way as the raspberry, but in a well kept garden it must be trained in some way on account of its straggling growth and terrible armour. A very pretty feature may be made by planting a lot of the *Lawton Blackberry* to ramble over a rough bank. This variety in a strong soil produces an abundance of fruit that is sure to meet with favour in the household, and is of great service to mix with damsons in tarts. There are about half a dozen sorts of American blackberries in cultivation, and they form a pretty collection for an amateur who cares about such things.

THE STRAWBERRY admits of literary treatment to almost any extent, as may be seen by the miles of essays that have been written upon it in the horticultural papers, and a few good books have been especially devoted to its cultivation. But to grow strawberries in any quantity and of quality *sans reproche* is such a simple business that we shall hope to sum up in a very few words all that need be said on the subject here.

The strawberry requires a deep fertile soil which may vary from a warm sandy loam to a cold tenacious clay. A shallow sand and a poor limestone soil are equally unsuitable, and therefore to produce strawberries on such, a made soil is required, and even then there are difficulties to be encountered as the price of a few good berries. Any soil that will produce a cauliflower will produce strawberries, but an open situation is absolutely necessary, and the purer the air the better for the fruit. We have seen nice samples of Black Prince grown in worn out soil in a London backyard, where such fine sorts as British Queen and Carolina would not produce a fruit at all. On the other hand, in one of our gardens which consists of stubborn clay that turns up in hard clods like quartern loaves, we can grow the finest strawberries ever seen by preparing the land in good time, planting in showery weather, and then leaving the rest to nature, for we do not give them a drop of water from first to last. To prepare the land, deep digging and liberal manuring are requisite.

Strawberry culture begins in August, when the early runners are nicely rooted. To promote rooting peg them down and put a little fine soil about them, and if the weather is dry water regularly. When the first runners are rooted take them off and plant them at once. It is customary to plant them rather close with a view to transplant when strong. It is better practice to plant them where they are to stand at a proper distance apart, and never after remove them until they are worn out, when you will dig them in with a good body of manure, and devote the ground to rotation crops. The proper distance will in some degree vary with the sorts and the strength of the land. From eighteen inches to two and a half feet may be the range, and the larger distance is the best if you can make it square with the general business of the garden. Little crowns dotted about at two feet apart make an appearance of waste of ground, but you can run in another crop, such as winter broccolis to begin with, or winter spinach, and all through the next summer you may crop between, taking care not to encroach too closely on the strawberries, but in the following year your plants will be too large to allow of any more stolen crops, and will pay their rent too well to permit of any such trifling.

The routine culture consists in keeping the ground clear of weeds, putting on a heavy top dressing of long green stable dung in January or February, so as to just cover the plants and compel them to push through, and cutting back runners from the time they appear unless they are wanted, in which case those that come first are the best. As to watering, it all depends. On a hot dry soil water must be given copiously during May, June, and July, but generally speaking strawberries do well without artificial watering, although systematic irrigation in a hot sunny season will pay well. The laying down of a good coat of manure in February answers several purposes. The rain washes in the alkalies and phosphates to the advantage of the crop, the roots are protected from the heat of the sun, which is another advantage, and the litter that remains, and which the plants push through, becomes well washed by the rains of spring, and serves to keep the fruit clean. If you can afford the time you may put slates or stones under bunches of fruit to prevent contact with the soil, or you may spread clean straw or cocoa-nut fibre, or you may tie the bunches to sticks, or you may use "crinoline" wire frames, or you may have strawberry tiles, which are flat and square with a semicircle cut out on one side, so that a pair of them form a clean square pavement with a hole in the centre for the plant.

A very important feature in strawberry culture is the periodical renewal of the plantation. As a rule, the plants are in their most vigorous and fruitful state in the third year, after which they decline in vigour and should be destroyed. Instances might be cited of plantations remaining in health and fruitfulness for ten years, being aided by heavy top dressings in spring and occasional drenchings with a hose from a stand pipe during summer. But such exceptional cases must develope themselves, they cannot be provided for in books. In every garden that includes the strawberry amongst its necessary productions, a plantation, large or small, should be made every year, and simultaneously after the routine is established, a breadth of old plants should be destroyed. It will happen however on strong lands that the plants will pay to keep to the fifth year, and although the fruit may be small, it will be useful for preserving and for other purposes that need not be specified.

A SELECTION OF STRAWBERRIES should include in the first instance those varieties that have proved to be suitable to the locality; but having secured two or three sorts on which you can rely, it is advisable to make a small collection for comparison of their respective merits, that the most useful of them may be taken into the routine cropping and the least desirable destroyed. The cost for so doing is next to nothing, the amusement of strawberry tasting is proper to the round of garden pleasures, and the discovery of a good sort that suits the soil and climate, is a great gain, and one to be ensured only by an *experimentum crucis.* The following, for a strawberry soil, constitute a fine collection, the most desirable being starred to distinguish them :—*Aromatic*, *Dr. Hogg**, *Elton Pine*, *Filbert Pine*, *Frogmore Late Pine**, *James Veitch*, *La Grosse Sucrée**, *President**, *Sir Charles Napier*, *Sir Joseph Paxton**, *The Amateur*, *Vicomtesse Héricart de Thury**.

CHAPTER XXIX.

REMINDERS OF MONTHLY WORK.

"There be some sports are painful ; but their labour
Delight in them sets off : some kinds of baseness
Are nobly undergone : and most poor matters
Point to rich ends. This my mean task would be
As heavy to me as 'tis odious : but
The mistress, which I serve quickens what's dead,
And makes my labours pleasures."

Tempest III., 1

THE "mistress" may be Flora, or Pomona, or Ceres, but perhaps in this connection her proper name is Hortensia, and for the personification we may even look to that daughter of Hortensius, who pleaded for the Roman matrons, and redeemed them from a burden that was heavier than they could bear. But to proceed with our proper work. Garden operations of every kind must of necessity be influenced by the season, the weather, local usages, and the peculiar needs and circumstances of the cultivator. The legitimate purpose of a calender is to remind the cultivator of the operations which require to be performed as the seasons revolve, and, making due allowance for the diversity of climates within the range of which the calendar is likely to be used, to add such precautions as may be needful to guard against accident and mistake. A calendar is of necessity framed on the supposition that the reader knows how to perform the various operations mentioned in it, and is more in want of direction as to the work to be done than as to the way of doing it. Immense advantages are to be derived from method in garden work ; the observance of a rule is essential to success, and generally it is safer to be a few days or a week too soon than too late in the sowing or harvesting of a crop, and also in other operations and details of garden work.

January.

"Blasts of January would blow you through and through."

During this month it is desirable to derive as much benefit as possible from the frost, and hence all unoccupied plots of ground, including flower beds, should be deeply dug and laid up in ridges. Composts, turf for potting, and other special soils should be turned, so as to get them frozen through. Planting cannot be prosecuted with so much success as in the autumn; but where there are arrears to be got up, the work must proceed during open weather, and the greatest care must be taken to secure the roots of trees while out of the ground from being attacked by the frost. During frosty weather work is sometimes scarce; then is a good time to char edge clippings and other such refuse, and spread the ashes as manure.

At any time this month, as opportunity occurs, there may be sowings made of peas, beans, two-bladed onions, collards, York cabbage, horn carrot, and parsnips. There is, of course, a certain amount of risk in early sowing, and the whole may be lost; but in mild and tolerably dry seasons, there is ample compensation for losses at other times in the earlier production or increased bulk and excellence of the crop. In the event of the perishing of the seed sown now, there is time to sow again as soon as weather permits, so that the seed is the only loss. Dry sheltered borders are invaluable for these early sowings. In the event of severe weather, it will be necessary to protect by shaking down dry litter and placing reed hurdles in suitable positions to screen off the wind. In mild weather slugs and snails will make terrible havoc with the seedling plants, and they must be kept in check by the use of lime, soot, or wood ashes. Rhubarb in the open ground may be forwarded by covering the crowns with seakale pots, or a lot of old boxes. The covering will be nearly as effectual without the help of hot dung as with it. Another very simple and effectual way is to drive in a few stakes round each stool, and tie them together at top, so as to form a sort of tent; then heap over them any dry litter, such as pea-haulm. Celery in trenches will need protecting during hard weather. It is best also to get up occasionally a good supply and place it in dry earth in a shed or outhouse, as in the event of frost after wet much of the crop may be destroyed.

This is a bad time to prune, but if this sort of work is in arrear, it may be carried on during mild open weather. Never prune during frost. Cuttings of gooseberry and currant trees and of quinces, doucin apples, and generally of sorts required for stocks, may be put in now, though it is full late. Trees on east walls had best be unnailed till the end of next month to prevent premature excitement. Manure bush fruits, and take care not to dig between raspberries. In planting, be careful not to dig in any frozen soil. Dress fruit walls and old trees with a mixture of lime, soot, and clay.

Give special attention now to cauliflowers, lettuces, &c., in frames, and dust them with lime occasionally. Make up a small hotbed for cucumbers and melons, and sow in pots, and when forward enough, make the fruiting beds. To force sea-kale, asparagus, and rhubarb, make up a hotbed in a pit or frame, and over the dung spread four inches of soil; then take up strong roots and put them in pretty close together, and cover them with leaves. Always allow asparagus to become green at the points before cutting; if completely blanched, it is completely spoiled. Sow peas on slips of turf for transplanting.

February.

"You have such a February face,
So full of frost, of storm and cloudiness."

There should be no delay in getting ready every inch of ground intended for summer crops. Get all plots requiring manure ready at once, as it is much better to have the ground prepared in advance, that the manure may be more completely incorporated with the soil, than to sow or plant immediately after manuring. Ground for peas, beans, onions, cauliflowers, and broccoli must be liberally manured and deeply stirred. Mark out the soil for onions into four-feet beds, and raise the beds six inches above the general level, and leave the surface rough. Choose for potatoes ground on which cabbage, or broccoli, or celery has been grown, and which for those crops was well manured last year. Make up sloping borders under warm walls and fences for early lettuce, radish, onion, horn carrot, and to prick out cauliflower and broccoli from seed-pans, &c. On dry soils plant potatoes as soon as possible; sets should be of moderate size, and with short stubby hard sprouts upon them; when the sprouts are long and white, it is scarcely reasonable to expect a sound and plentiful production. To raise a few early potatoes, the simplest method is to make up a slight hotbed, and cover it with old lights, or canvas on hoops, or even hurdles or mats will do, as by the time the haulm appears the season will be sufficiently advanced to allow of taking off the covering by day, putting it on at night, however, to keep safe from frost. If there is plenty of charred refuse, use it liberally in making up the bed, and cover the sets with some of it reserved for the purpose. The main crop of potatoes should be planted at greater distances between the rows than is usually allowed; two feet and a half apart, and nine inches between the sets, should be the least distance for moderate growers, and three feet to three feet and a half apart, and a foot or more between the sets, for robust growers. When cultivators complain that their potatoes have "run all to haulm," it may always be understood that they are planted about twice as thick as they ought to be. Sow *in the open quarters*, peas, parsnips, spinach, leeks. Sow *on warm slopes* radish, hardy lettuce, cabbage, parsley. Plant potatoes, garlic, shallots, chives, onions for seed.

Prune out-door vines, and lay in only the ripest of last year's shoots, at about eighteen inches apart, and not more than four eyes in length. Clean the wall, and nail firmly, using as narrow shreds as possible. Get ready netting or other protection for espalier and wall trees, and use it as soon as the buds begin to swell, during the prevalence of north-east winds. Strawberry beds bear well if made early this month, on rich, firm ground. Plant and prune bush fruits. Begin grafting as soon as the weather permits; scions thrust into the ground in bunches, with a tally to each, will keep a month, if necessary, and take better than if put on as soon as cut. See that all bearing rods are neatly trained; if any pruning is neglected, attend to it at once. Vines bleeding through being pruned too late may be stopped by cutting raw potatoes to fit over the wound.

Tender plants that have been wintered in cold frames must have very little water at present; but nothing should be allowed to get dust-dry; it is most injurious. Sow in heat, to transplant, Spanish onion, cos and cabbage lettuce, celery, tomatoes, capsicums, melons, cucumbers, and cauliflowers.

MARCH.

"Worse than the sun in March,
This praise doth nourish agues."

Wheel out manure to the plots that are to be sown or planted this month and next, and dig the ground over deeply, and leave rough. If the ground is well drained, plant at once the main crop of potatoes, but on damp soils wait till next month. It is not safe to manure for potatoes, but charred rubbish, old mortar, and other dry materials may be used to lighten the soil and nourish the crop. For main crops choose a plot that was well manured last year; for early sorts that are to come up before the autumn rain set in, manure may be dug into the trenches. Potatoes are best planted in trenches, and covered loosely with soil; dibbling is apt to cause rotting, by the holes getting filled with water. Make new plantations of artichokes. Horseradish may be planted in any spare corner, but the ground should be dug deeply, and the roots will come finer if the subsoil is well manured. The crowns should be planted fifteen inches deep and six inches apart every way, and the holes filled with fine coal ashes. Mark out onion beds, and let the soil be liberally manured. Get ready for all successional summer crops, so as to have the ground firm and well sweetened in time to receive them. Sow turnip, long radish, main crop of parsnips, horn carrot, cauliflower, cabbage, savoy, broccoli, main crop of onions, peas, beans, lettuce, leeks, spinach, parsley, and small salads.

Cuttings of bush fruits may still be put in. Grafting should not be delayed, as the sap is now rising. Pruning and cleaning ought to have been completed long ago; if not so, let your motto be, "Better late than never." Burn all the prunings and clipping of trees, hedges, etc., and use the ashes as a top-dressing for quarters of bush fruits. Mulch raspberries with half-rotten dung, and take care that they are not dug between. Lay down plenty of manure between strawberries.

Sow in pans or pots tender annuals, melons, cucumbers, capsicums, tomatoes, and a few pans of celery, lettuce, French beans, etc., etc., for planting out early on warm sheltered slopes. Many of the plants wintered in frames will now need repotting and other attentions. It will be well, towards the end of the month, to make a general clearance, and re-arrange the whole stock.

April.

"O, how this spring of love resembleth
The uncertain glory of an April day;
Which now shews all the beauty of the sun,
And by and by a cloud takes all away!"

The month of April is one which tests severely the capabilities of the gardener, as well as his ways and means. The weather may be summer one day, and winter the next; and inexperienced hands may easily be led astray by the temptations of warm showers and sunshine, to regret, afterwards, the havoc caused by sudden frosts, storms, and even snow and hail. In the general work of the garden, many of the directions—especially as to sowing—given last month, apply to this, and more particularly to those who live in exposed districts.

Successional sowings may be made of all leading vegetable crops, and where the work of the last month has been delayed, seeds got in early will not be much behind those sown last month. Sow Windsor, longpod, and Johnson's Wonderful beans; marrow, Auvergne, and dwarf mammoth peas, and a few rows of the earlier sorts to come in before the late peas are ready. In small gardens the dwarf kinds are always to be preferred. Sowings should be made of horn carrot, savoy, Brussels sprouts, Scotch kale, broccoli, cauliflowers, and cabbages, for autumn use, a succession of such things being preferable to a glut all at once for a private grower. Among cabbages, Atkins's Matchless, Shilling's Queen, Early York, and West Ham are good sorts to sow now, but the main crop of cabbages should be up by this time, and must be hoed between when the ground is in a fit state. Beet should be sown in the second week, in ground deeply dug, but not manured; the main crop of celery should be sown on a rich warm border, the surface to be made light and fine; sow thin, and merely dust the seed over. Sow also onions, lettuce, radish, small salad, seakale, and asparagus—the two last in drills, one foot apart, and one inch deep for asparagus, and two inches for seakale. Another mode of raising seakale plants is to sow in four-feet beds, the seed to be in patches of eight inches diameter, and two feet apart, and about eight seeds in each, the plants to be thinned to three plants in each patch; the ground should be rich, well drained, and deep. Beds may also be formed now by planting roots, but the best plantations are those raised on the spot from seeds. Those who purpose raising seedling rhubarb plants should sow about the middle of the month in shallow drills, eighteen inches apart, dropping the seeds in patches, six inches from each other. Potatoes not yet planted should be got in without delay, and towards the end of the month scarlet runners and French beans may be sown; the runners should have a warm dry position until the 1st of May, when they may be sown in almost any soil or situation without risk, but like most other things yield the best crops on ground well dug and manured. The main crop of carrots should be got in about the 15th of the month, and there is still time for a crop of parsnips, but they must be sown directly. Slips of kitchen herbs may be put in any time this month, and will root quicker if planted in a rather dry sandy border.

Wall trees must have protection from the cutting east winds, and the protection should be of a kind easily removed, so that the trees have free air upon them night and day, weather permitting, and be covered with the least possible trouble if the wind shifts to east or north. It will generally be found that those who exclaim against protecting have been in the habit of shutting the trees up as if they were muffled bells. In the open quarters, pruning and grafting must be completed quickly. Give abundance of water to fruit trees in pots, and see that the orchard-house is in an orderly state; if it is now crammed with plants from other houses, as is too often the case, there will be but a small crop of fruit. If bedding stock is still in request, put in more cuttings; a heat of 90 degs. may be used now if the cuttings are of stout young wood. China roses may be propagated now by taking off young shoots close to the old wood when four inches long, and plunging in a moderate heat.

MAY.

"As full of spirit as the month of May."

High culture should be aimed at now with all vegetable crops, frequent stirrings between the rows with the hoe to keep down weeds, and abundant supplies of water and liquid manure. It is hardly possible to give too much water, and in exposed situations and on thin soils grass mowings should be used as a mulch to keep the ground moist, but should be examined occasionally to guard against it becoming a harbour for slugs. Put sticks to rows of peas as soon as they require it; well bank up those that are forward. Thin parsnips and carrots to eight inches apart, and go on transplanting from seed-beds as fast as the plants are large enough to handle, leaving the smallest to get stronger before removing them. Choose showery weather, if possible, for transplanting, or else give shade for a few days, and gentle watering. Flat-hoe potatoes, and draw but little earth to their stems; the old method of moulding them up has proved to be of no benefit at all, rather an injury, as the heat of the sun cannot have too ready an access to the roots. Thin out celery, and make up small beds for the plants on very rich, hard ground. Trenches should now be made for celery, and six inches of rotten dung forked into the bottom of each. A dull or showery day should be chosen to put out the plants, and plenty of water given during dry weather. Look to seed-beds, and transplant; well hoe and clear the ground as may be necessary. The use of liquid manure and frequent stirring of the ground between growing crops, will hasten and improve the growth of all things. Sow beans and peas for succession; savoy for late crop. Cabbage, broccoli, kale, beetroot, kidney beans, both runners and dwarfs, lettuces, spinach, turnips, cucumbers, and marrows may now be sown in the open ground for a late supply.

Plums and pears, and indeed all bush and pyramid fruits, will want pinching in to the third or fourth leaf from the base. Where large crops of fruit are set, thin severely, but not all at once, as the more fruit the poorer will its quality be. Give strawberries plenty of water. If raspberries have not been mulched, give them at once a top-dressing of half-rotten dung. Do not dig it in. In the orchard-house renew the mulchings if needful; give plenty of water.

Pits and frames that have been emptied of their winter occupants will now be useful for hardening bedding plants previous to planting out. Cucumbers and melons must have good culture and regular stopping and training; they should be looked to daily. Always keep a canful of water in each frame, to have it tepid for use.

June.

"The cuckoo is in June heard, not regarded."

The ground will be now, for the most part, covered, and everything in full growth. The hoe must never be idle; weeds grow faster than the crops, and exhaust the soil rapidly, and, if allowed to seed, make the mischief worse. Next to keeping down weeds, the most important operation is that of watering. Plants lately put out should not be drenched to excess, or the chill will check them more than a drought would, and it is better to trust to moderate watering and shade combined than to keep the soil soddened about plants that have barely taken root. Cucumbers, gourds, tomatoes, and capsicums may be put out; the soil should be rich; and for tomatoes a sunny aspect must be chosen. Manure-water should be freely used to all crops in full growth, and especially to strawberries, but there should be two or three waterings with plain water to one with liquid manure. Sow beet, early horn carrots, scarlet runners, and French beans, turnips, lettuces, radishes, cabbages, spinach, endive, cauliflower, and peas and beans. All salad plants should have a shady position, or they may run to seed. In sowing peas and beans, it is best to depend on the earliest sorts at this time of year, as they are soon off the ground, but Knight's Marrow and Bedman's Imperial are good peas to sow now for late supply. Dress asparagus and seakale beds with one pound of salt to every square yard, and give asparagus beds strong doses of liquid manure from horse-dung.

Search among raspberries every morning for snails, which take shelter on the stalks and among the side-shoots. If large fruit are required, thin the blooms at once, and give liquid manure. Disbud and nail in. Pot trees to have plenty of water, and, if weakly in their new growth, pretty strong doses of liquid manure at intervals of a week each. Pinch, regulate, and where the fruit grows thick, thin it out.

Put in cuttings of alyssums, wallflowers, pansies, and a few other such subjects of choice kinds. Balsams, asters, cockscombs, and other tender annuals, must not be pot-bound or starved, which they too often are at this time. Give cucumbers and melons plenty of water; the latter must have the full sunshine.

JULY.

"As clear as founts in July, when
We see each grain of gravel."

A few remarks on watering may be useful here. As a rule, water should never be given until the further withholding of it would be detrimental to the plants. Plants left to battle with drought send their roots down deep in search of moisture, and when rain does come they benefit more by it than those that have regular waterings all along. If the ground is dug deeply, and kept in good heart, plants that have got once established will bear drought for almost any length of time; but things lately planted, and that have not had time to "get hold," must be kept supplied. Succulent vegetables, too, which ought to be kept growing quick, must have abundance; and of course plants in pots must have sufficient. There are two important points to be attended to in giving water: one is to expose the water to the sun before using it, to render it soft and warm; and the other is to give a thorough soaking at once, sufficient to keep the ground moist for a week. Supposing the supply to be limited but regular, the best way of economizing both water and time is to take the garden piece by piece, watering each piece thoroughly every evening, and then beginning again as at first. Surface sprinklings bring the roots to the surface in search of the moisture, which, when they reach it, is insufficient to nourish them, but, on the contrary, causes exhaustion, by inducing the growth of fibres within reach of the burning rays of the sun. Plants in pots, in windows, and on gravel paths are very much tried by the heating action of the sun, and to keep their roots cool it is advisable to drop the pots into larger ones, and fill between the two with moss. This is the proper way to use ornamental pots, and the dressing of moss may be made to hide the inside pot which contains the plant, by arranging it neatly over the surface of the soil.

Where early crops are coming off, clear the ground and dig it over at once; it is a folly to wait for the last handful of peas or beans. As soon as the rows cease to be profitable, destroy them, and clear the ground. Dig deep, and plant out Brussels sprouts, green collards, kale, savoys, cabbages, broccolis, etc. If the plants are crowded in the seed-bed, it is best to get them out at once. Have all ready, and in the evening put out as many rows as possible, and give a little water to every plant. Next morning lay a few boughs or mats over them, to shade off the sun, and the next evening get out more, till the planting is finished. This is better than waiting for rain, which may be so heavy as to render the ground unfit to be trodden on, and, if succeeded immediately by heat, the plants will flag as much as if put out in dry weather, whereas, being already in the ground, the smallest shower benefits them. Seed-beds for winter spinach should now be made up and well manured, and the seed got in without delay. In gathering French and runner beans, take all or none. If seed is desired, leave a row untouched. Never take green pods and seeds from the same plants. Take up onions, shallots, and garlic as they ripen, and store for winter. Give asparagus beds plenty of liquid manure, and use the grass mowings from the lawn as mulchings, to prevent the soil from cracking. Earth up celery for early use, but the rows that are not forward must be kept open and well watered, as the plants grow very slowly after being earthed up, the object of the earthing being to blanch it only. Also plant out the main crop of celery as soon as the ground can be got ready. Cut down artichokes. Hoe between all growing crops, and especially between potatoes. Top runners, and keep them well staked. Sow the last succession of runners and French beans; also lettuce, endive, Stadtholder and Mitchell's cauliflower, radish, small salads, spinach, peas, and turnips. Land laying high and dry may be planted with potatoes now, for use early next spring.

Keep gooseberry and currant bushes open in the centre, and leave on the bush fruits only as much wood as will bear a fine crop next season. Cuttings of gooseberries and currants may be struck now in a moist shady border. Mulch raspberries with half-rotten dung. Strawberry beds now want special attention. Strong-rooted runners should be taken off to form new plantations, and be pricked out into well-manured beds, pretty close together, to strengthen, preparatory to making new beds in September; or they may be laid in small pots, with a stone or peg to fix them, and will root directly. After three years, strawberry beds cease to pay, and should be broken up, and the ground trenched for winter crops. Tie in and train as needful and use the syringe to wall trees, if the weather should be dry, and especially with east winds. Continue to bud stone-fruit trees for orchard-house and pot culture. Thin out weak spray on all bush trees, and fore-right shoots on wall fruits. Maiden trees intended to be trained should be stopped, to make them into side-shoots, as a whole season's growth is thus saved.

AUGUST.

"You sun-burn'd sicklemen, of August weary,
Come hither from the furrow, and be merry."

Winter greens claim the first attention, and it is necessary to ensure at once a good supply, and a variety. By this time, Scotch kale, Brussels sprouts, broccolis, savoys, etc., ought to be strong, and where they have been planted between rows of peas, to stand the winter, should now be looked over, and every other plant taken out, to make fresh rows if they are at all crowded. Cabbages of most kinds may be sown in the second week of August; Shilling's Queen, Sprotborough, West Ham, and Red Dutch ought to have a place in every garden. Sow also prickly spinach on slopes in rich soil, and plenty of hardy green Hammersmith, and black-seeded cos lettuce. Sow cauliflower from the 7th to the 20th, to keep over winter in frames. The summer-sown endive will now be strong enough to plant out on slopes or raised beds. Give plenty of water, alternately with liquid manure, to celery, and do not earth it up until it is well grown, the earthing being only to blanch it for use. Give plenty of water to broccoli and cauliflower beds, and top scarlet runners. In good open situations, vegetable marrows for a late supply may still be planted. Use grass mowings to mulch the ground between crops that are likely to suffer from drought. Hoe between the rows of potatoes in dry weather. The foliage, where it remains green, should be injured as little as possible; those that are casting their haulm may be taken up. Earth up leeks; thin out the rows of parsley, so as to get rid of every plant not well curled. Throw nets over fruit bushes to keep off the birds, and give a little shade to keep a few bunches hanging for a late supply. Put wasp-traps about vines and peaches, or stick a few lumps of loaf-sugar among the branches, and as long as there is any sugar left they will not touch a single fruit. Nail in all good shoots on wall trees, that they may have the heat of the wall to ripen them. Encourage in every possible way the ripening of the wood of the season. If any trees have been allowed to get crowded, thin them a little now to admit the sunshine amongst the well-placed shoots and spurs. Windfalls to be sent into the house every morning for immediate use. Gather fruit in dry weather, and, as a rule, not till quite ripe. Plant strawberries.

September.

"Fruits that blossom first, will first be ripe."

The autumn hues, which increase and deepen as the flowers depart, give a peculiar interest and beauty to plantations and shrubberies; and in all arrangements in regard to planting, the autumnal effects of contrasted tints of foliage should be considered; and for the next two months we have every opportunity of observing how much variety and how many charming effects may be obtained by a judicious assortment and grouping of trees and shrubs. In regard to bedding plants, accurate estimates may be formed as to the suitableness of the kinds that have been used this season. Whatever alterations are to be made in garden plans, too, should be definitely determined at once, so that the ground may be trenched up, and deciduous trees got into their quarters before the earth begins to cool, and walks, excavations, etc., made before unfavourable weather begins to interfere with such operations.

The winter stock sown last month will now be coming forward for planting out. Where onions have been cleared off is generally the best place for cabbage for spring use, because the ground having been well manured for the onions, is in good heart, and yet so far relieved of manure by the onions, there will be no fear of a rank growth, such as will cause the plants to suffer from frost. Plant firm, and during damp weather if possible. Thin winter spinach to six inches from plant to plant; thin the rows of lettuce that are to stand the winter; but not severely, because, in the event of severe frosts, the plants protect each other, if somewhat close together; on the same principle, broccoli and cauliflowers left to risk it in the open ground should be not more than fifteen inches apart, and the ground for them should not at this season be very rich, or they may suffer in severe weather. Earth up celery as the rows require it, in dry weather; but if not well grown, give plenty of liquid manure, and postpone the earthing-up till the plants have made good substance. This is the best time to form new beds of horseradish, the crowns to be planted fifteen inches deep and six inches apart, in very rich and well-trenched soil. Continue to sow saladings, and gather seeds as fast as they ripen. Potatoes to be taken up as the tops wither; carrots and beetroot many remain till the frost cuts off the foliage, and no longer, but parsnips may be left in the ground, to be trenched out as wanted for use, unless the ground is required, in which case store them in sand.

It requires some experience to determine the right moment to gather any particular kind of fruit, and no fixed rule can be given, because seasons and soils differ so much that the same kind will be ripe in one place a week or a fortnight earlier than in another. When the pips of apples and pears acquire a dark colour is usually the signal for harvesting the crop, but in looking for this sign a sound fruit must be taken, not one that has been pierced by an insect. Have all fruit gathered with care, and stored without bruising. Wall trees in a gross state should be disleafed; the removal of a few leaves from vines, peach trees, etc., will often materially promote the ripening of the wood. Plant strawberries. Those to be forced should now be strong in pots; give them a shift, and in doing so use a firm rich compost, and ram it in hard. Give plenty of water, and let them have full sun.

October.

"Blessing of your heart, you brew good ale."

This is a busy month; nearly every kind of winter work may be commenced—and, indeed, completed—if weather permits. Deciduous trees and hardy fruits may be planted towards the end of the month, for there is no need to wait till every leaf has fallen. Get them into their places while the ground is warm, and a season is saved, and the tree will always be the stronger for it, for the fate of many a tree is sealed in its original planting. Earthwork, too, may now be commenced, and drains laid, turf stacked for forming composts, and deep soiling practised on ground suited to such treatment, so as to have it in ridges in good time to be acted on by frost. The whole of the arrangements should be determined from this time, and in taking up bedders and decorative plants from the borders, their good and bad qualities should all be noted down, so that things that have proved inferior, or that evidently do not suit the soil, or situation, may be substituted next season for objects of higher merit. Every soil has its peculiarities, and one great secret of success, especially in ornamental gardening, is to select varieties that have been proved to succeed in the place. Pits, frames, and houses ought now to be clean, and free from the smell of paint and putty. If any repairs have been neglected, see to them at once, and get all sweet and dry without a day's delay; for when we get to October, we are never sure for a week together but that our appliances and manual skill may have a sudden trial.

This is a time for earnest work in every department. Make a general clearance of the ground wherever there are vacant spaces, and ridge up all plots not to be planted on during winter. Get a waste corner clear for heaping up manures and composts, where they can be turned over during frosts; and if convenient, empty the muck-pit, and cover the rotted stuff with a layer of soil to throw off rain; the whole to be turned two or three times before using it in the spring. In preparing for next year's crops, trench over first the ground intended for root crops next season, and choose for potatoes, carrots, parsnips, and beet, plots that have been well manured this year. If the soil allows of deep digging, fork over the second spit, and if it is of a friable or fertile nature, bring it to the top, so as to turn the whole soil over eighteen inches or two feet deep. Plant out the August-sown cabbage; leave the weakest in the seed-bed for future planting. Plant out lettuce in a warm situation; take up potatoes, carrots, beets, and parsnips; earth up celery. Lay cabbages and broccolis that are forward with their heads to the north. In undrained soils it is a good plan to cut a few channels among standing crops, to enable the heavy rains to run off more quickly to an outlet, as dryness of the ground very much lessons the effects of frost. Fork over asparagus beds, and clear away all litter; remove the stems with a knife, and dress the crowns with manure, and a little fresh mould over all. This is the best time to make plantations of rhubarb for producing next season. Let the ground be deeply dug and well manured. Tomatoes not ripe should be cut with a length of stem, and put in a warm greenhouse, where they will soon ripen.

Towards the end of the month gooseberries, currants, and raspberries may be moved. New plantations should be made on ground deeply trenched and manured; gooseberries and raspberries need a richer soil than currants; and black currants and raspberries will thrive in more marshy ground than any other of the bush fruits. The black currant is the best of all fruits to grow in the shade. Currant and gooseberry canes may be put in to increase stock, and for this purpose two-year-old wood is better than the shoots of the season, if disbudded a foot or eighteen inches from the base. Drain and trench the ground where the fruit trees are to be planted next month. Moss on apple trees generally disappears when the ground is drained. Root-pruning and planting may be commenced the last week, but root-pruning should only be resorted to in the case of over-luxuriant, unfruitful trees. Get all plants of questionable hardiness, and any that are liable to suffer from wet or the attacks of snails, under cover. Pot or bed cauliflowers in frames for the winter. Remove decayed leaves wherever they occur, to prevent the formation of moulds about growing plants.

November.

"Fetch us in fuel, and be quick."

Planting is now going on in all directions. In this work delays are dangerous. Trees got into their quarters at once, even if they have not quite shed their leaves, will at once make fresh root, and get well established before severe frosts set in. Order at once whatever fruit trees, roses, etc., you may require, and have the ground prepared, so that they may be planted immediately on arrival. Laying in by the heels is a mischievous practice, and should never be resorted to except when unavoidable. Wherever digging and trenching are required, let it be done without delay; every additional day's exposure of the soil to the action of the weather is a benefit to it. Generally speaking, it is not well to manure in the autumn, because the winter rains wash the best of it away; but manure should have attention, and this is a good time to clear out the muck-pit, and pile the stuff in a heap, and throw over it a few inches of soil or burnt clay. In dry frosty weather it should be chopped down and turned, and again soiled over to preserve its virtues and at the same time sweeten it for use. Turf should be stacked, and clippings collected for burning to make dressings of manure for beds and borders. The general work of the kitchen garden is but a continuation of last month, to which we refer to avoid repetitions. Those who are inclined to venture a few speculative crops should sow Mazagan beans, Dillistone's Early, Sangster's Number One, and Early Emperor peas. If they get through the winter, they will produce a few early dishes, but there is the risk not only of severe weather, but of the attacks of slugs and snails, and where these vermin are allowed to riot on the ground, winter sowings have but little chance. Broad, well-drained slopes are of great value for winter sowings, and for bedding out lettuce, broccoli, and cauliflower for the winter; and with the help of reed or thatched hurdles for shelter, late and early supplies of vegetables and saladings may be secured, and will always pay well. Turn gravel walks, clean and turn plunging beds, make a clearance of corners devoted to rubbish, especially where there is an accumulation of old pea-sticks and timber, as it is among such stuff that the vermin take shelter, to issue forth in spring and destroy the seed crops, and bring disgrace upon the small birds.

Prune and plant as weather permits. Give special attention to wall fruit, and where standards have got crowded thin out the heads, but be very cautious about cutting large boughs off healthy bearing trees. Bush fruits should be pruned, and the ground forked over between the rows. Burn the pruning, and strew the ashes over the newly-forked surface. Red and white currants must be cut back to skeletons; the chief of the fruit-buds being at the junctions of the new wood with that of last year, leave only two or three joints beyond that point, and cut clear away to the base every branch that is ill-placed or that chokes up the centre. Black currants do not like the knife; trim the branches to regular distances, and shorten the longest back to good joints, but preserve plenty of young wood, leaving the plumpest branches nearly their full length, and cutting all weak ones clean away. Scrub old apple trees that are infested with blight with a strong brine, and stop the holes with a mixture of clay, sulphur, soot, and cow-dung, beaten together into a tenacious paste. Pits and frames will now be crowded; give air plentifully on fine days, and whenever practicable take off the lights; sunshine will do good, but rain will generally be mischievous, though during dry weather a shower will occasionally freshen up the plants and save the trouble of watering. Remove dead leaves, and keep all very clean as a preventive of mildew.

DECEMBER.

"Rain and wind beat dark December."

Make plantations of rhubarb, seakale, asparagus, and horse-radish. Roots of dandelion, packed together in leaf-mould and put into gentle heat, will furnish a delicate salad, in five or six weeks. Keep dung and all soluble matters under cover. Turn over manures, and put aside in heaps to be frozen rotted leaves and other materials suitable for potting, and when well sweetened and pulverized remove to bins in the potting shed to keep dry for use. Get sticks and stakes tied up in bundles ready for use; wheel turf and weeds to the muck-pit; get pots washed and sorted over, and crocks shifted into sizes for the potting-bench. This is a good time to make new drains, improve watercourses, and plant hedges. Sow early peas and beans on dry slopes; broccoli to be heeled over with their heads to the north.

Dig round old fruit trees, and lay down a layer of old dung six inches thick, in a ring, four feet distant from the stem of each, and the size of the fruit will be improved. Trees that are sufficiently luxurious should not have manure. Give protection to tender fruit trees, and lay boards in a slope over vine borders to shelter them from excessive cold rains. Unnail from the walls the younger shoots of tender wall-trees to prevent premature growth. Bush fruits properly taken up and properly planted out do not miss the move in the slightest degree, but you are sure to loose a whole season if they lay about waiting to be planted. Strawberry beds may be made this month, but it is not a good time to plant strawberries. Bush fruits should be planted, potted, pruned, and manured. Burn the prunings, and if the ashes are not wanted for any particular purpose, throw them round the roots of trees; they are powerfully fertilizing. Gooseberries and currants may be lightly forked between to mix the manure with the soil, but raspberries should have three or four inches of dung, not very rotten, laid over the piece, and the soil between them should not be dug at all. Orchard-house trees may be pruned at once, and washed with a solution of eight ounces of Gishurst to a gallon of soft water.

INDEX.

www.ingramcontent.com/pod-product-compliance
Lightning Source LLC
Chambersburg PA
CBHW021126270326
41929CB00009B/1060

* 9 7 8 3 7 4 2 8 9 2 5 7 7 *